Markets and Moralities

Markets and Moralities

Ethnographies of Postsocialism

Edited by
Ruth Mandel and Caroline Humphrey

Oxford • New York

First published in 2002 by
Berg
Editorial offices:
150 Cowley Road, Oxford, OX4 1JJ, UK
838 Broadway, Third Floor, New York, NY 10003–4812, USA

Berg is an imprint of Oxford International Publishers Ltd.

Library of Congress Cataloging-in-Publication Data
Markets and moralities: ethnographies of postsocialism / edited by Ruth Mandel
and Caroline Humphrey.
    p. cm.
Includes bibliographical references and index.
ISBN 1-85973-572-X (cloth) -- ISBN 1-85973-577-0 (pbk.)
    1. Free enterprise--Europe, Eastern. 2. Free enterprise--Former Soviet republics.
3. Post-communism--Case studies. 4. Europe, Eastern--Economic conditions--
1989- 5. Former Soviet republics--Economic conditions. I. Mandel, Ruth (Ruth
Ellen) II. Humphrey, Caroline.
    HC244 .M3445 2002
    380.1'0947--dc21

                                                                    2002002837

British Library Cataloguing-in-Publication Data
A catalogue record for this book is available from the British Library.

ISBN 1 85973 572 X (Cloth)
    1 85973 577 0 (Paper)

Typeset by JS Typesetting Ltd, Wellingborough, Northants.
Printed in the United Kingdom by Biddles Ltd, Guildford and King's Lynn.

Contents

Contents

A Note on the Cover:
Weiche by Neo Rauch

Neo Rauch, born in 1961, studied art in Leipzig (then the GDR), where he still lives. Drawing on archetypal figures characteristic of the utopian iconography of socialist realism, he creates a bleak post-industrial, postsocialist, landscape. His work has been described as resembling 'giant World's Fair postcards overcome by an Orwellian surrealism' (Max Henry). In *Weiche*, or 'Switch' (as in a rail-road switch), Rauch's socialist-era images, such as the woman's uniform and the panoptic watch-tower, confront a troubling dystopic uncertainty that encompasses the socialist past as well as the postsocialist present and future.

Acknowledgements

The chapters included in this volume began life as presentations at one of a series of annual workshops initiated by Caroline Humphrey, Deniz Kandiyoti and Ruth Mandel, held at University College London, beginning in 1996. These gatherings have brought together both graduate students and more established anthropologists and like-minded scholars primarily from Britain, but also from other parts of Europe and the former Soviet Union. Our idea has been to create an informal forum in which to present and discuss recent and ongoing research about postsocialist societies. The workshops have been sponsored in part by the Department of Anthropology, and the Graduate School, University College London; Centre for Democracy and Society, University College London; the British Museum's Ethnographic Department; ESRC's Transnational Communities Programme; School for Oriental and African Studies; and Cambridge University. This is the second publication emerging in part from the workshops: the first was a special issue of *Central Asian Survey*, December 1998, co-edited by Deniz Kandiyoti and Ruth Mandel.

Notes on Contributors

André Czeglédy is Senior Lecturer of Social Anthropology at the University of the Witwatersrand, Johannesburg. His main academic interests include the study of corporate culture, international joint ventures and national identity in business, and he has carried out research in Hungary and South Africa. Recently he has also focused on architecture and the built environment in the context of transitioning states. He also works as a management consultant specializing in corporate restructuring and international human resource development.

Adam Drazin has recently completed his PhD at the Department of Anthropology, University College London. He has published several papers on Romania, including one in another Berg collection, *The Material Culture of the Home* (2000). He is currently lecturing at Maynooth University, Ireland, and conducting research on the material culture of photography. He plans to carry out research on the material culture of migration and transnational communication in Dublin.

Faride Heyat is a writer and researcher on the Caucasus affiliated with SOAS, University of London. Her PhD research, published by Curzon Press, focused on the impact of the Soviet system on the position of Azeri women and the post-Soviet changes. Her previous research concerned Iranian women and the Islamic revolution.

Caroline Humphrey is Professor of Asian Anthropology at the University of Cambridge, UK and a Fellow of King's College, Cambridge. She has worked since 1966 in Asian parts of Russia, Mongolia, Inner Mongolia (China), India and Nepal. Among her publications are *Karl Marx Collective: Economy, Society and Religion in a Siberian Collective Farm* (1983, Cambridge University Press); *Barter, Exchange and Value* (ed., with Stephen Hugh-Jones, 1992, Cambridge University Press); *The Archetypal Actions of Ritual* (with James Laidlaw, 1994, Clarendon Press, Oxford); *Shamans and Elders* (1996, Clarendon Press, Oxford); *Marx Went Away, but Karl Stayed Behind* (1998, University of Michigan

Notes on Contributors

Press); *The End of Nomadism? Society, State and the Environment in Inner Asia* (with David Sneath, Duke University Press, 1999). Research interests include political, economic and social transformations in Russia, especially in the Asian regions, including 'democracy' and new political forms in the Russian provinces; leadership and authoritarianism; nationalist and ethnic ideologies; the effects of de-collectivization and privatization; de-monetization and barter; the emergence of racketeering; bribery and its institutionalization; poverty, social networks and household strategies; new and revived religions.

Deema Kaneff is a researcher at the Max Planck Institute for Social Anthropology, Germany. She has carried out fieldwork in socialist and postsocialist Bulgaria. Forthcoming is a book on this material, titled *Who Owns the Past? The Politics of Time in a 'Model' Bulgarian Village* (Berghahn). She is currently carrying out new research in the Ukraine where the focus is on property relations and social equality.

Ruth Mandel teaches anthropology at University College London. Her research interests include transnational migration, and media and development in postsocialist societies. She has carried out research in Turkey, Germany, and Kazakhstan; her most recent research, funded by the ESRC Transnational Communities Programme, has been among Volga German immigrants to Berlin, where she was a Berlin Prize Fellow at the American Academy in Berlin in 2000. She has published numerous articles about Turkish migrants in Germany; with Deniz Kandiyoti she co-edited a special issue of Central Asian Survey (December 1998) on recent anthropological research in Central Asia, and is completing a book on Turkish migrants in Germany.

Louise Perrotta trained in Social Anthropology at the London School of Economics, where she received her PhD in 1996, based on fieldwork carried out in Moscow. Since that time she has worked as a social and economic development consultant in the Ukraine, Kazakhstan, Russia and Albania. She currently works as a Social Development Advisor at The Department for International Development.

Frances Pine has been conducting research in rural Poland, and more recently in urban industrial areas as well, since the late 1970s. She is the author of many articles on kinship, local economy, work and related areas in socialist and postsocialist Poland and co-editor, with Sue Bridger, of the collection *Surviving Post-Socialism* (Routledge 1998). She is a Bye-Fellow of Girton College, Cambridge.

Sigrid Rausing received her PhD in Social Anthropology from University College London in 1997, having carried out research in rural Estonia in 1993–94; she has been an honorary fellow in the same department. Since then she has published numerous articles based on her Estonian fieldwork on a former collective farm. She currently is working on a book based on her fieldwork diaries.

Rosamund Shreeves has been conducting research on gender since 1990, when she completed a postgraduate dissertation on women's participation in *perestroika;* she has published articles on this theme. After conducting a research project for the University of Wolverhampton, she is currently working in Brussels and completing a doctoral dissertation on gender and rural development in Kazakhstan. Her current research interests include rural poverty, inequality and the interaction of local populations with NGOs and international organizations in Central Asia.

David Sneath lectures at the Department of Social Anthropology, Cambridge University, and is a Fellow at Corpus Christi College. He is the Assistant Director of the Cambridge University Mongolia and Inner Asia Studies Unit, and is the co-editor of the journal *Inner Asia*. His research interests include pastoralism, land-use and the environment, decollectivization and postsocialist social transformations, and the anthropology of development. Recent publications include *Changing Inner Mongolia: Pastoral Mongolian Society and the Chinese State* (2000, Oxford University Press); 'Sustaining the Steppe: The future of Mongolia's grasslands' (2000, in World Resources Institute, World Resources 1999–2000, Oxford University Press); *The End of Nomadism? Society, State and the Environment in Inner Asia*, (with C. Humphrey) (1999, Duke University Press); 'Mobility, technology and decollectivisation of pastoralism in Mongolia' (1999, in S. Kotkin and B. Elleman (eds) *Mongolia in the Twentieth Century: Landlocked Cosmopolitan*, Armonk: M.E. Sharpe Inc.) 'State policy and pasture degradation in Inner Asia', *Science*, 281(5380), 21 August 1998.

Julian Watts studied for his doctorate at the Institute of Social and Cultural Anthropology, Oxford University, and carried out ethnographic research in Archangel, northern Russia, between 1993 and 1995. He subsequently worked for the Bank of England and is now at the Financial Services Authority in London.

–1–

The Market in Everyday Life: Ethnographies of Postsocialism

Caroline Humphrey and *Ruth Mandel*

During the socialist period in Eastern Europe and Russia, making profits from marketing was illegal in most circumstances and state ideologies branded private trading activities as immoral.[1] Such judgements were widely, though of course not universally, shared by ordinary people (Pine 1996; Stewart 1996; Humphrey 1999a). From 1991 postsocialist governments, however, moved rapidly toward market reform. Ten years on, having survived Western market-oriented 'shock therapy,' taken on IMF and World Bank loans, and entered the global marketplace, the postsocialist societies still struggle to come to terms with the clash between deeply ingrained moralities and the daily pressures, opportunities and inequalities posed by market penetration. 'The market' confronts people in diverse contexts and is not experienced as a purely economic phenomenon: it might appear as a rural privatization programme, advertisements for Western cigarettes, daily observation of growing inequalities in poverty and nouveau wealth, or the sudden visibility of prostitution. Attitudes and practices even within one region are by no means uniform, yet we need to try to understand what patterns are emerging in the groundswell of everyday activities. It is just such confrontations, ambiguities and compromises concerning 'the market' that are described and analysed in this volume.

This collection represents original research, echoing in its variety and freshness the diversity of quotidian market activities of the people living in the new states and regions of the former Soviet Union and its eastern European satellites. Though not representative by any measure, the range of material assembled here covers a span of countries and continents, regions and topics, and collectively demonstrates the specificities of local responses to the introduction of market activities in the tumultuous last decade of the twentieth century. It is this broad span, combined with the focus specifically on 'the market', that differentiates this volume from the other collections on postsocialism that have appeared in recent years (Buckley 1997; Burawoy and Verdery 1999; Berdahl et al. 2000). Furthermore, unlike the literature in political science (e.g. Mau 1996; Urban 1997), sociology (e.g. Stark and Bruszt 1998; Szelenyi and Costello 1996) or economics (e.g. Boycko et al. 1995; Sachs 1993), this book takes an anthropological approach, and therefore differs in its contribution from the kinds of works that have dominated in Soviet and post-Soviet studies. Anthropologists specialize in long-term, on-the-ground, multi-stranded and reflexive research. Rather than analysis of statistics, mass surveys or interviews with elites, anthropologists tend to deal with the ordinary people in a wide variety of walks of life, including the marginal and dispossessed, and the resulting research confirms the rich insights this intensive, context-sensitive approach is able to offer (e.g. Mandel 2001; Hann 2001).

In this introduction we have placed 'the market' in inverted commas because a simple and common understanding of this concept cannot be taken for granted. There is no 'market' that exists outside and beyond the particular forms of it that appear in historical circumstances in particular countries and cultures (Dilley 1992). The specific version of the market introduced in the early 1990s, under the influence not only of American but also of indigenous economists attracted to Western liberalism (Lloyd 1996) became known as 'shock-therapy'. This doctrine emphasized rapid privatization, the freeing of prices, withdrawal of subsidies, and free trade, as distinct from state-supported and more regulated varieties of capitalism. What is often forgotten, however, is that this version of 'the market' did not land on unoccupied ground. In all the former-socialist countries, including even remote areas of the former Soviet Union, the 'market' was introduced into societies where there were already a variety of entrepreneurial or profit-oriented practices of one kind or another. Some of these were legal and had had a long-standing existence within the overarching state-run economy, as in Hungary (Lampland 1995). Others were illegal, like the underground workshops and racketeering activities that operated in Russia (Humphrey 1999b). And Gorbachev's *perestroika*, which began in the mid-1980s and enabled the emergence of a widespread, rapaciously commercial cooperative movement, also created a foreground of everyday economic practices that 'the market' had to encounter. In other words, we are not dealing simply with the clash of two mutually alien economic systems, 'the market' and 'the socialist planned economy', but with a much more complex encounter of a number of specific, culturally-embedded, and practical organizational forms.

The Market in Everyday Life

One phenomenon that emerges from the research presented here is a common set of complaints and reactions to the new economic and social challenges. These focus on the unfairness of economic differentiation and anger directed at 'the state' for its inability to provide services taken for granted in socialist times. Interestingly however, despite these common reactions, the countries that once shared a single socio-economic template are increasingly coming to diverge from one another (Kandiyoti 1996, 1998, and forthcoming). For example, some of the new Central Asian states have assumed highly authoritarian forms, complete with a near absence of civil rights or press freedom, and beset by new and widespread impoverishment, rising mortality rates, pervasive corruption and, in some cases, personality cults of their presidents. On the other hand, many of the countries of Central and Eastern Europe have experienced the vicissitudes of struggling proto-democracies. They face profound economic and political challenges, to be sure, but all the same have moved in an unambiguously 'Western' direction, so much so that they are applying for membership in the European Union. It is likely that the candidacies of Hungary, Poland, and the Czech Republic will be considered seriously in the near future.

Given these contrasting directions a persistent and implicit question necessarily arises from all these chapters: how long will it be tenable to speak of, write of, think of a category called 'postsocialism'? Given the quite substantively differing paths these countries took during the 1990s, the time has come already when to speak of 'postsocialist' processes and practices one must carefully qualify the context and content in question.

Despite these uncertain future trajectories, we feel that the 1990s represented a critical period that does have a certain unity. It was during this period that people living in these new states experienced the withdrawal of state surveillance and the collapse of accustomed social (as well as economic) institutions, while at the same time being brought face-to-face with the exigencies of a hard-edged variety of 'the market'. Of course, they were not alone in this. It was not just in the postsocialist countries that new junctures of globalization, the accountancy culture, and down-sizing took drastic effect. This is why the particular trajectories of the former socialist societies are so relevant for social scientists concerned with the pasts, presents and futures of political economies in general. It is with the aim of contributing to such discussions that these chapters have been brought together, illuminating as they do certain common themes emanating from postsocialist social spaces, despite the perhaps increasingly disparate realities these fascinatingly different places represent.

Thematic concerns

The chapters in this book address the priorities iterated endlessly by international development agencies and organizations active in the region (e.g. IMF, World Bank, USAID, DFID, EBRD, Soros), the multinational investors (e.g. international oil and gas companies), and myriad observers (media, academic, OSCE). These include privatization and decollectivization, inflation, unemployment, poverty, and alternative economic employment (notably in Chapters 9–11 by Perotta, Sneath and Shreeves, respectively), new work ethics (Czeglédy in Chapter 8 and Kaneff in Chapter 3), civil society and new patterns of consumption (Rausing in Chapter 7 and Drazin in Chapter 6), and entrepreneurship (Heyat in Chapter 2 and Pine in Chapter 5). However, anthropological insights on these exacting issues and processes depart in important ways from the macro-levels of analysis and description normally found in media, grey-literature reports, and the like. Furthermore, they introduce other themes not generally considered in the development literature, such as the ways in which ethnic identity and national affiliations can have an impact on economic activity (Rausing; also Watts in Chapter 4).

The anthropological contribution can upend commonly expressed and explained economic relations. Instead of studies of transactional outcomes abstracted from historical time and social context, an anthropological perspective may point out the importance of long-standing and culturally specific patterns of economic activity. Existing socially-constituted practices, such as the sexual division of labour, ethnic work specialization, or local entrepreneurial traditions, may significantly affect the way in which the postsocialist 'market' is encountered and engaged with. Our first four chapters take this approach, with each individually also touching upon other issues.

Deema Kaneff's Chapter 3 shows the explicitly ideological nature of market activity. Engagement in the market is not a moral-free activity but given value through the political-economic context in which it operates. In contrasting two women, Maria and Grigora, Kaneff looks at different ways in which sellers view their own participation in market trading – as either a shameful practice or one conferring pride. These different moral positions expressed by kin engaged in the same activity are rooted in an individual's location with respect to 'production' and 'work' – both terms having undergone revalorization since the 1989 postsocialist reforms. For Maria, once an official who upheld a work ethic grounded in state production, market trading was a shameful act with which she still does not feel totally comfortable, though one in which she engages as a coping strategy – her state pension no longer is sufficient. Her mother, never involved in political life to the same degree as her daughter, finds engagement in the market a cause for pride, as household production is much more central to her own identity.

Similarly, contrasting ideologies and moralities are at the root of Pine's study of the Górale of southeast Poland. A population tracing their roots to transhumant Vlachs, they operated as petty traders and international migrants in the socialist period. Their understanding of money, value and labour contrasts with that of their more sedentary neighbours. Money per se is not viewed negatively by Górale; rather, it is the provenance of money that is valorized. For the Górale the salient distinction is shown to be between different types of labour and exchange, producing differently valorized types of money. Pine describes how during the socialist period money and labour articulated with Górale beliefs about the primacy of the household and their hostility to the state. Earnings from entrepreneurial practices or from economic migration were liable to be displayed proudly; on the other hand, earnings associated with waged labour, dependency and inequality – all characteristic of state-related labour – were disvalued. A tension emerges in Górale ideology, namely the opposition between a collective morality of the house and community, and individual autonomy and individualism. In a persuasive account, Pine suggests a parallel in the contrast between capitalism and communism and how those of the Górale community integrate the two in practice if not in ideology. However, the situation shifted, and after a period in the early 1990s 'when everything seemed to be out of focus, in reverse or slightly wrong' the Górale have changed their attitude toward the state and money. Always politically charged, money, and the commodities for which they can be exchanged, now have assumed a new inflection. Instead of the state, the new focus of their hostility has become the Western business and governments operating in Poland. Foreign money, once prized, has assumed negative associations, and Polish złoty are explicitly preferred, still reflecting an anxiety about autonomy, but at a different level and scale from earlier. Now fears expressed are concerned with economic and cultural encroachment from the West. Thus for Górale, money, always heavily social, has also become national.

As with Pine's case, Watts's study describes a group who maintained an alternative, viable value and moral system throughout the socialist period. In Watts's analysis of new entrepreneurs in Archangelsk in northern Russia, a region inhabited by a distinctive group of Russians known as Pomors, he demonstrates precisely the unique perspective and insights an anthropological study can offer. Disputing the findings of standard political accounts and opinion surveys on the one hand, and the dead end of culturalist-reductionism on the other, he shows that a more nuanced understanding of indigenous notions, symbols and practices of entrepreneurship, historically contextualized, can lead to quite different conclusions. Drawing on historical studies of the region, he traces the mytho-ethnogenesis adhered to by the Pomors and seen not only in their own expressive culture but also in works written about them over the past centuries. The Pomors, having achieved a reputation as self-sufficient fishermen and entrepreneurs in Tsarist times, experienced a devastating transformation of their way of life with the Soviet Revolution. Condemned as 'primitive' on the one hand, and 'petty bourgeois' and 'kulak exploiters' on the other, they, like so many others, suffered appallingly under Stalinism. After their rehabilitation under Gorbachev they, along with the rest of the country, experienced the shocks of post-Communist Party rule.

Again, as in pre-Revolutionary times, a new entrepreneurialism has taken hold in the region. However, unlike the imagery of the pre-Revolutionary pomor entrepreneurs, whose pride derived from their industrious independence, having 'pulled themselves up by their own bootstraps', the postsocialist entrepreneurial variant has been the notorious New Russians. Their entrepreneurial success derives not from hard work, but from the social capital accumulated during the Soviet period – their already existing networks and connections. The former Party and State nomenklatura, undaunted by the new market order, instead exploited it, capturing for themselves the state resources in the privatization sweepstakes. In some regions of the former Soviet Union, this practice has been cynically termed *prikhvatizatsia* (from the Russian word *prikhvatit'* 'to grab'), a play on the Russian word for privatization, *privatizatsia*. Watts describes the negative popular reactions to the instant windfalls gained by an elite few, an attitude informed partially by a perception that the nouveau wealth was not *productive* – the pre-Revolutionary local magnates had given back to the region with their mills, factories, shipping fleets and railroads. Thus, not totally unlike the Gorale analysed by Pine, wealth was differentially valorized depending on its source and the labour associated with it. Meanwhile, the term and concept *khozyain* has undergone redefinition. An interesting polysemy has taken hold, as it refers both to literal ownership in a privatized sense and also to valued personal qualities, such as wisdom, fairness and stewardship – the very things denied the new *khozyains*.

Entrepreneurialism is again the theme in Farideh Heyat's Chapter 2, a historically informed portrayal of current market opportunities in the context of an Islamic society. Heyat analyses the activities of women entrepreneurs in post-Soviet Azerbaijan and the changing social values that surround them. Women had always played some role in Azeri trade, which was a respected profession in pre-Revolutionary times, usually as assistants to the male members of their families. During the Soviet period, however, trade was ideologically associated with 'speculation', and became a despised activity, especially by contrast with the high value then accorded to the intellectual professions. This meant that petty trade, which was mostly located in the market area of Kubinka in the capital city of Baku, was denigrated and hidden, carried out largely by women in nearby private apartments. This pattern continues in post-Soviet times. It is still dominated by women and still considered somewhat shameful, while the more prestigious sphere of large-scale business (i.e., well-capitalized and multinational concerns linked to government interests) is dominated by men. Yet this division of 'the market' into two gendered spheres may change, as some women are now penetrating into big business and there is a growing mid-level of market activity (street stalls, services such as hairdressing, etc.) in which Azeri women are visible. Condemnation of economically-active Azeri women is lessening, for a number of reasons, such as the absence of many Azeri men searching for jobs elsewhere, the impact of Western media portrayals of independent women, and the growing social acknowledgement of the importance of women's incomes to family budgets.

The advent of 'the market' has brought sudden changes in the field of consumption, and this is the theme of our second section. Not only what is consumed, but also people's attitudes to the whole set of activities that comprise consumption are in the process of transformation. These range from urban shoppers' strategies concerning price and value to the decisions of the poor about whether to buy something or produce it oneself. With the end of socialist distributional methods, in which consumption was closely aligned to allocation (Humphrey 1995), people are now suddenly presented with far greater choice, and here the shift in the values and signification of iconic markers of goods has been particularly evident. This is not simply a matter of the 'reading' of brand names along with the fantasies displayed by advertisers, but involves the active articulation of such signs with the pre-existing (and new) social practices that are involved in the encounter with marketed goods.

Adam Drazin (Chapter 6) and Sigrid Rausing (Chapter 7) focus on this aspect of consumption, the former in a provincial Romanian town, the latter on a former collective farm in Estonia. Drazin's study of Romanian domesticity brings together themes of gender relations as well as the gendering of the materiality of the home itself. The ethnographic analysis addresses the deeper cultural meanings attached to the ideal of the household, for example in hunting for pernicious invading domestic moths which symbolize dirt and disorder attacking from outside and threatening the home. Yet the changes in postsocialist attitudes to, and practices of, cleaning and decorating the home are also shown to be related to international markets and influences. The direct-selling organization Amway, peddling a range of hitherto unseen cleaning products – both personal and household – has penetrated into provincial Romania, along with foreign magazines and catalogues. Drazin demonstrates how such products and ideas, associated with modernity and progress, can be understood in one sense as transforming the domestic interior but in another as still related to the socialist period, when similar practices were employed but using different products and with different symbolic connotations. He shows thus that the work of cleaning is historically and socially situated, and he argues that it 'works' in provincial Romania today as a re-interpretation of the past. The symbol of cleanliness is explored in its full polysemic range of meanings and, as these meanings shift, we learn how public and private techniques of cleanliness are transmitted intergenerationally.

In her suggestive study, Rausing's keen eye is turned on the local symbols of the West, the concept of 'normality', and its relation with Western consumer goods. She analyses the pivotal role played by Western consumer products in the process of what the people of this depressed region of Estonia envision as a 'return to normality'. An explanation is needed for the patterns of consumption Rausing discovers, as people are spending far beyond their means in order to acquire a brand name and foreign packaging. The concept of the 'normal', she argues, is related to the very notion of 'Estonian-ness', which with all its attendant characteristics is situated in direct opposition to 'Russian-ness'. In other words, consumption is shown here not to be simply a matter of the satisfaction of individual desire, but is implicated in issues of collective identity and national aspiration. Importantly, Rausing criticizes the simplistic conclusions others so easily proffer, namely that a certain deliberate agency on the part of Estonians either located them in a newly achieved postmodernity or, simply by virtue of their equation of 'normality' with Western goods, guided their trajectory automatically towards neoglobalization. Rather, their pattern of consumption reflected a very conscious articulation with their Russian/Soviet past; this is the source animating the complex layers of normalcy, normative, and normalizing practice in this region.

Czeglédy's Chapter 8, by contrast, presents an account of the basically outward-looking orientation of people involved in the introduction of a Western-type institution into Hungary, the fast-food restaurant. One useful aspect of this chapter is that it analyses market innovation not only from the point of view of consumers but also from that of the people involved in manufacturing and selling the new products. Czeglédy shows that there was a traditional concept of fast-food in Hungary, which, although it was produced domestically rather than industrially, may have facilitated the acceptance of the new Americanized variants. The Yankee Chicken chain allowed its licensees to adopt deep-fried, breaded recipes that suited existing local tastes. The transformative effect of 'the market' in this case was more evident in social organization than in eating habits. Notably, the new restaurants changed labour practices and attitudes to customer service. By circulating work tasks in the kitchen and service areas, not only was it possible to relieve the stress and boredom of repetitive, high-pressure work, but also the restaurants were able to counteract the tendency to establish status hierarchies of labour. So, despite the persistence of earlier gender stereotypes (men in production, women in customer service), the chain was able to generate new attitudes to employer-employee relations and a certain enthusiasm for inter-nationalized commercial enterprise as a way of earning a living. This success, Czeglédy suggests, is related to the popular imagination of 'Amerika', and the way that fast-food – both in its status-signifying packaging and in its ability to become emblematic of a more youthful and democratic society – directs Hungarians' gaze outward, toward the arena of international shared culture.

With the final section of the book, the chapters take on the issues raised by the institutional transformations brought about by, or necessary to, the operation of 'the market'. The debate on whether 'shock therapy' has succeeded or failed, whether it is a species of 'economic vandalism' and 'soft imperialism' or a necessary painful transition to an economic turnaround, may not be quite over.[2] But it is generally acknowledged that even where it has been undertaken only partially, as in the Ukraine and Russia, the result has been immensely increased poverty in agricultural regions (for regional comparisons see Bridger 1997; Humphrey 1999a). The introduction of 'the market' in its shock-therapy guise crucially involved the elimination of collective and state-funded institutions and their replacement with privatized variants, and this involved not only shops and services, but also institutions in social life, from clubs to crèches. It is because none of these institutions can be seen simply as economic units that anthropological insights into the ways they constituted social relations and intertwined with local values is so important. The ways in which people now engage with their market replacements, and deal with the gaps where there are no replacements, are the direct consequence of such involvements.

The privatized market variants also are the subject of Rosamund Shreeves's Chapter 11. She casts her eye on the effects of decollectivization of a former *kolkhoz* on gendered practices, showing that women and men are apt to stand in different positions in relation to the retraction of the state and the advent of the market. Through careful historical and ethnographic attention Shreeves shows precisely the ways in which women have become particularly vulnerable, as market reform in the agricultural sector has forced them out of the labour market and into the domestic domain. Moreover, she describes how Kazakh family obligations and expectations come into sharp conflict with new bottom-line priorities, further disadvantaging women, who are discouraged from active participation in new economic ventures. But the new market order and its celebration of the new 'hero-entrepreneurs' who are supposed to conquer the market proves traumatic for men, as it is an all but unachievable fantasy, nurtured in part by local media (Mandel, in press). This creates a situation where rural men are unable to perform the expected masculinity. Ironically, unexpected continuities emerge, stemming from the socialist modes of rural economy to today. The 'rural gender contract' associates men with the 'outside' and women with the 'inside' economy, linking men with market production and women with subsistence and the domestic domain. Finally, Shreeves illustrates how the macro-economic and local models misrecognize the value of women's work, in terms of both their actual contribution to production and the added value of their reproductive labour, raising critical questions concerning women's property rights, the formal recognition of their labour, and access to resources. Along with other recent work considering implications for gender of postsocialist transformations (e.g. Gal and Kligman 2000a and 2000b; Pine 1998; Buckley 1997; Kandiyoti 2001) Shreeves's research begins to address what until recently has been a lacuna in the study of postsocialist societies.

Chapter 10 by David Sneath, 'Mongolia in the "Age of the Market"', addresses the Euro-American concepts and values underlying the market reforms and development discourse. He contrasts these ideas (for example, that the economy should be separate from political structures, that it is necessary to introduce private property, and that economic actors should be envisaged as individuals rather than collectivities) with the concepts of the Mongols. The latter are more holistic and combine economic and political categories. Sneath demonstrates how the Mongolian concepts (for example about custodial property) were related to the pastoral political-economy at different historical periods. He argues that pastoralism operates best with common, as distinct from private, rights to land, and that this fact makes it difficult – and even in many situations inadvisable – for Mongolians to adopt a private property regime. During the Soviet-dominated period the merging of political and economic structures and the presence of common property were maintained, so the present 'age of the market' is attempting to overturn deeply ingrained practices that have worked reasonably well in different political regimes. Sneath explains in detail why the market reforms have resulted in widespread poverty and unemployment in Mongolia. Importantly, he shows how the reforms were undertaken without regard for the non-market state-organized institutional structures that had sustained the transfer of agricultural and pastoral products to the large urban population. 'The market' has not managed to create viable alternatives either for these crucial links or for the large-scale (recently collective) organizations that enabled the production of a sufficient amount of meat, grain, etc. to feed the population as a whole. Mongolia is now dependent on aid and imports in spheres where it was earlier self-sufficient.

If Sneath's work addresses the disjunction between 'shock therapy' and indigenous concepts of economic life, Louise Perrotta in Chapter 9 provides a detailed study of its effects on rural society in the Ukraine. Perrotta's work is a rare example of a study that attempts both quantitative and qualitative analysis. In some ways her message is the opposite of that found in Sneath, since she documents the inadequacy of maintaining large-scale collectives in the current economic situation. Focusing on household incomes, she shows that the attempt to retain collective-type farms with large workforces has resulted in the insolvency of these enterprises, and consequently their inability to pay wages and the unwillingness of people to provide labour in them. Households suffer at the same time from the problems described by Sneath (drastic price rises, debt, and the difficult of marketing small surpluses). Perrotta describes the retreat to subsistence farming on small plots, and shows how and why it is almost impossible for households to develop new small businesses, a ploy which might otherwise have been a solution. The present situation in many agricultural regions of the Ukraine is unsustainable, she argues. There is a disaster waiting to happen, possibly even threatening famine unless there are significant changes in policy and practice.

Conclusion

This volume explores some common experiences of the market and reactions to it. From these discussions, as well as earlier publications (Humphrey 1999a, 1999b; Bruno 1998), we can see how the category called 'the market' has in practice differentiated into spheres of different scale (international chains and joint ventures; large indigenous businesses; wholesale and mid-range retail shops; kiosks and shuttle trade; street selling and reselling by non-professionals). Such marketing patterns mirror the economic differentiation of the population, which has markedly increased throughout the former socialist world. At the same time, though in different degree in various countries, market enterprises are involved with 'protection' and racket businesses, to the extent that state security has declined. All of this has given rise to common anxieties and (in many places) anger, as accustomed channels of provision to ordinary people have melted away.

It is well known that during socialist times political and economic structures were indissolubly tied together. Now it seems that they may be splitting apart, in that the complex economic consequences of the reforms (for example of privatization) appear to be evolving in their own unpredicted directions. This is where the different countries studied here provide evidence of diverse trajectories. Poland, Hungary, Kazakhstan and Mongolia undertook similar policies in the 1990s (radical privatization, freeing of prices, withdrawal of state subsidies) yet the consequences have been very different. As Sneath's Chapter 10 indicates, changes of government in Mongolia, from socialist to democratic and back to a variant of socialist again, have been unable to halt the deepening economic crisis unleashed by the initial 'reforms'. Meanwhile, Perrotta's material shows that a different policy in the Ukraine, which retained collectives and preserved bankrupt enterprises through (minimal) state subsidies, has resulted in an equally disastrous growth of poverty. Undoubtedly any persuasive explanation for such unforeseen patterns would be extremely complex and would have to take account of macroeconomic factors that lie beyond the scope of this book. Yet a part of the explanation must lie with the everyday practices of ordinary people participating in the economy according to their own priorities, social pressures and values. It is at this level that we hope this book can make a contribution. The studies presented here show that people take part in 'the market' as social persons, that they are already participating in a variety of relations (with families and household members, friends, workmates, bosses, administrators and officials, and so forth). In this sense, we cannot support the idea that 'economics' has split away from 'politics', for relational persons are inevitably also political actors and subjects in whatever power relations surround them. As Kaneff argues, 'the market' itself may be experienced as having brought a reduction in economic freedom as compared with the state-dominated system of socialist times. In other words, a new economic system can appear as (and therefore in effect be) a regime of power. But as these chapters show, it is not only the politics that is involved in the practices that make up market actualities.

Thus we see from Heyat (Chapter 2) and Watts (Chapter 4) how locally specified historical identities, and also ethnicity, can be a factor in the social input to marketing. Closely linked to ethnicity is the way that *identity* is formed in contradistinction to other groups. Here Rausing (Chapter 7) paper argues that negative contrasts with Soviet Russians and positive identifications with Scandinavia have been central to the sense of identity of people in northeast Estonia that informs their consumption patterns. Sneath (Chapter 10) shows how Mongolian *indigenous concepts of property* have conflicted with those introduced by international economists, subverting privatization programmes. Meanwhile, Pine (Chapter 5), Kaneff (Chapter 3) and Czeglédy (Chapter 8) show how yet another 'cultural factor', *local understandings of labour as distinct from commerce*, have interacted positively or negatively as the case may be with 'the market' in those regions. It is clear from several of these chapters that *gender constructs* are deeply involved in each of these social spheres. Though some of the articles do not deal with gender directly, it is evident that it is an integral part of the social determination of who takes part in trading and in what manner (Heyat), on the ideational forms of identity (Watts) and common property (Sneath), and on labour hierarchies (Czeglédy). Finally, we could mention *areas of culture usually neglected in economic analyses*, such as ideas of privacy, cleanliness and idealized 'modernity' (Drazin, Chapter 6), ideas of 'a normal life' (Rausing), local conceptualizations of social distance (Kaneff), or the fantasy of 'Amerika' (Czeglédy), that interact with identity and gender to influence the ways in which ordinary people react and contribute to 'the market'. And perhaps we should be more specific, for that is the nature of ethnography. These 'cultural factors' influence how people set their prices (Kaneff), how they address customers (Czeglédy), what they choose to buy (Drazin), how they calculate what income consists of (Perrotta Chapter 9), and how they work in market settings (Heyat). A myriad of economic decisions and practices are influenced by such matters, and it behoves us to try to understand them as they contribute to the abstraction we call 'the postsocialist economy'.

Notes

1. For discussion of the situation in the various countries of Central and Eastern Europe and Russia, see Lampland 1995, Verdery 1996.
2. For an example of this debate, see John Lloyd's 1996 argument with Peter Gowan in *New Left Review*, 216, 119–40.

References

Berdahl, D., Lampland, M. and Bunzl, M. (eds) (2000), *Altering States: Ethnographies of Transition in Eastern Europe and the Former Soviet Union*, Ann Arbor: University of Michigan Press.

Boycko, M., Shleifer, A. and Vishny, R. (1995), *Privatizing Russia*, Cambridge, Mass.: MIT Press.

Bridger, S. (1997), 'Rural women and the impact of economic change', in M. Buckley (ed.), *Post-Soviet Women: from the Baltic to Central Asia*, Cambridge: Cambridge University Press.

Bridger, S. and Pine, F. (eds) (1998) *Surviving post-socialism: local strategies and regional responses in eastern Europe and the former Soviet Union*, London: Routledge.

Bruno, M. (1998) 'Playing the Cooperation Game', in Bridger and Pine, pp. 170–87.

Buckley, M. (ed.) (1997), *Post-Soviet Women: from the Baltic to Central Asia*, Cambridge: Cambridge University Press.

Burawoy, M. and Verdery, K. (eds) (1999), *Uncertain Transition: Ethnographies of Change in the Postsocialist World*, Oxford: Rowman & Littlefield.

Dilley, R. (ed.) (1992), *Contesting Markets*, Edinburgh: Edinburgh University Press.

Gal, S. and Kligman, G. (2000a), *The Politics of Gender after Socialism*, Princeton: Princeton University Press.

Gal, S. and Kligman, G. (eds) (2000b), *Reproducing Gender: Politics, Pulics and Everyday Life after Socialism*, Princeton: Princeton University Press.

Gowan, P. (1996), 'Eastern Europe, Western power and neo-liberalism', *New Left Review*, 216: 120–40.

Hann, C. (ed) (2001), *Postsocialism: Ideals, Ideologies and Practices in Europe and Asia*, London: Routledge.

Humphrey, C. (1995), 'Creating a culture of disillusionment: consumption in Moscow 1993, a chronicle of changing times', in D. Miller (ed.), *Worlds Apart*, London: Routledge.

—— (1998), *Marx Went Away, But Karl Stayed Behind*, Ann Arbor: University of Michigan Press.

—— (1999a), 'Traders, "disorder", and citizenship regimes in provincial Russia', in M. Burawoy and K. Verdery (eds), *Uncertain Transition: Ethnographies of Change in the Postsocialist World*, Oxford: Rowman and Littlefield.

—— (1999b), 'Russian protection rackets and the appropriation of law and order', in J.M. Heyman (ed.), *States and Illegal Practices*, Oxford: Berg.

Kandiyoti, D. (1996), 'Modernization without the market? The case of the "Soviet East",' *Economy and Society*, 5(4), 529–42.

—— (1998) 'Rural livelihoods and social networks in Uzbekistan: perspectives from Andijan', *Central Asian Survey*, Special Issue on Market Reforms, social dislocations and survival in post-Soviet Central Asia, eds D. Kandiyoti and R. Mandel, 17(4), 560–78.

—— (2001), 'How far do analyses of postsocialism travel?', in Chris Hann (ed.), *Post-socialism: Ideals, Ideologies and Practices in Europe and Asia*, London: Routledge.

Lampland, M. (1995), *The Object of Labour: Commodification in Socialist Hungary*, Chicago: University of Chicago Press.

Lloyd, J. (1996), 'Eastern reformers and Neo-Marxist reviewers', *New Left Review*, 216: 119–28.

Mandel, R. (in press), 'A Marshall Plan for the Mind: The Political Economy of a Kazakh Soap Opera', in L. Abu-Lughod, F. Ginsburg and B. Larkin (eds), *The Social Practice of Media*, Berkeley: University of California Press.

—— (2001), 'Seeding Civil Society', in C. Hann (ed.), *Post-socialism: Ideals, Ideologies and Practices in Europe and Asia*, London: Routledge.

Mau, V. (1996), *The Political History of Economic Reform in Russia, 1985–1994*, London: Centre for Research into Communist Economies.

Pine, F. (1996), '"The cows and pigs are his, the eggs are mine": women's domestic economy and entrepreneurial activity in rural Poland', in C.M. Hann (ed.), *Socialism: Ideals, Ideologies and Local Practice*, London: Routledge.

Pine, F. (1998), 'Dealing with fragmentation: the consequences of privatization for rural women in central and southern Poland', S. Bridger and F. Pine (eds), *Surviving Post-Socialism: Local Strategies and Regional Responses in Eastern Europe and the former Soviet Union*, London: Routledge.

Sachs, J. (1993), *Poland's Jump to the Market Economy*, Cambridge, Mass.: MIT Press.

Stark, D. and Bruszt, L. (1998), *Postsocialist Pathways: Transforming Politics and Property in East Central Europe*, Cambridge: Cambridge University Press.

Stewart, M. (1996), 'Gypsies, the work ethic, and Hungarian socialism', in C.M. Hann (ed.), *Socialism: Ideals, Ideologies and Local Practice*, London: Routledge.

Szelenyi, I. and Costello, E. (1996), 'The Market Transition Debate: Toward a Synthesis', *American Journal of Sociology*, 101(4), January, 1082–96.

Urban, M. (with V. Igrunov and S. Mitrokhin) (1997), *The Rebirth of Politics in Russia*, Cambridge: Cambridge University Press.

Part I
Trading Cultures, Market Ambiguity and Historical Transformation

–2–

Women and the Culture of Entrepreneurship in Soviet and Post-Soviet Azerbaijan

Farideh Heyat

The mechanisms involved in transition to a market economy, the process of privatization, and the evolving business culture in Azerbaijan bear many parallels to, as well as some distinctions from, those in other FSU republics. This situation is also reflected in women's entrepreneurial activities and their participation in the transition economy. The introduction of the market, as in the other republics, has given rise to a strongly male-dominated business environment. In this environment, given the breakdown of the welfare system, high rates of unemployment, and drastic cuts in income levels for many women, as indeed for men, engagement in entrepreneurial activities has been more of a survival strategy than an informed choice. This is as much true for the village women lining the streets of Baku offering fresh produce as it is for those running stalls with clothes, cosmetics, footwear, and other personal consumables imported individually in what is euphemistically called the 'suitcase trade'.

Higher up the economic ladder, some of the professional women, and others with access to capital through their husbands, fathers or lovers, have engaged in business activities ranging from lending out and brokering high-interest loans, to wholesale imports of consumables, and provision of educational and cultural services. But many spheres of commercial activity such as import/export of industrial goods and raw materials, ownership of leisure facilities and stores, construction business, transportation, and factory production are not open to women entrepreneurs. Their operations are closely controlled by power groups in league with top state officials. Since independence in Azerbaijan, access to sizeable capital and ownership of newly privatized companies have been mostly attained by those previously holding high- ranking positions in the Communist Party, the regional soviets, or the state-run distribution and retail sector. With Heidar Aliev's accession to power in 1993, his extended family and those of his associates in key posts are the latest category of the new rich. More generally, in Azerbaijan today the political elite largely overlaps with the economic elite, a pattern not so different from that of the late Soviet period. Hence the wealthiest sector in the country includes not only those in charge of privatization programmes and major industries, in particular oil and cotton, but also many of the public prosecutors and heads of law enforcement in key regions, as well as leading members of the parliament and the government.

Direct political power has always been, and still is, mainly a male prerogative. Networks of corruption and large-scale informal dealings in the economy have also been a masculine domain, organized through male patronage and kinsmen. This is not to say that there are no women near the top of the political pyramid. One of Aliev's four presidential advisors and two of his cabinet ministers are women, some of whom have been accumulating small fortunes in their own right. Nevertheless, a strongly patriarchal ethos governs the world of big business in Azerbaijan. The women of the new economic elite are very much identified with the domestic arena, in charge of the family affairs, organizing lavish hospitality at home, and running a busy social life. While daughters are still encouraged to attain university education up to the post-graduate level (a legacy of the Soviet system), in the present circumstances of pitiful wages, outside employment is considered economically meaningless and not sought after. Instead, wealth and social status for these women is derived directly from fathers and husbands. In the small- to medium-sized business sector, on the other hand, there is active involvement of women, either as partners to their husbands or in their own right as single, divorced or widowed women.

This chapter examines the cultural values associated with entrepreneurship, and its gendered dimension, in Soviet and post-Soviet Azerbaijan.[1] It discusses some of the ways in which Azeri women are engaged in entrepreneurial activities, and how this relates to their involvement in the alternative economy in the Soviet era. It shows that, just as Azeri women's closer association with domestic life afforded them greater cover for the observance of religious practice, a high degree of domesticity also facilitated their involvement in the underground supply of consumer goods and informal trading. This was in turn reinforced by the gendered cultural division of labour in the Soviet Azeri society. In the post-Soviet market economy, women entrepreneurs have to contend with a strongly male-oriented business culture, in addition to problems of deep-rooted corruption and lack of supportive legal framework. Nevertheless, many women have been successful in establishing small businesses in the trade and service sectors. This has been facilitated by changes in Azeri women's employment patterns and public activities brought on by the departure of women of other ethnic communities (Russians and Armenians), coupled with the prevailing Western cultural influences.

Women's role in underground trading in the Soviet era

In Azerbaijan up until the oil-related industrialization of the late nineteenth century, trading (*tijarat*) was the most predominant and high-status profession among urban Azeris. This related to the region's strategic position on the trade routes between Iran, Turkey, Russia, and Central Asia. In Baku, the oil centre of the Russian Empire, Muslim Azeris dominated the commercial sector, though they formed less than 40 per cent of the city's population (Altstadt 1992). The pre-Soviet ethnic Azeri culture was marked by a strong tradition of entrepreneurship. Among the women, despite the Islamic prescription on their seclusion and veiling, involvement in entrepreneurial activity was not uncommon. This was especially the case at the village level and among wealthy widows. A rare ethnography of pre-Soviet Azeri women revealed: 'If village men come to town to sell they bring their wives with them to oversee the transaction. When women are buying they count very precisely and it is very hard to cheat them' (Zakharov 1894). Interestingly, this is also the pattern today, but more often village women come to town unaccompanied and sell their fresh produce directly, huddled in groups along the street pavements.

Following the Soviet revolution and collectivization in the countryside, individual trading was mostly banned. Then in the aftermath of the Second World War a second-hand market was established in a large square in Baku, called Kubinka. To ease the severe shortages, individuals were permitted to set up stalls offering used goods for exchange. However in the following few years transactions in this market increasingly involved cash payments and sales of new goods, including imported cigarettes and alcoholic drinks. The authorities then closed down the market in 1953. But this did not stop unofficial dealings in the area. A black market in consumer goods continued to operate from individuals' homes in the surrounding streets and alleyways. In the 1960s with growing affluence in the republic and the economic development that accompanied the post-war reconstruction and post-Stalin liberalisation, this Kubinka trading flourished, as described below.

For Azeri women, who had by now entered paid employment, en masse, there was increased purchasing power. Western fashions were being introduced through access to the Russian media, in particular women's magazines (McAndrew 1985), and greater ease of travel to Eastern Europe where consumer goods were more readily available. Consequently, ideas of modernity, *muasirlik*, were associated with one's pattern of consumption and styles of personal wear, as well as with the liberalization in gender and inter-generational relations. Generally in Soviet society, acquisition of Western goods by the elite and their association with power and privilege became a marker of elite identity. But the majority of professional women with financial means did not have access to hard currency stores reserved for the Party elite and had to resort to the black market in imported goods. A number of my women informants reported episodes of great planning, effort, and manoeuvrings in the past to clandestinely purchase items of prestigious foreign-made clothing, footwear, and accessories. This was done either by locating the appropriate suppliers across Baku through one's personal network, or a trip to the Kubinka district. Here dealers, normally boys and men, would be cruising the streets in search of customers who would then be directed to a nearby home where the desired goods were on sale by their mothers or wives. Elsewhere in the city, suppliers were also very often women, operating from their home premises.

According to my informants' accounts, women and men who got involved in this form of trading (*al ver*) were those on low incomes and without higher education. The women were often housewives with a number of children and their families did not wish them to work in a factory or other industrial sites. Such establishments, with the exception of textile and food-processing outlets, were associated with the Soviet state and its female labour force with the Russians and Armenians. The service sector was also ethnically divided with regards to its female workforce. Armenians dominated skilled jobs such as dressmaking, beauticians and hairdressing, while Russian women predominated in jobs serving the public such as in catering, hotels and stores, and in the entertainment business. The Muslim Azeri community did not approve of its women serving male strangers. Even secretarial and nursing jobs were considered low-status and not particularly desirable. Private trading in consumer goods, on the other hand, entailed working from home serving women, as they were mostly in charge of the household's shopping.

The strong association between women and domesticity, reinforced by the Islamic prescription on the seclusion of women, had prevailed in the pre-Soviet culture of Azerbaijan. Following the Soviet revolution religion was denounced as a remnant of the backward past. Hence from around the mid-1920s the religious establishment was increasingly under attack and public display of religion was banned. This shifted the site of Islamic rituals from the public to the private sphere. The ceremonies of *marsiyeh*,[2] for example, could no longer be held in the mosques, the majority of which were closed down in the 1930s. Instead they were only conducted at home, organized and attended mostly by women. Another example was the wake/funerary ceremony, *yas*, which retained its religious content far more in the case of the female *yas*. These events are still sexually segregated, as is generally the Muslim custom. However, while the female *yas* has always been held at home, often in the presence of a mullah reciting from the Koran, the male *yas* was a more secular event. During the early Soviet decades when most Azeri women still did not have a public role that would expose them to the scrutiny of state officials, religious practice could be conducted by them with some impunity.

Similarly, in the later Soviet era, women's close association with domestic life could afford them a cover for involvement in the underground supply of consumer goods and informal trading. The housewife was often indeed a prime example of this activity (trader, *al verji*). At the same time there was a definite social stigma attached to such an occupation since it was an illegal activity, ideologically denounced by the state. In the public discourse the character of an *al verji* was associated with cunning, sleaze, and vulgarity. The stereotype depicted in the literature and the media was a poorly educated woman of dubious virtue, with premodern attitudes and village values.[3] The condemnation of the *spekuliant* in Russian was indeed echoed in the Soviet Azeri society in its characterisation of *al ver* (petty trade) as a demeaning occupation. But informally, as a number of my respondents confirmed, the positive side to these women was also recognised. In the words of a member of the Azerbaijan Women's Association:[4]

You had to be a smart (zirang) individual to do this kind of work. A timid and incompetent type (ajiz) could not engage in such an activity. These women needed a lot of initiative and always had to be on the look out for customers and new supplies. These would come from people returning from trips abroad, or they were goods siphoned off at the source somewhere. They had to constantly urge husbands and sons to do errands for them; to fetch and deliver goods.

Indeed the caricature of an *al verji* in the official media does not reveal the importance of this marginal group to the Soviet Azeri society given the shortages of consumer goods. In many ways their role in the alternative economy paralleled what has been described by Pine (1993) for rural Polish women whose entrepreneurial activity was elemental to the alternative domestic economy under the Communist regime.

Post-Soviet entrepreneurial activities among women

Since 1991, with the introduction of market economy in Azerbaijan, as elsewhere in the FSU (Humphrey 1998), trading activity began to replace employment in industry and agriculture as the main source of income generation. This trend has been somewhat modified since 1994–95 due to increase in investment in the oil and construction industries (constituting over 80 per cent of total investments in the country), and the subsequent spill off leading to the growth of the service sector.[5] Most consumer goods, including food, with the exception of fruit and vegetables, are imported, and the FSU republics as the suppliers have been increasingly replaced by Iran, Turkey, Syria, Dubai, and EU countries.

As mentioned earlier, women's entrepreneurial activity is mostly connected with trading, either as creditors or in the shuttle trade, or as individual sellers. On the credit side this became widespread during 1992–95, though it has subsided since the bankruptcies of 1994–95 that followed the war in Chechniya and the crash of the rouble and the *manat*. Given the highly underdeveloped banking system, small traders in this period turned mostly to individuals who were members of their personal networks for short-term loans to finance their business activities. These loans were negotiated with extremely high interest (15–20 per cent per month) and, as in the alternative Soviet economy, they were underwritten by personal trust rather than any formal contracts. In Azerbaijan major trust is only invested in one's network of close kin, neighbours, and intimate friends. Since women occupied a central position in maintaining such networks, it followed that many became actively involved in brokering short-term loans and their supply. While some had accumulated capital through their high professional positions and access to bribery, most others were handing out their small family savings to generate a supplementary income for survival.

Furthermore, since the Brezhnev era, in a similar vein to the Russian women commented on by Marta Bruno (1997), the urge to provide emotional and material support for the family pushed many women to adopt and develop broad entrepreneurial attitudes toward life. Given the shortages and the de facto low buying-power of money, women invested their efforts in constructing complicated systems of barter of goods and favours and in cultivating insider networks of knowledge and information. However, the nationalist element manifested in the Russo-centric vision of production that Bruno observes for the Russian women entrepreneurs does not seem to have a parallel among Azeri women, nor the general demeaning of commerce and trade as something not very genuine and akin to a scam (1997: 65). Nevertheless, among the Azeri intelligentsia there is a deep sense of regret at the breakdown of the productive sector and industry. As an academic Azeri friend commented, 'Look at what we have gained from getting rid of the Soviet system: our youth want nothing more than engaging in *al ver* and just getting rich. Instead of preparing engineers, scientists and managers we are becoming a nation of *al verji*'.

The derogatory connotations of the concept of *al ver*, though somewhat diluted, still persists in the present entrepreneurial climate. This is especially the case in contrast to the social category *ziyali* (academics and other highly educated members of intelligentsia) who stood at the top end of the Soviet spectrum of social status and respectability. The distinction stems from the diametrically opposed value systems associated with intellectual and commercial activity under the Soviet system. Consequently there is great embarrassment and personal dilemmas for those former academics and employees of research institutes who since the breakdown of the economy have had to resort to selling in shops or engage in the 'suitcase trade'. A typical case is that of Dilbar, a 57-year-old unmarried woman who was formerly a chemist. Since 1993 she has made a living from shuttle imports, initially food from Iran and later women's clothing from Turkey, Syria, and Dubai. Most women who engaged in this form of individual trading came from poorly educated backgrounds and no access to prestigious jobs. Many of them may have done private trading in the later Soviet period. Unlike these women and others of the younger generation who were not as deeply conditioned by the Soviet ideology, Dilbar felt rather demeaned by her new occupation and was not forthcoming about it in the early period of our acquaintance. Eventually she explained her feelings as follows.

I am not proud of what I do, it affects me badly. Here, buying and selling, al ver, is considered spekuliant *which is shameful. When I carry these big bags of clothes or whatever I am selling, and then I am travelling along or negotiating with some vulgar upstart type of woman of much lower level than myself, I really feel bad about it. Many of these women are low-level,* ashagha saviyye, *who have married wealthy men, basically thieves, who are now trading with their husbands' money. I didn't tell my family about it for some time. When my mother first heard about it she just sat down and cried. She said 'Oh my God, my daughter, a chief scientific worker. After 31 years at the university she is now involved in al ve'. My father was in the hospital for some time and we have never told him about it. But he doesn't realize that all the good care he had in the hospital from the doorman to the doctors and nurses, every step of the way I had to pay for it. How could I, an unemployed woman without an income, manage such a thing? Well, it is life, kismat [destiny], that has forced me into this. I have to help my parents who are old and needy.*

Dilbar, however, as with my other informants, drew a distinction between this form of individual trading and work in the corporate business sector which she considered a respectable occupation. Being employed by a large company with foreign connections was considered especially prestigious. Given the relatively high salaries paid by multinationals and the kudos of Western business and other organizations, secretarial work is now considered a desirable profession for a young woman. At the same time it is only open to young people from the professional and the formerly elite families, mostly in their 20s or even late teens, who have had the educational means and the family support to acquire a Western language required in such environments. What is more, such opportunities are very much confined to Baku where international organizations, foreign businesses and NGOs are concentrated. For the great majority of the population the level of salaries are far below the cost of living and have to be supplemented by a second income.

Given this economic imperative, there is great interest in entrepreneurial activity and a positive valuation of private business. In Baku, with the expansion of the service sector since the mid-1990s, there has been a proliferation of catering services (cafés, restaurants, take-aways) and personal services for women (fitness centres, beauty salons and hairdressers),[6] many of which are owned and run by women. A few enterprising women have also established larger businesses such as maternity clinics and factories producing building materials. But in the case of medium to large business ventures the question of patronage and support from someone high up the political structure is vital. Whether it is in obtaining licences, dealing with the tax authorities, or any other official dealings, utilizing personal networks and bribing the relevant officials is very often a prerequisite for the successful running of a business.

For women entrepreneurs, however, access to start-up capital and know-how is further hindered by the strongly male-dominated business culture. Obtaining credit from commercial banks is particularly difficult given the prevailing stereotype of women as street traders, or running a shuttle trade, and not suited to business management. This was confirmed by a recent survey of 1,000 women across Azerbaijan. The survey found that the great majority of the respondents (86 per cent) were unwilling to consider establishing a business, in the first place because of lack of access to initial capital and then because of their lack of knowledge about bureaucratic procedures concerning registration and running of a business.[7] In general, major monetary transactions are considered a male domain, exemplified by the common phrase '*pooldan danishmak kishinin ishi dir*' (talking money is a man's job). Even on a personal level such as purchasing an apartment, it is the man who is expected to negotiate the price. If there is no husband present, the father, brother, or brother-in-law would commonly step in to conclude a deal. Then there is the ubiquitous practice by government and municipal officials of demanding bribes. posing greater problems for women entrepreneurs as they may be more easily intimidated. Nevertheless, some shrewd business-minded women have been successful in dealing with these difficulties and have established profitable small businesses.

A good example of this is Gulnar Hassanova whose networking skills. business acumen, strong drive, and abundant energy have enabled her to succeed in establishing a profitable beauty and fitness salon for women. Gulnar is a lecturer at Baku University and in addition works for the government department for women's affairs. She is 48 and married with two children. The salon was set up in 1996 in partnership with her sister. Most of the initial capital was raised from the sale of an apartment they jointly owned. Gulnar is the overall manager and was able early on to build a sizeable clientele through her contacts, both locally and among the foreign women in Baku. She employs a staff of ten including a hairdresser, two beauticians, a masseur, and an aerobics instructor. The following is Gulnar's account of the difficulties she had to face in establishing her business.

When I first decided to set up this salon everyone warned me against it. My husband told me: we are a ziyali *family, none of us have ever been involved with business, you will not know what to do. Other people said that it would be too difficult combining the jobs I do with running this place. Or they would say: you are a woman, in every organization you contact there will be men in charge, sceptical of you managing by yourself. But I thought, if men could do it, so could I, and I began this venture with a lot of faith and enthusiasm.*

The first two years were very difficult. I had to hire and fire many of my workers. Because of the Soviet mentality, people here are not accustomed to serious hard work. They used to get paid anyway, whether they worked or not. But in the capitalist system it doesn't work that way. If somebody doesn't do their job properly you dismiss them. People say to me: but don't you feel pity, yazigh, for that person? I tell them that market economy, bazaar ekonomiyasi, is not about pity, but profits and productivity. Of course I have to provide suitable working conditions and pay adequately. At the same time, my staff have learnt that they must turn up on time and work seriously.

Then there is this problem of dealing with the municipal officials. Every few months there seems to be a change of staff and the new guys feel at liberty to come and knock on our door, demanding to investigate us. But we are not doing anything illegitimate. We abide by all the laws and regulations. We keep a high standard of hygiene. Still they keep coming and bothering us. Well, now I have found the language to deal with them. First of all I tell them that this is a women's salon and we don't welcome men in the premises. The staff know they should not let anybody snoop around the place. I deal with all the enquiries on the phone. Secondly, I have a wide network of friends and family, both myself and through my husband who works for the public prosecutor's office. If necessary I can contact somebody in charge and ask for their help. They then realize that just because I am a woman they can not easily intimidate me.

The problem is, what these guys are really after is receiving bribes. But we don't have such a big turnover in this business and cannot make payments to new officials every few months. What is more, there are a lot of unexpected expenses. For example, last year the owners of the apartment above us left the water running and went out. It caused a lot of damage to the ceilings and the walls. The repairs were a big expense. There was no compensation; we don't have an insurance system for this, and the family above could not pay anything. They are very poor, a family of six living in two rooms. Their relatives kept phoning me, asking me for forgiveness. I was very angry at first, but then thought there was no point in suing them, we were not going to get anything, anyway.

The underdeveloped state of the insurance industry in Azerbaijan and difficulties in enforcing protective legislation are in fact very significant in hindering the development of small and medium sized businesses. In many legal disputes it is often the party with greater political muscle, larger bribe, or both, who ultimately has the law on his or her side. The problem of ubiquitous corruption in Azerbaijan is indeed a legacy of the Soviet system, common to other FSU republics, further accelerated since the transition to market economy and the impact of the wealth created by the oil industry. One reason for the perpetuation of demands for bribery by public employees, commented upon by Gulnar, is the price tag often attached to a job as a state official by those in charge of the appointment. This in turn generates the need for raising an income from such employment, beyond the legitimate remuneration the employee would receive. It is a pattern that goes all the way up to the highest levels of government, but is never publicly articulated.[8]

In considering the proliferation of Azeri women's entrepreneurial activities, it is worth noting that this is taking place alongside significant changes in their employment patterns. The large-scale entry of women into the retail, catering, leisure and entertainment sector jobs reflects a degree of culture change in popular attitudes regarding female public activities. Occupations in these areas were the niche for the Russian, and to a lesser extent Armenian, women. However, since the departure of the non-indigenous ethnic communities, following the break-up of the Soviet Union, their places have been taken up by Azeri women. Although many Azeris I questioned maintained that the young women working in clubs, restaurants, hotels and places of entertainment were half-Russian, my own observations did not confirm this. The claim of a Russian descent only confirmed the still lingering Azeri community's disapproval of females serving or entertaining a male public. At the same time, the predominance of Azeri women as shop assistants and stallholders has now led to greater public approval of such employment for women, though still considered of low social status, *ashagha saviyye* (literally, 'low level').

It is clear that the transition to market economy in Azerbaijan has encompassed a whole array of social and economic changes. This is manifested most clearly in the city of Baku where the oil industry and most of the foreign community are based. In the absence of an all-encompassing state doctrine as in the past, barriers have been lifted to varied cultural influences that shape women's lives, and more generally the youth, in significant ways. The Western images of women projected through the media (especially the Russian, Turkish, and independent Azeri television channels), and contact with Westerners and travel abroad, have somewhat broadened the perceptions of feminine identity and female propriety. For example, in the city of Baku women driving cars, wearing trousers or revealing clothes, and smoking in public are far more evident today than they were a decade ago. They also call for a degree of autonomy and mobility that go beyond what was expected by women under the Soviet system. All this has been further reinforced by departure from the country of large numbers of Azeri men in search of jobs, mostly for Russia and other FSU republics (Heyat 2002).

In the 'free market' Azerbaijan of today, the changing cultural perceptions regarding women's public activity, along with the increased economic opportunities, are promoting the tradition of entrepreneurship among women. This may in time undermine the strong male bias in the business sphere that inhibits women's access to credit and training. However, what is also needed for Azeri women, as indeed for the men, to succeed in entrepreneurial activities is a more rational system of government and legal reforms that would ensure a reduction in the level of corruption in the public sector. This could in turn promote the establishment and running of efficient businesses in Azerbaijan in the years to come.

Notes

1. This chapter is based on fieldwork carried out during 1994-95, and intermittently in 1996 and 1997, initially for a PhD research, and later in the spring of 2000. All the names and some personal details regarding the informants have been altered to protect their privacy.
2. The *marsiyeh* ceremonies, held by the Shiites during the holy month of Muharram, commemorate the martyrdom of Imam Hussein, the grandson of the prophet Mohamed.
3. A prime example of such characterization of a woman *al verji* is in the play Hijran, a popular musical comedy in Azeri, regularly performed in Baku since the 1970s.
4. Prior to 1991, the Azerbaijan Women's Association was the official women's organization, affiliated to the Azerbaijan Communist Party. Following independence it changed its charter, registering as an independent charitable organization.
5. See 'Economic Trends Quarterly Issue, Azerbaijan July–September 1998', report prepared by TACIS, European Commission, Brussels.
6. The mushrooming of fitness centres and beauty salons in Baku in the late 1990s may be linked with the rapidly growing Western cultural influences in the city that promote slim fashionable looks for women, in contrast to the overweight stuffy Soviet images.

7. The survey 'Women and Economy' was carried out by the GID unit of UNDP, Azerbaijan, and SIGMA Survey Centre, 1999, to be published by Sada Nashriyyat.
8. Since the lifting of censorship in 1998–99, in an attempt to project a liberal image of the regime and gain greater acceptance from Western governments, there has been public debate on the question of *korruptsiia*, though in very general terms, in the independent non-governmental media.

References

Altstadt, A. (1992), *The Azerbaijani Turks: Power and Identity under Russian Rule*, Stanford: Hoover Institution Press.

Bruno, M. (1997), 'Women and the culture of entrepreneurship', in *Post-Soviet Women: from the Baltic to Central Asia*, Cambridge: Cambridge University Press.

Heyat, F. (2002), *Azeri Women in Transition: Women in Soviet and Post-Soviet Azerbaijan*, London: Routledge Curzon.

Humphrey, C. (1998), 'Traders, "Disorder", and Citizenship Regimes in Provincial Russia', in K. Verdery and M. Burawoy (eds) *Uncertain Transition: Ethnographies of Change in The Postsocialist World*, Lanham, MD: Rowman and Littlefield.

McAndrew, M. (1985), 'Women's Magazines in the Soviet Union', in B. Holland (ed.), *Soviet Sisterhood: British Feminists on Women in USSR*, London: Fourth Estate.

Pine, F. (1993), 'The cows and pigs are his, the eggs are mine': women's domestic economy and entrepreneurial activity in rural Poland', in C.M. Hann (ed.), *Socialism: Ideals, Ideologies, and Local Practice*, London, New York: Routledge.

Zakharov, A. (1894), 'Domashnyi i sotsialnyi byt zhenshchin u zakavkazskikh Tatar' (family and social life amongst the Tatar women of Transcaucasus), in *Sbornik materialov dlia opisaniimestnostei i plemen Kavkaza* (Collection of Writings on the People of the Caucasus), vol. 20, Kavkazki Uchebnik Okrug, Tiblisi.

The Shame and Pride of Market Activity: Morality, Identity and Trading in Postsocialist Rural Bulgaria

Deema Kaneff

One sunny but cool autumn morning in September 1997, I accompanied Maria, an inhabitant of the village Talpa, to the local markets in the district township of Nekilva, northern-central Bulgaria.[1] Standing behind the stall, sipping coffee and trying to keep warm, Maria described the shame she experienced the first time she came to the markets to sell her produce. On that first occasion in 1993 she had accompanied a friend from Talpa. They had travelled to Nekilva by bus, Maria carrying two bags of onions to sell. She recounted how on the bus she had tried to hide her produce under the seat, so that no one could see where she was bound. Walking from the central bus station to the markets she said that she had 'felt like a criminal', thus indicating the shame and embarrassment that she experienced. At the market, she stood for the whole morning behind her friend, who sold the onions for her. 'But' she continued, 'from the two bags I received 300 leva, which was as much as my monthly pension at the time'. And so, the following week she went again, this time selling the produce herself. But at the beginning, she concluded, '*Beshe mi izsram*', that is, 'I was ashamed'.

Here, an explicit moral commentary was attached to market activities that was not evident during other exchanges in which Talpians engaged. To make sense of this, we need to recognize that 'the market' is a site which carries special significance, in both the socialist and postsocialist periods. The 'market' ('*pazar*' in Bulgarian) delineates a particular space for a particular form of economic activity which in turn carries implications of morality. In contrast to former times when market activity was not encouraged, since 1989 it has been a favoured and central domain of state reforms. The ideologically laden nature of 'the market' in the context of a changing political-economic environment has resulted in openly charging market relations with a morality: a morality which finds expression in villagers' conversations such as the one that I have just provided. The shame described by Maria underlines the point that engagement in the market is not a moral-free activity but is given value through the political-economic context in which it operates.

In this chapter I explore market activities as a site in which local mores and identity are expressed.[2] I shall suggest that engagement in market activity is associated with a particular form of production (household) and this in turn is deeply rooted in particular understandings about 'work'. It is only in considering market exchanges within a wider social context – particularly in terms of notions about 'work' and 'production' – that an appreciation can be gained of the moral views associated with such activities.

Market Activity and Household Production

The market is a 'political icon' (Carrier 1997: 1) which holds strong ideological connotations (Holy 1992) and has played a central role both symbolically and practically in the postsocialist reforms. Creating a market economy has become synonymous with the move toward demo-cratization.[3] The market is perceived – at least by pro-reformers – as a 'civilized' place characteristic to 'modern' societies and as a symbol of rationality (see Carrier 1997 for a general discussion, Hann 1992 for a Hungarian example, Holy 1992 for a Czechoslovakian case and Smollett 1993 for a Bulgarian example). The positive value attributed to the market in the 1990s in postsocialist Europe is in contrast to the way it was viewed in a socialist economy, where it held an ambiguous, even negative position. While the negative view of the market can be traced back to Marx (see Parry and Bloch 1989), it was developed by Lenin in his discussion of the peasantry as 'petty commodity producers' (Lenin 1968: 495) who engaged in market activities. In this way the peasantry was represented as an antagonistic class to the proletariat, that is, to that class which held the historically leading role in the realisation of Communism.[4] Applying Marxist-Leninist ideology, Bulgarian political ideologues developed a similar line. For example, see the writings of the long-term head of State who led Bulgaria over the greater period of the socialist era – Zhivkov (for instance 1985:185).

During socialism, market activity was carried on largely outside the domain of the state public sphere. In fact, in a situation where prices and values were centrally determined,[5] the market was viewed as deeply problematic to the socialist system's 'inner logic' (Verdery 1996: 30). This was for two reasons. The first explanation relates to socialist ideology. A central tenet of socialist policy, along with industrialization, was the concern to 'upgrade' rural life. The considerable investment in rural infrastructure (electricity, running water, improvement of transport and other forms of communication), but even more importantly the collectivization of land, was ultimately about transforming 'peasants' into 'workers': that is, transforming petty commodity producers who traded at the local markets into collectivized producers engaged in state production and acting in accordance with the egalitarian goals of the socialist state. The socialist work ethic implied a strong moral association between the individual who was expected to engage in productive state work and the paternalistic responsibilities of the state toward its workers (Pine 1998: 120). On the other hand, markets – centres that could not be easily controlled by the Party – provided sites where individual interests could be played out in a competitive environment. Local market activities were therefore marginal, indeed they were seen to run counter to the ideologically more acceptable collective forms of state production/marketing.

The second reason the market was viewed as problematic has to do with the centralized structure of state socialism. In a socialist system goods moved vertically toward the centre (from where they were redistributed), not horizontally as in market oriented systems. This feature Verdery calls the drive to maximize allocative power, contrasting it with capitalism's drive to maximize surplus (Verdery 1991: 420–1). Controlling resources fortified the centre's capacity to redistribute goods (Verdery 1996: 24); thus local market activity ran against the system's logic. As Verdery concludes, it is 'Because these horizontal movements and individualising premises subverted socialism's hierarchical organization, [that the] market mechanisms had been suppressed' (Verdery 1996: 30). Local markets such as the one that I will be discussing, while under some degree of control, were nevertheless outside direct influence of the state. Local markets were a place where villagers could engage in second-economy activities and the competitive, individualistic pursuit of interests could 'fester'. This functioned against central Party control and also countered the paternalistic relationship set up between the state and the socialist citizen.

It is here that I must make explicit another important consideration: the fact that the market intersects with particular forms of production. During the socialist period two types of agricultural production dominated the Bulgarian landscape. First, there was state-controlled production based on land that was amalgamated after 1944 and worked cooperatively.[6]

Collectivization changed villagers' pre-Second World War relationship to this land, breaking emotional and financial bonds of dependency upon it. The transformation was clearly evident after the introduction of the land privatization bill, in the early 1990s. To the surprise of reformers, Talpians – as well as many other villagers in the region – did not enthusiastically take up private farming but instead re-established the liquidated state-run cooperative into initially two but then (late 1990s) into three new privately run cooperatives (see Kaneff 1995 and 1996 for the early phase). This points to a central assumption of my argument, that land – and what is produced from it – holds significance only when invested with labour and work. It is 'work' that determines an individual's sense of rights over ownership, both of the land and of the produce created from it. Since land is given significance through work, then the collectivization of land was an important way of breaking the emotional bond between villagers and their specific land holdings located outside the village.[7]

The second form of agricultural production was private production based on household plots. In contrast to the situation with collectivized land, Talpians' relationship to household plots have continued uninter-rupted throughout the socialist and postsocialist periods. Irrespective of whether villagers worked in the agricultural cooperative or not, all were – and still are – involved in the production of food on their household land. A wide variety of produce is grown – vegetables and fruit. Animals are also raised for meat. Decorative plants (mainly roses) cultivated for beautifying parks and gardens constituted the only crop tended specific-ally for cash profit. Such activities have gained importance as a means of surviving the increasing economic hardships resulting from postsocialist reform.

The relationship between these two forms of production – household and state – was complex and often fraught with tension and ambiguity. In socialist Bulgaria, many resources from the state-run cooperative were either officially or informally channelled toward the aid of household production. In the mid-1980s, for example, the state cooperative con-tracted out calves for fattening by households. Apart from being paid for the meat per kilogram, the households also gained in other, less direct monetary ways, such as access to free veterinary services. At times household production was seen by officials as a threat to state-sponsored economic activities. Thus at village meetings which I attended during the socialist period, a common complaint by officials was that agricultural cooperative workers claimed to be 'too ill' to come to work on particular days and yet were spotted on the same day digging in their own household gardens. Certainly there was cause for such concern. I know of one senior schoolteacher who would regularly take days off work in order to tend her large cash crop of decorative roses. Private household activity was therefore both encouraged and yet also seen as a threat to the state-controlled economic domain. It frequently entailed involvement in the market that was the site, as far as socialist state officials were concerned, of relations of inequality, a sphere of social life that had to be confined and restricted. Nevertheless both state production and household production existed jointly and individuals often, if not usually, engaged in both (see also Creed 1998).

While the balance between state and private production underwent vast transformation in the late 1990s, with the state withdrawing from agricultural production, the presence of newly established private cooperatives maintains a similar balance between large mechanized farming and household production. In many senses the latter has suffered from the new conditions: households can no longer depend on assistance from the private cooperatives to the same extent that they could from the previous socialist organization. Household farming has, therefore, become both more 'risky' and more burdensome. But despite these difficulties production has not been reduced. Indeed in a context of economic hardship, householders have become far more dependent on what they can produce from their plots.

The Nekilva Market

It is surplus stock from household produce that is sold at the local market in the district administrative capital of Nekilva – population of approximately 14,000 in the mid-1990s – eight km from Talpa. Every Tuesday there is a market in the town that attracts people from the surrounding district (the home of approximately 30,000 inhabitants) and even beyond. The market is operated by the municipality, which makes charges for the stalls that are arranged in a large rectangle, sellers standing on the inside facing outward to their customers. An official walks around the stalls collecting the cash fee from those occupying stall space. There are 122 available fruit/vegetable stalls, and on any Tuesday, approximately one-half to two-thirds of the stalls are occupied, sellers grouped together along two or three of the sides of the rectangle.

Talpians have been participating in the local Nekilva markets for many years. From my own experience the type of goods sold by the villagers has not changed since the socialist period. Villagers sell whatever is in season; in spring this is largely restricted to cucumbers and spring onions, while early autumn yields the most stock and participation in the local market reaches its peak during this period. The day I accompanied Maria to the markets, she had a wide variety of goods for sale: parsnips, beans, cucumbers, carrots, cabbages, leeks, tomatoes, apples, aubergines, eggs, capsicums and walnuts. As most sellers, she only carried a few kilograms (sometimes less) of each item. In part this restriction was one of a practical nature: villagers take no more produce than they can carry on the bus or, as in our case, the amount that could be accommodated in the back of the car.

Since the 1989 reforms, market activity has dramatically increased. But this increase is not so much in terms of villagers selling their food produce, although there has been an increase in activity here too. Rather, the expansion is in non-consumable goods – clothes, spare car parts, cassettes and kitchen utensils. In the early 1990s the markets took on an international character – with 'Russians' from Moldova and Ukraine,[8] Bulgarians and Roma all represented. The former arrived quite literally in bus loads from the closer regions of the former Soviet Union. They sold, to quote some friends from Nekilva, 'just about anything that they could lay their hands on': primarily Russian-made goods ranging from glasses to crocheted children's booties to Lada and Moskvich car parts, blood-pressure measuring kits and children's toys. The items were arranged on plastic sheets on the ground. Since the value of the rouble varied widely during this time – in early 1993 there were twelve roubles to the Bulgarian Lev and the latter held a more stable value with respect to the US dollar – Russians sold their goods in Bulgarian leva and converted their earnings into US dollars before returning home. I was informed by locals from Nekilva that often the Russians, having traded their goods for local currency, would continue south to Turkey, buy goods there, selling the produce in Bulgaria before returning home, thus making a return trip selling goods in both directions. Such activities continued until the mid-1990s when changes in the law deterred Russian traders from coming to Bulgaria.

Market expansion also involved ethnic Bulgarians: not only locals, but traders who followed a circuit, travelling to different towns every day of the week in order to participate in the respective district markets. These people sold exotic fruits (citrus, bananas), clothes, car parts and a variety of Western-made goods (watches, biros, soaps, shampoos, clothes). Such items were displayed on fold-away tables or on the bonnets of their cars. The Roma focused their trading on jeans and other Turkish-made clothes – frequently imitations of famous labels.

Ethnicity served as one point of orientation in terms of who sold which goods.[9] Despite the non-participation of Russians in more recent times, a demarcation is still evident between Roma who sell jeans and Turkish-made clothes, and the Bulgarians who deal in most other goods (local villagers with food produce, other 'professional' traders from the region with all other goods). Apart from ethnic delineations, the market is also spatially divided. Non-consumable goods are generally sold outside the fenced area of the market place proper – reserved for the fruit/vegetable stalls – in the adjoining streets where sellers set up their own make-shift stalls.

Occasionally produce from the Nekilva markets was bought by 'middle men' who sold the goods at a profit in larger city markets. Maria told me that one week a customer had bought all her eggs for 160 leva each and sold them at the Veliko Turnovo markets – a nearby city of approximately 80,000 inhabitants – for 230 leva each. (Prices indicate the high figures reached before the re-evaluation of the Bulgarian currency in 1999.) Her mother, Grigora, similarly informed me that at a previous market day a Sofian had bought all her tomatoes with the intention of selling them at other markets for a profit. She added, 'you can do this if you know where the good markets are [in terms of price] and you have the transport'. Most villagers did not fall within this category.

Two Moral Positions

Shame

Unlike her mother, standing in the stall next to ours, or many of the other 20 or 30 Talpians with stalls on market Tuesday, Maria had not started selling until after the 1989 reforms. In fact, in 1986–88, when I first met her, Maria was a senior teacher in the village school, teaching science and music. In 1990, having reached retirement age, Maria gave up her teaching position at the school. Since then she has concentrated on running her half-hectare household garden – growing a wide variety of fruits and vegetables, raising geese, chicken, a pig and lambs for meat, and producing decorative plants (mainly roses) for cash. For Maria such activities have become increasingly a matter of survival, as steep inflation and meagre pensions have encroached on her previously comfortable standard of living.

Maria's prominent public position in the previous socialist period is central to understanding her present feelings of shame when participating in market activity. Apart from her teaching responsibilities, she had also been a member of the Communist Party, Head of the Teachers' Union, Deputy head of the Fatherland Front (an organization of non-party and Party citizens mobilized to implement government policies), and a member of the Council running the *Chitalishte* (the cultural house of the village). As a prominent figure in socialist society, Maria did not engage in local market activity. Indeed her non-engagement was a way to publicly convey her ideological and economic support for the socialist state – ideals that she reinforced in her official capacity as a teacher, Party member and other related public positions. Having espoused beliefs all her life which negated market activity and supported a work ethic based on engagement in the sphere of state production, her relatively recent participation in the market came at a cost, namely feelings of shame and guilt. I suspect that this is why she constantly displayed her relative inexperience in, and discomfort with, trading. For example, by seeking advice from her mother as to what price to ask for a particular good she emphasized her position as a newcomer to this 'business'. On one occasion, Maria did not know the current price of carrots and asked her mother, Grigora, in front of the enquiring customer, how much she should charge. Maria's discomfort in engaging in market trading was accentuated whenever political colleagues, many of whom have not abandoned their prominent public profile, stopped to talk to us during the morning's trading.

Such was the situation, for example, with Petur Pashev, a distinguished-looking gentleman, who had worked in Sofia as a senior civil servant, retiring in Talpa in the early 1990s. He headed the contemporary village Socialist Party (previously known as the Communist Party) and was also a prominent figure in the new socialist-type cooperative (see Kaneff 1995 and 1996). On seeing me, Pashev immediately launched into the topic of world politics. We finished the conversation with him jokingly inviting me to come and help pick grapes on cooperative lands as I had done the previous year. In so doing he sent a clear message, to those listening, of his and my engagement in cooperative activities. That is, he underlined his activeness in economic relations that were of benefit to the community rather than to the individual. His clearly stated support for, and involvement in, the cooperative, which while no longer in state ownership was still perceived to be based on collective rather than individual interests, revealed his preference for one type of production over others. In addition, Pashev's well-dressed appearance, in contrast to the less smartly attired village traders, served to visually emphasize his non-involvement in market trading activities. The 'civilized' non-trader and the 'less sophisticated' trader presented a visual critique to the current positive value given to market activity by pro-reformers.

The negative value attributed to engagement in trading activities was also expressed by another passer-by, Nadia Nateva, elected village mayor (Socialist Party) during the mid-1990s. When I asked her what she was doing at the markets, her response was 'to look, not to buy or sell'. Her attendance at the market just 'to look' was a clear statement indicating her distance from this form of trading; she was here as an observer rather than as an active participant. The presence of such people clearly caused Maria some discomfort, underlining her personal moral dilemma resulting from her previous involvement in state production and relatively recent participation in market activities (associated with a form of petty commodity production – household). Such a change in status still disturbs Maria, even after a number of years of selling at the markets.

Pride

At one point during the morning's trading I commented to Maria's 84-year-old mother Grigora that a considerable number of the market stalls seemed to be manned by Talpians. She agreed. When I asked why, she responded 'it's because we are closer to Nekilva and are more hard-working'. The point of practicality is well taken: with the increasing costs of fuel, the longer bus or car trip from more distant villages would certainly have made trading at the Nekilva markets less worthwhile. However, it is the other point made by her that particularly interested me, for it indicated that unlike her daughter Maria, Grigora did not have the same association of market exchange as being 'shameful'. Rather the tone of pride in her response indicated that for her market trading was a source of positive achievement, part of an identity that marked, her as, 'hard-working'.

Despite having laboured many years in the agricultural cooperative – her services having been recognized through awards for diligent work – Grigora was never a prominent figure in state-sponsored production. While Maria had been a state representative whose work identity came primarily from participation in public life, Grigora was not a Party member nor was she particularly ambitious in establishing a public career. As a pensioner she devoted her retirement years to building up household production. Her very different position with respect to state production accounts, I believe, for the contrasting view she expressed concerning market participation. Again, it is engagement in a particular form of agricultural production and the influence of this in terms of identity that appears central when considering the positive view held by Grigora in respect to market activity.

The food sold at the local markets is produced in the private land plots. Households are largely self-sufficient in the production of meat, fruit and vegetables. The majority of the produce is consumed by Talpians and extended family living outside the village. All family members benefiting from the food contribute their time and labour to its production. City-dwelling family members return regularly to Talpa on weekends and spend most of their summer vacations helping in the garden. Village statistics reflect this, as the permanent population of 615 swells to approximately 750 in the summer months when there is the greatest amount of work to be carried out in the garden.[10]

Maria's situation is common in this respect. She is a widow and her only child – in her late 30s – is married and lives in the city of Veliko Turnovo, some 40 km from the village. The daughter, Tanya (who works in a chemical plant), son-in-law (an officer in the army) and teenage grandson, spend alternate weekends in the summer months with Maria; every other weekend they are with the son-in-law's parents who live in another village. From early morning until sunset they work together on numerous garden tasks. Tanya helps with the weeding, watering and harvesting of the vegetable and fruit crops. Together with her mother, she makes pickles and fruit preserves for the winter. There is also the chore of looking after the animals. The son-in-law usually helps with the heavier work associated with gardening and with caring for the animals. The slaughtering of livestock at the appropriate time is a job that concerns the whole family. Most of the meat is preserved in jars for the winter.

The family's involvement is not only vital in the preparation of the produce; it is also the main recipient. For example, the majority of the 500 jars of stewed fruit made in the summer of 1996 were transferred by car to Tanya's apartment in Veliko Turnovo for consumption by the couple and their teenage son. A year later, Maria told me that of these preserves, fewer than 100 jars remained uneaten.[11]

Grigora's situation is similar. Her married son who lives in Nekilva (he is some 10 years younger than his sister Maria), daughter-in-law and two teenage grandchildren are in Talpa every weekend; the son and daughter-in-law are also frequently in Talpa on weekdays, after work. As Grigora's age gradually limits what she can do in the garden, so the son and his family spend more time tending the garden. Most of the produce is, after all, for their household, including profits from Grigora's market trading.

The important point is that food produce from household land provides the foundation for regular interaction between kin; food production is a joint project through which kinship relations are constituted and reproduced. It serves to cement the ties between household members, despite their physical separation between village and city. In fact, apart from the odd festive occasions – birthdays and new year which Maria frequently spends in Veliko Turnovo; Grigora usually prefers to remain in Talpa – family interactions are focused on the production of the food in the village. Food sharing and production have always had symbolic, as well as practical, importance in maintaining kinship ties (Smollett 1989) and have gained a new impetus following the economic hardships of the 1989 reforms (Czeglédy 2002; Kaneff 1998).

Further, many of the day-to-day exchanges between villagers themselves – kin or not – are also focused on the production of food. Maria regularly rings her mother, who lives at the other end of the village, to discuss the progress of a certain crop or to seek advice as to when to plant particular seeds. Such conversations are not restricted to her mother, however. Comparisons, advice and shared knowledge make up most of the discussion between non-kin villagers: between neighbours and other villagers when they meet in the streets or across boundary fences and in informal chats at local meetings. They ask each other whether they have started transplanting the tomato seedlings or whether they have pruned the grape vines, or compare recipes for preserving fruit. Neighbours and friends often help each other in labour-demanding tasks, such as in ploughing the corn which is cultivated to feed household animals.

Thus the preparation/production of household food, as well as its exchange, is the cornerstone of interaction between kin, neighbours and other villagers. Relationships are constituted through reciprocity in labour and produce. Here we see another concept of work that is not associated with state-sponsored production, but is bound up with the notion of the reproduction of the household. To use Kopytoff's term (1986), the object (food) has a 'biography'; in this case it is a biography embedded in kin and village relations through work. 'Work' invests objects, land or the produce resulting from it, with meaning. It can be viewed as a metaphor for a whole range of social relations that are constituted in the course of household food production. Significantly, only a very small amount of household produce reaches the market; namely the surplus produced once obligations to kin or to other village and neighbourly relations have been fulfilled. Thus while food production has a variety of functions – from biological to symbolic maintenance of a wide range of social relations – only the 'surplus' becomes saleable at the local markets.

The sale of home-grown produce does not eliminate an object's biographical importance. Rather it is precisely because food is central to social interactions (embedded in relations of familiarity) that when it becomes exchanged in the market place it plays out another role – as a marker of identity boundaries. The produced object – food – signifies 'work' and in Grigora's opinion at least, delineates those who are diligent, hard workers. Since household food production is not normally intended for market exchange, the surplus that is sold is an important indicator of those who have fulfilled all social obligations to family, friends and neighbours and been left with an excess that can be converted into a commodity. This for Grigora, as for other more elderly villagers present, was clearly an issue of pride, that their hard work was not only visible, but could be converted into something – cash – which would further benefit the household and family.

It is because market produce was bound so closely to village relations that its exchange was also a means of creating social distance. The association between exchange and social distance has been well documented by anthropologists (for example, see general discussion by Gudeman 1992: 284 or Davis 1992). The reproduction of social distance, with goods being sold at different prices to different customers depending on whether they are kin, friends or strangers was something that I also observed at the markets. One example concerned the sale of Maria's tomatoes. Because it had been a bad season for tomatoes in the region and because Maria's tomatoes were of high quality, she could demand a high price.[12] For this reason her mother instructed her to charge 1000 leva/kilogram – most tomatoes fetched 650–750 leva/kilogram. But because of the high asking price, the tomatoes remained unsold in the first few hours of trading. Maria, impatient to return to Talpa, would have weakened and lowered the price except for her mother's insistence that she should not accept less: 'You mustn't sell them for less, they are of such high quality and also in deficit this year'. Just as Maria's patience was running out and she was quietly discussing with me – out of earshot of her mother – the possibility of reducing the price to 900, a Nekilva friend passed and Maria sold her the tomatoes for 800 leva/kilogram. The friend also bought beans from Grigora at 550 leva/kg, a reduction of 50 leva on the price quoted to strangers.

While friends were sold goods at a reduced price, there was little concern to look after the interests of strangers in the same way. At one point a man was interested in Grigora's packaged garlic. She told him each bag contained one kilogram of strung garlic, but when at his request she put one of the bags on the scale, it was shown to contain just under the specified weight. The man was further annoyed when he pointed out to her that the bags contained not only the garlic head, but also the dried stem, by which means the heads were plaited together. Before leaving, he asked her indignantly 'Do I eat the stems?' Grigora sold the garlic to a less demanding client some minutes later. A similar situation was replicated in terms of the quality of the produce: the best was kept for kin and the household, and what remained was sold at the market with the worst quality produce being sold to strangers.[13]

The selling of produce at different prices – showing an indifference in short-changing strangers and alternatively selling at reduced prices to friends – served to recreate boundaries of social distance between the traders and their customers. The market was a space in which relations of different degrees of social distance were reproduced through exchange. However, market activities as a symbolic construction of community did more than just mark degrees of familiarity between individuals (family, friends and strangers). They also denoted boundaries between Talpians and other villagers. Grigora's response to my question as to why many of the market sellers were Talpians, that 'we' – meaning the Talpians – are hard-working, was a means of distinguishing themselves from other villagers. Local identity was thus expressed through participation in market exchange.

Again, evidence may be sought in terms of the price-setting strategies. Grigora and Maria were asking a high price for onion bulbs – 2000 leva/ kilogram. They were aware that if they reduced this price they could obtain a sale, but as Maria explained to me, they were prepared to return home with this commodity unsold if necessary, as it could still be sold the following spring. Grigora's in-laws who had the stall on the other side of her were in agreement and also asked this same high price. At one point another Talpian woman from some stalls away came to confirm with Grigora how much she was charging for the bulbs. Grigora advised the woman to sell them for the same price as her own and also told her to pass this message on to the others. I realized then that the Talpians had formed a verbal agreement between themselves not to lower the price. (Communicating joint pricing arrangements was made easier by the fact that Talpians chose positions next to each other, at the same end of the market stalls.) Sellers from other villages were not part of this arrange-ment. This became clear when a potential customer, after enquiring about the price, stated that 'they are selling it for 1500 down there', and he pointed to further down the line of stalls where no Talpians stood.

In their solidarity to create a joint price strategy, Talpians were marking a boundary between themselves and traders from other villages.

The creation of such an alliance, as well as the high price they gave their produce – with the knowledge that in so doing they may not sell the bulbs – revealed the considerable value Talpians placed on their produce and therefore on their social relations and local identity. It was not something they were willing to negotiate, except on their terms, for the 'right price'. Again, it is the relations embedded through the objects, through 'work', which enabled the foundation of such an alliance. Market exchanges of food were therefore entwined with local identity: between the 'hard-working' Talpians, and others. In this way, village identities were recreated in the local market place.

Conclusion – Market, Identity and Morality

In Talpa an explicit moral commentary was attached to market activities that was not expressed during exchanges in other contexts. It was in the market place – a public site of considerable political and ideological significance both during the socialist period and also since the 1989 reforms – that issues of morality were vocalized and given prominence. As Dilley aptly notes 'moral evaluations of trade must be viewed as arising from a context of changing politico-economic relationships' (1992: 4).

In contrasting the two women, Maria and Grigora, I have attempted to highlight different moral positions expressed by kin engaged in the same activity: views which are rooted in an individual's position with respect to 'production' and 'work' in the context of political-economic reform. For Maria, once an official who upheld a work ethic grounded in state production, market trading was a shameful act, with which she still does not feel totally comfortable. For her mother, who previously worked for the agricultural cooperative but was never involved in public life or the Communist Party to the same degree as her daughter, engagement in the market was cause for pride – household production being much more central to her own identity. The contrast is based on identities rooted in two different notions of work: 'work' as engagement in the public sphere of state production and 'work' as the labour performed upon household land. The women's identities are therefore rooted in terms of their participation in, and preference for, one form of production over another. In short, engagement in the market provides the domain in which local identities – founded in complementary but distinct forms of production/ work and on the basis of territorial (Talpa versus other villages) difference – and various degrees of social relatedness are played out. Such identities, expressed through market participation, are laden with moral undertones that are rooted in ideologically valued forms of production made meaningful by the political-economic context.

Assumptions about the market, such as that it consists of 'free' individuals who act in instrumentally 'rational' ways, are of questionable relevance in the case that I have examined above. Many other ethnographic studies make a similar point, one that essentially reminds us that market activities are embedded in social relations. Perhaps in finishing, therefore, I need to address the question of what makes my example particular to the postsocialist Bulgarian context. In response I offer three trains of thought.

First, it appears that a socialist valuation of the market still influences current social practice – Maria's shame at engaging in trading activities may not be as pronounced now as it was the first day that she went to sell her goods, but it is still a consideration. In fact as the state withdraws from the public domain, many of those who were once largely dependent on its protection, or who were engaged in its ideological reproduction, have been forced to participate in market trading. A consequence has been the renegotiation of individual moralities and identities, as participants like Maria are driven to engage in activities they once devalued or at least made a public show of rejecting. An individual's moral stance with respect to market activity is influenced by his or her biography, in terms of his or her previous position with respect to state production. The implication is that even in the late 1990s, socialist values concerning production, the market and morality still held some force, at least among the older generation in rural areas.

Secondly, the above discussion reminds us that the socialist economic system was not a monopoly purely under Party control. While it is true that the Party did not directly support the market, the symbiotic relationship that existed between state and household production made possible market activities. The market provided a trading outlet for household produce. This raises questions: is this simply an example of a contradiction in the socialist system – as Verdery suggests, see above – or does it underline the complexity and variety of economic practices existent in the socialist system? Or both? It also raises additional questions with respect to the present postsocialist context: do individuals really have greater economic freedom now that the market is 'dominant' and state production in decline, or have some individuals engaged in market relations experienced a reduction in their economic choice? (I suspect Maria would reply in the affirmative to this latter question.)

Which brings me to the final point. It is debatable whether the present growth in the local Nekilva market can be held up as a positive sign in terms of capitalist development. Grigora may be proud of her engagement in the market, but she is not the economically rational 'free' actor that the capitalist market purportedly espouses. Nor has she swallowed the particular American version of the market that young Sofians were sold in the early 1990s (see Smollett 1993). Indeed the provincial market that I witnessed held little of the idolization of the United States or of American goods. While any comparison with provincial markets must remain speculative, pending more research on urban markets such as Sofia, what is indicated is a general contrast between rural and urban markets. Such regional differences reflect unequal Western influence and investment in postsocialist Bulgaria with urban areas attracting far more Western attention and resources. Meanwhile, in provincial areas such as Nekilva, local mores and identity remain prominent features of market activity.

Notes

1. An earlier version of parts of this chapter is published in French in *Ethnologie Française*, XXVIII(4) 1998, under the title 'Un jour au marché: Les modes d'échange dans la Bulgarie rurale'. It should also be noted that the names of people, of village 'Talpa' and of the district capital 'Nekilva' are pseudonyms.
2. While protracted fieldwork carried out in Bulgaria in both the socialist and postsocialist periods provides much of the setting for this chapter, the primary ethnographic data was collected on the particular day at the markets that I spent with Maria.
3. For an extreme version of such a view see Marsland, who equates freedom and virtue with the market to such a degree that '. . . other than in free market societies, genuine freedom is infeasible better than occasionally, partially and accidently' (Marsland 2001: 34).
4. For example: 'In order to abolish classes it is necessary . . . to abolish the difference between worker and peasant, to make workers of all of them . . . It can be solved only by the organizational reconstruction of the whole social economy, by a transition from individual, disunited, petty commodity production to large-scale social production' (Lenin 1968: 497).
5. 'Artificially' determined from the perspective of those who consider the market as existing outside a political or social framework.

6. Actually, state production can be divided into two types: cooperatives (where land was legally still owned by individuals but farmed collectively) and state farms (where land was owned by the state and, again, farmed collectively). But for the purposes of this discussion, the two may be considered together.

7. This was not appreciated by exponents of the land privatization law: a law which required land to be returned to pre-1944 owners, thus ignoring the last 50 years of resettlement and internal migration during which time new relationships to the land were established. I should also add that while individual/household links to the land were broken, the land retains collective importance for the local community, as I have argued elsewhere (Kaneff 2000 and 2002).

8. I was unable to discover whether these traders were ethnic Russians or simply labelled in this way by the Bulgarians, who at this time (1992–1993) so soon after the collapse of the former Soviet Union, did not make distinctions between ethnic Russians, Ukrainians and Moldovans. For an insight into who such Russian traders might be, see Humphrey (1999). Hann and Beller-Hann (1998) also discuss post-Soviet traders in yet another context.

9. For an example of ethnic divisions being reinforced as a consequence of socialist economies of shortage in the Romanian case, see Verdery (1993).

10. The figure was provided by Mayor Nateva, in 1996.

11. The city-based family members are also the main recipients of the cash produced from the growing of decorative plants which are exported to nurseries throughout Europe. The profit is used to buy a variety of consumer goods aimed at improving the city apartment, or less often, the village house.

12. The generally poor crop throughout the region was a topic much discussed throughout the summer and blamed on acid rain as a result of pollutants from western Europe.

13. Increasing economic hardship during the 1990s led to a detectable shift in the boundary: a reduction in gift-giving and price discounting for distant kin, friends and neighbours and a correspondingly greater pursuit of individual economic interests.

References

Carrier, J.G. (1997), *Meanings of the Market: The Free Market in Western Culture*, Oxford: Berg.

Creed, G.W. (1998), *Domesticating Revolution: From Socialist Reform to Ambivalent Transition in a Bulgarian Village*, University Park: Pennsylvania State University Press.

Czeglédy, A. (2002), 'Urban Peasants in a Post-Socialist World: Small Scale Agriculturalists in Hungary', in P. Leonard and D. Kaneff (eds), *Post Socialist Peasant? Rural and Urban Constructions of Identity in Eastern Europe, East Asia and the Former Soviet Union*, Basingstoke and New York: Palgrave.

Davis, J. (1992), *Exchange*, Buckingham: Open University Press.

Dilley, R. (1992), 'Contesting Markets: A General Introduction to Market Ideology, Imagery and Discourse', in R. Dilley (ed.), *Contesting Markets: Analyses of Ideology, Discourse and Practice*, Edinburgh: Edinburgh University Press, 1–34.

Gudeman, S. (1992), 'Markets, Models and Morality: The Power of Practices', in R. Dilley (ed.), *Contesting Markets*, Edinburgh: Edinburgh University Press, 279–94.

Hann, C.M. (1992), 'Market Principle, Market-place and the Transition in Eastern Europe', in R. Dilley (ed.), *Contesting Markets*, Edinburgh: Edinburgh University Press, 244–59.

—— and Beller-Hann, I. (1998), 'Markets, Morality and Modernity in North-east Turkey', in T.M. Wilson and H. Donnan (eds), *Border Identities: Nation and State at International Frontiers*, Cambridge: Cambridge University Press, 237–62.

Holy, L. (1992), 'Culture, Market Ideology and Economic Reform in Czechoslovakia', in R. Dilley (ed.), *Contesting Markets*, Edinburgh: Edinburgh University Press.

Humphrey, C. (1999), 'Traders, "Disorder", and Citizenship Regimes in Provincial Russia', in M. Burawoy and K. Verdery (eds), *Uncertain Transition: Ethnographies of Change in the Socialist World*, Oxford: Rowman and Littlefield.

Kaneff, D. (1995), 'Developing Rural Bulgaria', in D.G. Anderson and F. Pine (eds), *Surviving the Tradition*, special edition, *Cambridge Anthropology*, 18(2), 23–34.

—— (1996), 'Responses to "Democratic" Land Reforms', in R. Abrahams (ed.), *After Socialism: Land Reform and Social Change in Eastern Europe*, Oxford: Berghahn, 85–114.

—— (1998), 'When "Land" Becomes "Territory": Land Privatisation and Ethnicity in Rural Bulgaria', in S. Bridger and F. Pine (eds), *Surviving Post-Socialism: Local Strategies and Regional Responses in Eastern Europe and the Former Soviet Union*, London: Routledge, 16–32.

—— (2000), 'Property, Work and Local Identity', *Max Planck Institute for Social Anthropology Working Papers*, Halle/Saale, 1–16.

—— (2002), 'Work, Identity and Rural-Urban Relations', in P. Leonard and D. Kaneff (eds), *Post Socialist Peasant? Rural and Urban Constructions of Identity in Eastern Europe, East Asia and the Former Soviet Union*, Basingstoke and New York: Palgrave.

Kopytoff, I. (1986), 'The Cultural Biography of Things: Commoditization as Process', in A. Appadurai (ed.), *The Social Life of Things: Commodities in a Cultural Perspective*, Cambridge: Cambridge University Press, 64–91

Lenin, V.I. (1968), *Selected Works*, Moscow: Progress Publishers.

Marsland, D. (2001), 'Markets and the Social Structure of Morality', *Society*, January/February, 33–8.

Parry. J. and Bloch, M. (1989), 'Introduction: Money and the Morality of Exchange', *Money and the Morality of Exchange*, Cambridge: Cambridge University Press, 1–32.

Pine, F. (1998), 'Dealing with Fragmentation: the Consequence of Privatisation for Rural Women in Central and Southern Poland', in S. Bridger and F. Pine (eds), *Surviving Post-Socialism*, London: Routledge, 106–23.

Smollett, E.W. (1989), 'The Economy of Jars: Kindred Relationships in Bulgaria – An exploration', *Ethnologia Europaea*, XIX(2), 125–40.

—— (1993), 'America the Beautiful: Made in Bulgaria', *Anthropology Today*, 2(2), April, 9–13.

Verdery, K. (1991), 'Theorizing Socialism: a Prologue to the "Transition"', *American Ethnologist*, 18(3), August, 419–39.

—— (1993), 'Ethnic Relations, Economies of Shortage, and the Transition in Eastern Europe', in C.M. Hann (ed.), *Socialism. Ideals, Ideologies, and Local Practice*, London: Routledge, 172–86.

—— (1996), 'What Was Socialism, and Why Did It Fall?', in *What Was Socialism and What Comes Next*, Princeton: Princeton University Press, 19–38.

Zhivkov, T. (1985), *The Komsomol Youth of Bulgaria*, Sofia: Sofia Press.

-4-

Heritage and Enterprise Culture in Archangel, Northern Russia

Julian Watts

The hostility of the Russian public toward the 'New Russians' and the market economy more generally became a commonplace of journalism and opinion surveys during the 1990s. Such enmity was hardly a new feature of Russian life, since for at least three hundred years the Russian aristocracy, bureaucracy, clergy, intelligentsia and peasantry had often been united in their profound dislike of businessmen (Owen 1999: 115).[1] Unsurprisingly therefore, both popular and scholarly discussions some-times attribute contemporary attitudes to the powerful work of history and culture, with Soviet ideology seen as merely reinforcing more ancient prejudices.[2] With the majority of adult Russians just two or three generations away from the egalitarian culture and communal organization of the peasantry, it is assumed there remains intact a mentality, or more euphemistically a 'political culture', which instinctively opposes the individualism inherent in entrepreneurial activity.[3] Critics of this view, however, argue that it fails to explain either the significant differences in attitude which exist between generations and social categories within Russian society, or the rapid rise and fall in the level of support for market reforms between 1990 and 1994, and so they suggest instead that people's attitudes are more readily explained in terms of their own instrumental calculations about whether the market has brought them personal benefit, or promises to do so (Reisinger et al. 1994, 1995).

This debate has tended toward sterility, since a crudely depicted 'culture' of antipathy to initiative and inequality is opposed to an equally implausible economistic view excluding cultural influence. In contrast, social anthropologists working in postsocialist states have been far more successful in exploring the ways in which people deploy and adapt their cultural inheritances in order to respond to the changing circumstances and predicaments of 'transition' (e.g. Creed 1998; Grant 1995; Humphrey 1998; Verdery 1996). This success rests on two main intellectual differences from political science: a willingness to tease out the indigenous under-standings of key concepts and value terms, and the recognition of 'culture' as highly fluid and dynamic, more repertoire or tool-kit than hard-wiring. In this chapter I wish to consider the views about entrepre-neurs which I encountered during my fieldwork in the city of Archangel (hereafter Arkhangelsk) in Northern Russia between 1993 and 1995. Though inevitably these were varied, I argue that one can identify a coherent popular critique of the new entrepreneurs which is far more subtle and morally informed than anything as simplistic as 'collectivism' or 'envy'. I explore the sources of this discourse, since it does have roots in the culture of the Russian North. As I shall stress, however, this is a culture which has been continually shaped by invented traditions, state-sponsored heritage, and contests over politicized symbols.

The North under the Tsars

In terms of metaphysical orientation, Peter the Great sought to drag Russia away from its backward theocratic 'Eastern' past to a modern secular 'Western' future. By the late eighteenth century however, a growing nationalist consciousness had come to resent this aping of the West. Influenced by the climatological doctrine of Montesquieu (which contrasted the hardy, sincere and freedom-loving peoples of the North with the sensitive but deceitful, indolent and slave-like people of the warmer South) and by the Romantic discovery of Scandinavian and Celtic barbarian life as an alternative to Greco-Roman culture, nationalist writers began to create a distinctive conception of Russia as being 'of the North' (Boele 1996: 18–35). Increasingly comfortable with the idea of Russia's own 'Otherness', they deployed the wildness of the North and the severity of its winter as defining tropes for the essence of Russia, viewing them as the fount of manliness and patriotism, a vision cemented by Napoleon's great defeat at the hands of 'General Winter':

> Born under the cold northern star,
> Pampered since childhood
> By the severe grey winter,
> We detest foreign luxury,
> And, loving our fatherland
> Even more than ourselves,
> Considering it the promised land
> That gives milk and honey,
> We will not exchange,

For all the bliss of southern nature,
Our snows, our national ice.

S. Zirinski-Zhikmahtov
(quoted in Boele 1996: 58).

Boele argues that such poems contributed to an increasingly sturdy national self-image which was grounded in the following binary oppositions (ibid.: 63):

North–South (West)
winter–spring
manliness–effeminacy
hardiness–weakness
courage–fear
melancholy–volatility
independence–slavery
authenticity–imitativeness.

The logic of this metaphysics implied that the people of the freezing Arkhangelsk region, the northernmost area of the country, should be the most independent, hardy and authentic Russians of them all, and their way of life indeed appeared to justify such a view. The region, known as the Pomorye (or coastal area), drew its name from its most celebrated inhabitants, the Pomors, who had settled the White Sea shores in the twelfth and thirteenth centuries and, uniquely among ethnic Russians, adopted deep-sea fishing as their way of life. In their small wooden boats the Pomors ranged far and wide across the polar waters, fishing in the hostile Barents Sea and Arctic Ocean and travelling thousands of kilometres east to explore the mouths of the great Siberian rivers. The Pomors were the pilots and crews for the first Russian fleet which Peter constructed in the wharfs of Arkhangelsk, and they enjoyed great military successes against the Swedes and French, and fought off English attempts to storm Arkhangelsk during the Crimean War. During the eighteenth and nineteenth centuries the Pomors also became inveterate traders, with hundreds of boats sailing each spring to the northern provinces of Norway to exchange fish and grain for Norwegian goods. This heroic and picturesque way of life attracted the attention of metropolitan society. Pushkin wrote a popular ode celebrating the bravery and simple nature of the northern fishermen, while the great scholar Lomonosov, himself born in the region, secured the Tsar's backing for the Pomors' Arctic explorations and made their heroic seamanship widely known through his writings.

In the wake of the emancipation of the serfs in 1861, scholars and political activists began to look more closely at peasant life throughout the country, and there soon appeared glowing accounts of the work practices of the Arkhangelsk peasantry. S.V. Maksimov, in his widely read 'A Year in the North' of 1859, described how his initial discomfort in the wild environment gradually passed to a feeling of familiarity and even affection, as he began to appreciate the immense labours undertaken by the Pomors to render their environment inhabitable:

> What gladdens the soul most are the successes achieved here by indefatiguable human labour, which enters into a battle to the death with the hostile forces of unwelcoming nature and has somehow wrested a good and healthy life from it, growing potatoes and beetroot and cabbage (Maksimov 1984 [1859]: 98).

Other writers noted that the Pomors' steadfast labour was helped by their shunning of alcohol and tobacco, which in turn stemmed from the prevalence among them of Old Belief, a strict dissenting sect of Orthodoxy.

As studies in ethnography and folklore developed, the view emerged that because of its geographical remoteness, the Arkhangelsk North had preserved intact the lexicon, ancient epics and folk culture of medieval Russia, which elsewhere had been contaminated by Mongol and other foreign influences. It was also believed that the Pomors were the descendants of migrants from Novgorod, the great city state which was the trade and manufacturing centre of old Rus. For the revolutionary Decembrists and radicals such as Herzen, Novgorod embodied principles of freedom, commerce and popular sovereignty which were quite opposed to the autocratic tradition of the Muscovite tsars who conquered it in the fifteenth century. Putting these two notions together, some scholars thus argued that the spirit of the independent and enterprising Novgorodians had been preserved only in the remote Pomorye. Muscovy had never established feudal estates there (due to the extremely poor soils), and so the Pomors had always remained free men, quite innocent of vassalage or serfdom.

As a result of these various influences and fancies, by the turn of the twentieth century Russian society had developed a powerful representation of the Pomor as 'a special type of Russian person, with distinctive features of character: enterprising, courageous, independent in action and judgement . . . Self-sufficient fishermen, voyagers and explorers, proud and free-spirited, they impressed every observer with their qualities'

(Bernstham 1978: 167, 3). Tsar Alexander III no less was said by his Chief Minister to have felt 'a deep attachment to the Russian north and thought of its peasantry as the proto-typical, real, and primordial Russians by virtue of their origins, ancestry and history' (Witte, quoted in Nielson 1992: 39).[4]

The North under Stalin and Brezhnev

Both the lives and imagery of the Pomors were turned upside down by the Soviet revolution. In 1930 Stalin began a distinctive style of collectivization in the North, herding the peasantry into logging camps where they were forced to work in murderous conditions to produce timber for export. They fled whenever possible to the growing factories and building sites of Arkhangelsk and to the new trawler fleets being established there and in Murmansk, and this great and rapid out-migration, compounded by the heavy losses of the war, shattered the Pomor villages and old way of life. Meanwhile, a vicious intellectual assault saw the Stalinist media condemning the pre-revolutionary North as hopelessly primitive and in desperate need of the industrialization being wrought by the new five year plans. The Pomors were reproached for their petty bourgeois trading instincts, their kulak tendencies (as demonstrated by the widespread ownership of the means of production – i.e., their fishing boats!) and their cut-throat individualism (as manifested in the traditional competitions to secure the best fishing locations). Soviet power promised to transform them into new men concerned only with the well-being of their peers. Meanwhile the Arkhangelsk Society for the Study of the Russian North (which had been formed in 1910 and had a fortnightly journal containing all manner of ethnographic, historical and geographical studies) was disbanded and its leading members repressed. The very name 'Pomor' virtually disappeared during the 1930s, incompatible as it was with the ambition to create a uniform socialist society and suppress local difference. The city of Arkhangelsk was castigated for its exploitative mercantile past and truck with foreign capitalists, and most of its historic buildings, including its magnificent eighteenth-century cathedral, were torn down in 1930–31. If the brutality eased somewhat under Krushchev, the underlying intellectual and political postures of the State did not, and so for more than forty years, generations of Northerners were raised in substantial ignorance of the pre-revolutionary history and culture of their region, and indoctrinated with the idea that the North had been no more than a squalid wasteland brought to life by the Promethean breath of the Party.

However, with Brezhnev's advent to power in 1964, the representations of the North began to become more positive, and this reflected the regime's eschewing of millenarian communism in favour of a growing accommodation with Russian nationalism and militarism. Rather than the Stalinist discontinuity with the pre-revolutionary past, pedagogy and propaganda now stressed elements of continuity. In 1965, the All Union Society for the Preservation of Cultural and Historical Monuments was established, and exemplars of craft and architecture were now praised as demonstrating the eternal genius of the Russian folk (*narod*), with the great wooden churches described as the *sputniks* of their time. Throughout the 1970s there was official encouragement for the creation of local history societies and amateur museums in schools and clubs, and young people were urged to learn about the pre-revolutionary life of their village, town and county. Ideological workers argued that patriotism evolved in subtle and complex ways, stemming not merely from the example of past heroism, but from a knowledge and love for one's own local area and native region, the *maliya rodina* or 'little motherland'.

In 1974 a large open-air museum was established on the outskirts of Arkhangelsk, bringing together the finest examples of wooden architecture from around the region, and it was soon receiving hundreds of thousands of visitors a year. Later, it opened a Pomor section, complete with interiors and portrayals of life in the old fishing villages. Endless press articles explained and praised the distinctive genius of the folk creations of the North, with everything from churches to wooden toys and oral epics purportedly sharing a purity and austerity that reflected the harsh Northern climate, and the region was constantly described as the 'treasure trove' of Russian culture. These accounts also revived the notion of the distinctive Northern way of life and resulting personality which had been so prominent at the turn of the century:

> After its Slavic settlement in the eleventh to fourteenth centuries, the formation of classes in the north was slow. Its limitless land and harsh climate gave the opportunity to peasants to flee feudalism and remain free and independent. As a result, the laying down of culture in the north was different from that in middle Russia, since the north never knew the tartar yoke, or estates or feudal oppression. And in their constant struggle with harsh nature, its people developed a strong will, independence and bravery. They conquered its resources, fishing, hunting, organized salt and iron production, and created various crafts and cottage production, and laid down a special way of life and custom and unique beliefs (*Kommunist*, 30.8.1966).

Always referring to the seas as their fields, the citizens of the Pomorye were a special breed of people, able to bear any deprivation with a smile and joke, look any torment or danger straight in the eye, unconcerned by isolation and being alone, with fear unknown to them, and possessed of an internal sense of curiosity and sharpwittedness. Genuine fishermen were entirely honest, never taking fish from another's net. Thieving was unknown among peasants in the Pomorye, and taking from others was regarded as a terrible sin. The cast of life in Pomorye, with its dangerous fishing occupation, created an ethic of fraternity and hospitality.[5]

As the Soviet economy began to stagnate, the regime gave increasing emphasis to trying to inspire people to work through imagery, symbolic awards, and newly created industrial rituals (Lane 1981: 109–30). Rather than stressing the discontinuity between the modern trawlerman and the old Pomors, as Stalin era writers had done, the North's Soviet fishermen and sailors were now firmly positioned as the rightful inheritors of the Pomors:

Yes, hard was the lot of the pre-revolutionary Pomor, but in the single-handed struggle with ice and storms was laid down the Pomorski character. Now we have a highly modern trawler fleet – but the Arctic remains the Arctic and the sea remains the sea. The dangers, heroism and romance persist. We are proud that the high human qualities and sailing expertise distinguishing our northern sailors and fishermen absorbed the best traditions of the Pomors. The North's youth still yearns for this arduous and honourable profession, the salty tang of the sea and northern winds, the romance of its hard and manly path (*Pravda Severa*, 5.9.1972).

This celebration of heritage reached its peak in the 400th anniversary of Arkhangelsk in 1984, when the city saw a great outpouring of regional feeling, some of it officially staged, but much of it genuine. A scale model of the pre-revolutionary city, complete with cathedral and churches, was displayed to thousands of visitors. There were re-enactments of the arrival of Peter the Great, flanked by Pomor helmsmen, while the verses of a celebratory cantata gave as much prominence to the Pomors as to Lenin. Images of the Pomors were also enshrined in the large mosaics and murals which adorned the new library and airport buildings built for the celebrations. Thus, while few physical Pomor communities actually remained, the city appeared to embrace the Pomor spirit and sense of identity, and Party officials duly deployed it in the service of patriotism and industry:

You are Arkhangelogorodski! Not for nothing has the title Pomor – an Arkhangelsk Northener – long been known as quite indivisible from the very highest qualities of the Russian character. Manly and honest, work-loving and loyal to comrades, to native region, to the Motherland . . . You, the young citizen of the capital of the North have received a rich inheritance. So be worthy of it. Protect the honour of the Arkhangelsk mark on any item of production. Let 'Made in Arkhangelsk' be a guarantee of reliability, solidity and durability . . . Continue the glorious revolutionary and working traditions of your fathers and grandfathers! (*Severni Komsomolets*, 11.3.1982).

The North during Perestroika

Under Gorbachev, images of the North became more complex and debated. As many people must have known, and as *glasnost* now admitted, the heritage-based hype was in stark contrast to the reality, since the society and economy of the North, particularly in its rural areas, was in fact in a parlous state, with a dwindling, ageing and increasingly demoralized population, and hundreds of ancient villages now lying abandoned. In the new spirit of self-criticism, local journalists contrasted the much-vaunted labour traditions of the past with those of the present:

> The village of Kimzha arose at the beginning of the sixteenth century, founded by enterprising migrants from Novgorod. No little danger awaited the newcomers to this uninhabited area, but they celebrated their safe passage by erecting the fine five-towered church of Odigitrii to the saint of travellers and fishermen . . . But now one has a gloomy feeling when encountering the church, with its broken door frames and collapsing timbers strewn around the ground. The fate of the monument depends above all on the attitude toward it of the citizens of the village – the building needs a master, and a master who will work (*Pravda Severa*, 14.1.1987).

Gorbachev was sympathetic to this kind of critique, and it was precisely such passivity, indifference and idleness among the rural population, and Soviet workers more generally, that he was determined to end. Proclaiming the slogan of Social Justice, he argued that under Brezhnevite stagnation wages had become unjust, with pay and bonus rates failing to reflect differences between hard workers and lazy ones. He thus proposed to reverse such levelling and give people more opportunity and incentive to work hard and demonstrate initiative, thereby helping to revitalize the moribund economy. This view struck a chord with many Russians and contributed to the widespread optimism during the early years of perestroika. The prevailing ethic of 'we pretend to work and they pretend to pay us' had become frustrating for those people who did want to work properly and skilfully and be rewarded for it, and there was widespread resentment that payments were often set not according to merit or effort, but rather *blat* (personal favouritism), or Party membership, or simply creativity in filling out the work sheet.

In the agricultural sphere, Gorbachev promoted a scheme which allowed small groups of family or friends to take responsibility for an area of land, farming it more or less as their own, freed from the collective farm bureaucracy. As it turned out, this new breed of 'Soviet farmer' came to be known throughout Russia as '*Arkhangelski muzhiki*' (Arkhangelsk peasants), a circumstance which reflected the story of one Nikolai Sivkov, who lived in Arkhangelsk oblast and was one of the first to take land in this way. Initially, he was systematically impeded and persecuted by the local Party structure which opposed such reforms, and condemned as a would-be kulak. However, he then received support from Moscow, and national newspapers such as *Pravda* discussed his progress at length, presenting it as an index of the course of perestroika and the struggle between reformers and reactionaries. A film crew made a glowing film about him which was shown twice on national TV during 1987 to huge audiences, and was awarded a Lenin prize. With his endearing personality and earthy humour, optimism and stubbornness in confronting the bureaucracy, and relentless sixteen-hour working days, Sivkov became a cult figure among supporters of reform throughout the country, and a hero of the times. He was gradually joined by others, most of them first- or second-generation proletarians whose forebears had been driven to the towns by collectivization, and who described their frustration at not being able to use their initiative and creativity in their factory jobs:

> These 'Arkhangelsk muzhiki' are all endowed with a certain obstinacy and caprice. They don't tolerate any coercion or goading or moral admonitions, and firmly adhere to their right to make independent judgements and pursue self-sufficient activity. Precisely such characters make excellent farmers. They aren't angels, but don't ask for the garden of Eden. They simply ask for land so that they can do good with it, growing vegetables and raising cattle to feed people (*Pravda Severa*, 15.2.1991).

This then was an interesting exercise in image creation, as older myths were recycled and the new farmers portrayed in ways which clearly mirrored the accounts of the firm and unyielding Northern character of yore. The North thus came to symbolize both the starkest problems of the Soviet rural slump, and the best hope for regeneration.

At the heart of the vision for reforming rural and urban workers was the notion of the *khozyain*. The word *khozyain* is an ancient and rich one, grounded in the world of the peasant household and feudal estate, and means variously owner, proprietor, master, boss, manager, husband, and host. A derivative adjective, *khozyaiski*, can mean proprietary, but more usually solicitous and careful, while the verb *khozyainichat* is to manage, and to keep house, but also has connotations of being commanding, confident, thrifty and economical. Many believed that the North had once been full of such men, since only genuine *khozyains* could wrest a living from the harsh climate. In the reformist discourse of the perestroika period therefore, the *khozyain* was someone who would once more work with feelings of true commitment to the land or factory, and with a sense of stewardship and responsibility that would search for constant savings and efficiencies. The farmer Sivkov happily declared that he was now:

> undoubtedly a khozyain, making all decisions, pouring all strength into work, constantly concerned about how work is proceeding, counting every last kopek, nursing every last cow. He told with pride how much meat he had given the country, how such work would soon cure all deficits! (*Pravda Severa*, 9.8.1989).

Meanwhile, in the industrial sphere, particularly in heavy industry such as the coal mines, a similar vision had developed of the need for a 'real *khozyain*' to run such enterprises. Tired of incompetent and arbitrary managers, the workers hoped Gorbachev's reforms would bring new bosses who were firm but fair, in control but beneficent and consultative, genuine stewards who could balance production and profit with the interests and well-being of the workers, thereby inspiring them to work (Ashwin 1999: 74–80).

The Approach to the Market

By 1991, the increasingly acute shortages and queues indicated that Gorbachev's attempts to reform the planned economy had merely brought chaos, and that a more radical move to embrace free prices and trade was inevitable. Responding to this prospect, local historians and writers poured out enthusiastic accounts of the North's pre-revolutionary economic life. They described in detail the Pomor trade with Northern Scandinavia, and stressed the contribution it had made to the prosperity of both regions. They also described the various *yarmarki*, or trading fairs, that had been held around the North, notably the great fortnight-long Maragaritskiya Fair in Arkhangelsk, where foreign and Russian merchants mingled among the Pomors and peasants, agreeing large-scale contracts for timber and shipping amid the stalls of craftsmen and the exuberance of folk festivities. Given the current shortages, it was proposed to revive the fair to improve trade flows into the region.[6]

In similar vein, there began to appear numerous articles, often in publications sponsored by new commercial organizations, describing the mercantile and entrepreneurial traditions of the North:

> For 75 years the government sought to erase the idea of business and entrepreneurship from our minds as something alien and associated with our enemies. We have good reason in this time of transition therefore to look back to our past, to search for our roots, the historic experience of our own remarkable forebears and the centuries-old tradition of the business world of the north (*Pravda Severa*, 18.1.1992).

A typical example was the remarkable tale of Ignaty Ivanovich Burkov, a Pomor born in 1861 who began with a small fishing boat, and gradually built up a passenger and freight fleet that by 1917 had made him one of the three richest ship-owners in the North and then the manager of the Arkhangelsk docks. He refused to flee after the revolution, handing over his property and putting his skills at the service of the Bolsheviks, but was eventually executed as a very old man in the 1937 purges:

> The strong and deep roots put down in the northern soil by Burkov have unfortunately withered. But we don't want to believe that they have disappeared completely. They ought to be an example to us – the energy and determination of the Pomor Burkov is a fine example of unselfish service to the fatherland (*Delovoi Nedelnik*, 2.4.1993).

Such articles stressed that, rather than being the exploitative villains of Soviet ideology, the entrepreneurs had worked very hard for often modest turnovers, while plagued by bureaucrats and bandits. They were men of honour whose word had underpinned transactions, and they were generous to their workers and philanthropic to their local communities. Above all, they were self-made men who through sheer endeavour had built up shipping lines or brick factories and brought employment and benefit to their native region, and were thus worthy of imitation:

> We have faith that in the present generation of Northerners is still preserved and has not been finally extinguished that spirit of healthy enterprise and trading ability which drove their forebears (*Arkhangelsk*, 27.9.1991).

As Clarke and Fairbrother rightly comment (and as survey results from that time confirm), the initial transformation of the socialist system into a market economy did have deep and genuine roots in the consciousness of the Russian people and was not something artificially imposed from without (Clarke et al. 1993: 57–90). Many people in Arkhangelsk entered the post-Soviet period with high hopes of the new market, and while the desire for improved supplies and higher living standards was certainly part of this, there were also moral and political aspirations. By ending the rule of the Party and its control of the economy, many hoped for a more just distribution of resources, whereby far less would go to the innumerable bureaucrats and functionaries and to the lazy and indifferent, and more to those who worked hard and conscientiously. It was hoped that these ambitions, which perestroika had raised but not achieved, would now be delivered by the market mechanism, providing incentive to everyone – farmer, industrial worker, manager or businessman – to become real *khozyains*, showing industriousness, skill and stewardship and reviving the enterprising spirit of the Pomors, the northern peasantry and the Arkhangelsk merchants, thereby renewing the life of the Pomorye itself, the essential soul of Russia.

The Popular Critique of Entrepreneurs

In assessing the subsequent negative views of the market economy, it is therefore vital to see in them an acute disappointment that such hopes have remained largely unfulfilled, the idealistic images of the market belied by the reality. The city's new trade did not resemble the festive and bucolic images of the old fairs with their hearty Pomors and handicrafts. Instead, petty traders, intermittently bullied by minor mafiosi, line the streets or occupy nooks and crannies in public buildings, more often than not selling cheap foreign clothes, cigarettes and chewing gum, and contributing to the mountains of cardboard and organic debris which pile up, blocking entrances and tram stops and provoking endless complaint. Meanwhile inflation and macro-economic instability have brought the collapse of whole swathes of local industry and agriculture. Afflicted by low food prices, high fuel prices, foreign competition and high interest rates, few in the North have chosen to follow the path of the Arkhangelsk *muzhiki* and become independent farmers, while many of the original ones have become bankrupt.[7]

Meanwhile factories stand idle, lacking materials, tools or orders, and even when the staff do work, the hard-working and lazy alike receive low wages, often many months late. Despite holding a handful of shares in their enterprises (which are worthless, given the absence of profits or dividends), few Northern workers feel they have gained an increased sense of ownership or control. Amid such a collapse, to retain feelings of responsibility for one's factory is simply to torture oneself, and so absenteeism and drunkenness persist and increase. While some managers certainly strive to sustain their enterprises, most remain far removed from the workers' hopes of a 'real *khozyain*', instead being prone to use intimidation and the manipulation of shareholdings and voting rights to increase their own power and privileges.

Nor do many entrepreneurs appear to live up to the idealistic images of their pre-revolutionary forebears. Consumers face a minefield of dodgy weights and measures, forged trading licences, food that is well past its safe trading date, fake vodka full of industrial spirit, shoes that fall apart on first wearing and televisions that catch fire, while millions have lost money in the various investment schemes whose founders pledged to renew Russia's economic strength. In the larger enterprises, managers complain they can no longer trust one another, and many flirt with criminality, with the heads of both the Arkhangelsk Fishing Fleet and Arkhangelsk Cellulose Plant being investigated in 1994 on various charges of tax evasion and fraudulent activity.

A key element in the imagery of pre-revolutionary entrepreneurs was their ability to rise from humble backgrounds and create something from nothing, but much of the New Russians' activity appears predicated on simply getting one's hands on the fruits of the privatization programme, and the Party-State nomenklatura, far from being undermined by the advent of the market, have flourished by virtue of their connections and access to capital. For example, one of the most successful Arkhangelsk banks was set up by the former head of the oblast Komsomol, who is generally presumed to have utilized its funds. As one irate citizen put it:

> To have opened a counting-house on the street corner when everything is falling into your hands, to simply close your fist in order to grasp what is handed to you by your patrons higher up as the Partyocracy transforms itself into businessmen – these are not exactly the dynamic qualities of business initiative which are going to raise Russia up out of poverty! (*Pravda Severa*, 26.11.93).

Popular critiques are also alert to the implausible rates of return achieved by the new millionaires. Old Soviet slogans repeatedly stressed to workers that real wages could not rise faster than improvements in productivity, and so Russian citizens are just as aware of this linkage as those in Western countries. Given that the economy was in free fall, how could such wealth possibly be made in other than illegal or fabricated ways?:

> Think what a hard-working farmer or garage owner can accumulate in his life, even in Western Europe: his farm and buildings, cars, tractors, some savings. That's about all. How is it then that our businessmen, so-called entrepreneurs, have been able to accumulate so much money so quickly? (*Pravda Severa*, 23.12.94).

The main popular criticism of the post-Soviet entrepreneurs is that they appear not to be contributing to developing the region's productive capacity. Where the pre-revolutionary magnates had built timber mills and brick factories, shipping fleets and railway lines, the New Russians preside over economic slump and unemployment. Those who have prospered have mostly been traders importing goods and food from abroad,[8] or else financiers who have benefited from the high interest rates which have helped cripple industry:

> The authorities claim to be pursuing the rapid inculcation of the doctrine of capitalism, but in practice this is simply involving the sale of state enterprises and creating a 'third layer'. But no one is thinking about how to bring to order the workings of industry. Our 'capitalists' aren't at all interested in production, only in making money out of thin air. A. Sorokin (*Pravda Severa*, 28.8.92).

> What is the basis for the creation of wealth for a country and its people? Only productive labour, that is, labour producing some kind of product. Our material and productive base is day by day getting worse, but the non-productive sector of banks and voucher investments grows like weeds. Our laws work not for workers but only favour buyers and resellers and provide no support for those producing material value. (*Pravda Severa*, 23.12.94)

The idea that only 'production' constitutes real economic activity deserving of reward is a widespread and deeply held one in Russian society, and stems from several sources. Inspired by Marx's labour theory of value, Soviet ideology and education not only surrounded labour with a sacred halo, but conceived of it in a very concrete way, with plans framed always in terms of tons of coal and litres of milk. While this framework typically disadvantaged health workers, teachers and shop assistants, it appealed to industrial workers. When the miners went on strike in 1989 and 1990 in support of market reforms, they explicitly argued that as the producers they should keep more of the surplus value generated, rather than having it seized by the unproductive bureaucrats of the Party-State (Crowley 1997: 196–7). The Soviet view was also concordant with Russian peasant culture which had its own labour principle, whereby only physical labour produced wealth, with the value and use rights of land rightfully determined only by the labour invested in it (Smith 1999: 144–5). This conjunction of the peasant and Marxist view should not seem so surprising, for as Steven Gudeman (1986) has shown, the agricultural 'house model' of early modern Europe influenced Marx himself via the Physiocrats and their mercantilist critics, while in Russian the word for the 'economy' is directly derived from that of the peasant household (*khozyaistvo*). In any case, there is little need to put too much weight on ancient peasant ethics since, as I have indicated, under Brezhnev and Gorbachev there were plentiful heritage images of the productivist ethos, with the Pomors and their trawlermen descendants battling the Arctic waves for fish, and the old northern peasantry and new Arkhangelsk muzhiki wresting vegetables and meat from the unpropitious soil.

Against this background, it is understandable why so many people should complain that whereas they had worked hard for long years in timber mills or shipyards 'creating material value for the state', the new entrepreneurs had not. Thus it is not simply that the new entrepreneurs fall short of the supposed standards of honour and grace of their predecessors. Rather, in the eyes of many, they are simply not entrepreneurs at all, since they are not helping to foster or organize production. This in turn is consistent with the frequent critical assessment of the aberrant nature of the Russian market as 'not really a market at all', but rather a primitive bazaar:

> We are not going to a market in our country. It is just a grand bazaar, a parody of a market, a facade for criminal activity. The businessmen are pillaging the country, raw materials are being sold abroad for next to nothing, capital is flowing out of the country. The country has become poor, and the narod with it, apart from the businessmen who enrich themselves at the expense of the *narod* (*Arkhangelsk*, 23.4.1992).

Accordingly, many people, including supporters of the transition to a free market, view most Russian businessmen as 'so-called' entrepreneurs within a 'bazaar' economy, and they thus resent the material rewards and official veneration bestowed upon them.

However, amid all the criticism, the people of Arkhangelsk also talk and write letters about businessmen whom they *do* consider to be genuine entrepreneurs. Generally, these are people running small-scale operations, often of an artisanal character, who have successfully addressed a particular need or shortage (either producing it themselves, or sourcing it from local producers) by selling decent quality goods at fair prices. Thus, in a typical example, someone praised to me (as 'a positive exemplar of the renaissance in Russia of the trading point of view') a milk merchant who bought and transported milk from local farms, and who had set up a small facility in his garage to produce milk cartons (from local cardboard), allowing him to sell milk in convenient form. Here then, both consumers and local producers benefited, while he himself made a modest return. In similar spirit, an old man urged the city's entrepreneurs to fulfil his dream of once again seeing throughout the city small private bakeries where he would be able to buy the kinds of cakes and pies his mother had made before collectivization, noting that:

> Many people today, especially from my own generation of older people, retain negative judgements about today's emerging merchants and entrepreneurs. Certainly they are a mixed bunch and not without their swindlers, but such was the case in Peter the Great's time also. But many are honest enterprising people, concerned about sustaining trade at a particular level, best deploying their means, organizing capital, and attracting the attention of buyers (*Pravda Severa*, 21.5.93).

In his analysis of Thatcherite rhetoric in 1980's Britain, Norman Fairclough discusses the slippery nature of the word 'enterprise' (Fairclough 1991). Standard dictionary definitions cite a disposition to engage in bold, arduous or momentous undertakings, or alternatively, in conjunction with 'private' or 'free', a more specific kind of business activity. While the context would normally resolve the meaning in everyday use, government speeches tended to glide ambiguously between the general sense of hard work, risk taking and responsibility, and the more specific business sense of spotting a niche opportunity and improving one's own financial position. Fairclough suggests that consciously or unconsciously, the ministers used such ambiguity and elisions to encourage the revaluation of a discredited private business sector by associating private enterprise with culturally valued qualities of 'enterprisingness' (Fairclough 1991: 38–58).

There is a similarly closely knit family of words in Russian (*predpriimchivost* – initiative; *predpriyatye* – undertaking or adventure; *predprinimatel* – entrepreneur; *predpriimchivi* – enterprising) and the official proponents of market reform also sought to play on such ambiguities. Building on perestroika's calls for a renewed spirit of enterprise, they equated this with the need for laissez-faire capitalism and entrepreneurship. Similarly, the new businessmen of the North sought a positive public evaluation of their activity by associating it with culturally and historically valued qualities of enterprisingness, as enshrined in the continuing popular images of Novgorod traders, the Northern peasantry and the Pomors. However, as I have suggested, many Northerners refuse to accept this association, comparing the new entrepreneurs unfavourably to the traditional figures they seek to identify with, and denying to them the claimed virtues of enterprise. Rather, people remain more likely to ascribe 'enterprise' to those who, though lacking in any capital, work hard to ensure that the track is always cleared of snow, or who break their backs on a tiny dacha plot to ensure they can feed their family.

There is a similar ambiguity over '*khozyain*'. The proponents of the privatization programme used the term to convey notions of private property, ownership and control over the production process. As I indicated earlier however, in popular usage the sense of the word was typically quite different, focusing not on aspects of contract or property, but on personal qualities of responsibility, wisdom, fairness and stewardship, virtues once more refused to the entrepreneurs who claim them:

> Now we have returned to the word '*khozyain*', and *khozyain*s we have in abundance, their businesses called 'joint stock company with limited liability'. They had said to us: soon the shops will be full, with everything of high quality. In fact the quality is now worse and the prices far higher. So all in the end depends on the man, his honesty and morality, and not on the name of his system, socialist or capitalist (*Pravda Severa*, 30.4.1993).

To sum up, I would suggest that in the Arkhangelsk region at least, there is not a widespread condemnation of entrepreneurship. Rather, those (few) individuals who are accepted as genuine entrepreneurs, as *khozyain*s who demonstrate enterprise by building up a small productive operation after starting with nothing, receive praise, not opprobrium. Similarly, there is not a blanket rejection of entrepreneurial wealth and income inequality, since the genuine entrepreneur is entitled to earn his money (while swindlers and speculators are not). It is an inequality, however, whose extent is logically limited by the prevailing view of genuine entrepreneurship as something not too far removed from peasant or artisanal activity,[9] where returns are modest and demonstrably connected to the sweat of labour:

> They say money doesn't smell. But the viewpoint of the soul perceives it differently. The working ruble smells of milk and onions, metal and timber,

soil and sky. The soul of such a business and such a businessman is clean and clear. So why not praise such a merchant? (*Pravda Severa*, 24.7.94)

Lastly, I would suggest it is inaccurate to talk of general Russian hostility to the market. There is hostility to the aberrant bazaar or 'so-called' market which many people consider they have, but there is also a clear vision of what a genuine market would be. On the one hand, it would allow those who wished to become genuine entrepreneurs to do so, participating in what Solzhenitsyn has called healthy, honest, wise private trade, enlivening and supporting society. On the other, it would allow and encourage those who did not wish to be entrepreneurs to nonetheless realize the virtues of enterprise and stewardship in whatever factory, farm or office they should find themselves:

> We are urged to get busy, be enterprising. Quite right, no time for delay. But what we must do is all get to work, not trade but work, work and more work. Then later we can think about trading what we have made. We must follow the example of the 'Arkhangelsk muzhik', who only sells what he breaks his back producing. Only an atmosphere of general and mutual respect between workers, farmers, kolkhozniki, engineers, and entrepreneurs – real ones that is – can bring the salvation of Russia (*Pravda Severa*, 7.2.92).

Conclusion

As political scientists have themselves admitted, despite the huge number of surveys conducted on Russians' attitudes toward economic and political questions, we remain unsure about fundamental aspects of public opinion. This is due to the significant variations in results between surveys, and the often confusing and contradictory outcomes within single ones (Alexander 1997: 107–27). In considering this predicament, some scholars have concluded that such results reflect the confusion and even *anomie* of this great ideological upheaval. While there may be something to this, the braver conclusion voiced by some is that the relevant ideas and moral notions are simply too complex to nail down with the standardized questions of a survey, particularly if it is designed to assess such crude factors as whether respondents are 'individualist' or 'collectivist', 'democrats' or 'authoritarians'. As I hope I have conveyed even in this short discussion, the popular critique of the market is more articulate and complex than such statistical constructs can allow. Some surveys for instance have been puzzled by the fact that many Russians respondents say 'yes' to freedom of economic activity, but 'no' to economic inequality, a combination which makes little sense according to the dominant American perspective. In the light of my discussion, however, we can perhaps see why this is nonetheless plausible and cogent in the context of Russians' wider views about entrepreneurs, views which in turn are caught up in a dense web of meanings taking in *khozyains*, enterprise, labour and production, and which have emotional and symbolic content and are infused by rich local historical imagery. This is not to call for the abandonment of questionnaires, but simply to speak in support of those who are now stressing the importance of first undertaking locally based ethnography in order to establish the vital synoptic and semantic foundations for more nuanced survey work (Alexander 1997: 125; Fleron 1996: 225–60).

Finally, and to return to the debate with which I began, the North's regional culture and traditions clearly *do* inform citizens' contemporary evaluations of entrepreneurs. However, as I have tried to show, this is the result not of some shadowy collective memory or peasant ethic which has stayed mysteriously intact, but rather reflects images and tropes which have been continuously invented, suppressed, revived and inverted during decades of ideological shifts and stormy cultural politics.

Notes

1. This chapter refers to letters and articles in the following Russian newspapers published and distributed in Arkhangelsk oblast (all of which are archived and available at the Oblast Reference Library in Arkhangelsk):
   Arkhangelsk – launched in late 1990 and published in Arkhangelsk by the press and media department of the Arkhangelsk city administration.
   Delovoi Nedelnik – a commercial newspaper launched in 1993, published in Arkhangelsk, sponsored by leading local banks and businesses.
   Kommunist – the main newspaper for Kargopol raion, published in Kargopol by the raion Communist Party Committee and raion Soviet of People's Deputies. In 1992 changed its name to *Kargopol*.
   Pravda Severa – the main newspaper for Arkhangelsk oblast since the 1920s, published in Arkhangelsk by the oblast Communist Party Committee and oblast Soviet of People's Deputies. Since 1992 published by the oblast administration.

Severni Komsomolets – formerly the organ of the oblast Komsomol, the paper continues to be published out of Arkhangelsk by the oblast administration, though now as a separately branded mainstream newspaper rather than a youth one.
All translations from these newspapers and from other Russian texts are my own.

2. 'The public looked askance at the profiteers . . . and objected vociferously to the high earnings of some entrepreneurs whom they compared invidiously to the "nep-men" and "bourgeois" of popular mythology. The transition to a free market awakened deep-rooted egalitarian sentiments. Envy of those who had made good had been the foundation of mass support for Stalinism' (Keep 1996: 395–6).

3. The idea is that traditional Russian peasant life continues to influence the Russian outlook by strengthening a distaste for individual achievement or distincton – better that all suffer equally than one gets ahead. The influential medievalist Ned Keenan stresses the anti-individualist ethos of village life and the strong tendency to maintain stability and a kind of closed equilibrium in order to avoid risk and suppress individual initiatives, and the striving for unanimous resolution of potentially divisive issues. Such attitudes, he suggests, were brought to the towns and cities through peasant migration after the 1861 emancipation and 1929 collectivization (Keenan 1986).

4. Witte appealed to this sentiment when he convinced the Tsar to build the new northern naval base on the Murman, rather than the more expensive base on the Baltic which the Admirals desired.

5. The poet and novelist Dmitri Lichutin, writing in the 1980s (quoted in *Pravda Severa*, 18.3.1993).

6. 'We are gradually coming to realize that no one is going to give us abundance, not the government, nor extraordinary committees; no one will feed and clothe the narod. We see rising prices, deficits of goods and the beginning of unemployment and our hearts quake. We will not wave our arms in despair in face of these difficulties, however. Instead we look to the history of our Russian North. This gives us a chance to be convinced that our forebears for the most part were well clothed and fed, on the basis of their profitable and useful trade with their neighbours, above all with the Northern provinces of Norway. Today as never before we ought to be turning our attention to the experience of the past generation, in particular to their organization of trade at fairs which was so precipitately and thoughtlessly abolished in the first years of Soviet power' (*Arkhangelsk*, 27.9.91).

7. The end of market optimism was seen to be symbolized by the death of Sivkov himself in 1994: 'Aged 62, full of ideas and plans for the future, he has died. A Man with a capital letter, glory of our Arkhangelsk soil. Along with Sivkov an entire epoch has quietly left the stage, a fine-souled and naive one, When he began, there was the conviction that if only on high they could be pushed in the right direction, within a year there would be a new life, with full shops, kindly leaders, fertility and abundance. On high they heard us it seemed, but we have ended up with only rackets, corruption, inflation and unemployment. Now we await no rural miracle, and have quietly moved on to the import of Snickers and Whiskas . . . So the death of the Arkhangelsk muzhik and his era is perhaps the saddest date in the whole of this last battle-filled and anxious year' (*Arkhangelsk*, 15.1.94).

8. 'Now people only want to trade – and where this is leading is clear. The wallets of our competitors grow fat while Mother Russia grows ever weaker, and the narod completely forget about our own products. This should make us think it's time to grow our own grain and meat once more' (*Pravda Severa*, 25.3.94).

9. This helps make makes sense of the survey findings from 1991/92 that showed strong support for the privatization of small-scale businesses such as shops, services and light industry, but opposition to that of major enterprises in heavy industry and finance (Wyman 1997: 188–92).

References

Alexander, J. (1997), 'Surveying Attitudes in Russia: A Representation of Formlessness', *Communist and Post-Communist Studies*, 30, 107–27.

Ashwin, S. (1999), *Russian Workers: The Anatomy of Patience*, Manchester: Manchester University Press.

Bernstham, T. (1978), *Pomori: formirovanie gruppi i sistema khozyaistvo*, Leningrad: Academy of Science of the USSR.

Boele, O. (1996), *The North in Russian Romantic Literature*, Amsterdam: Rodopi BV Editions.

Clarke, S., Fairbrother, P., Burawoy, M., and Krotov, P. (1993), *What about the Workers? Workers and the Transition to Capitalism in Russia*, London: Verso.

Creed, G.W. (1998), *Domesticating Revolution: From Socialist Reform to Ambivalent Transition in a Bulgarian Village*, University Park: Pennsylvania State University Press.

Crowley, S. (1997), *Hot Coal, Cold Steel: Russian and Ukrainian Workers from the End of the Soviet Union to the Post-Communist Transformations,* Ann Arbor: University of Michigan Press.

Fairclough, N. (1991), 'What might we mean by "Enterprise Discourse"?', in R. Keat and N. Abercrombie (eds), *Enterprise Culture,* London: Routledge.

Fleron, F. (1996), 'Post-Soviet Political Culture in Russia: An Assessment of Recent Empirical Investigations', *Europe-Asia Studies* 48, 22–60.

Grant, B. (1995), *In the Soviet House of Culture: a Century of Perestroikas,* Princeton: Princeton University Press.

Gudeman, S. (1986), *Economics as Culture: Models and Metaphors of Livelihood,* London: Routledge & Kegan Paul.

Humphrey, C. (1998), *Marx Went Away – But Karl Stayed Behind,* Ann Arbor: University of Michigan Press.

Keenan, E.L (1986), 'Muscovite Political Folkways', *The Russian Review,* 45, 115–81.

Keep, J. (1996), *Last of the Empires: a History of the Soviet Union 1945–91,* Oxford: Oxford University Press.

Lane, C. (1981) *The Rites of Rulers – Ritual in Industrial Society: the Soviet Case,* Cambridge: Cambridge University Press.

Maksimov, S.V. (1984 [1859]), *God na Severa,* Arkhangelsk: North West Press.

Nielson, E.P. (1992), 'Russian danger for Norway?', *Journal of the Museum of Tromso,* 192, 33–41.

Owen, T.C. (1999), 'Entrepreneurship, government, and society in Russia', in G. Hosking and R. Service (eds), *Reinterpreting Russia,* London: Arnold.

Reisinger, W., Miller, A. and Hesli, V. (1995), 'Political Norms in Rural Russia: Evidence from Public Attitudes', *Europe-Asia Studies,* 47, 1025–42.

Reisinger, W., Miller, A., Hesli, V. and Maher, K. (1994), 'Political Values in Russia, Ukraine and Lithuania: Sources and Implications of Democracy', *British Journal of Political Science,* 24, 183–223.

Smith, S. (1999), 'Popular culture and market development in late Imperial Russia', in G. Hosking and R. Service (eds), *Reinterpreting Russia,* London: Arnold.

Verdery, K. (1996), *What Was Socialism and what Comes Next?,* Princeton: Princeton University Press.

Wyman, M. (1997), *Public Opinion in Postcommunist Russia,* London: Macmillan.

–5–

Dealing with Money: Złotys, Dollars and Other Currencies in the Polish Highlands
Frances Pine

Introduction: money or monies

One day in 1979, I went with a small group of people from the village in south-western Poland, where I was living and doing research, to another village nearby to attend a wedding. At that time there were only two or three cars in the village, and we were travelling by horsedrawn cart. The trip was slow, over a rough dirt path, and there was a lot of time to talk. The conversation began with gossip about the bride, the groom and other guests and then moved on to money. Piton asked casually what the exchange rate between dollars and pounds was. Naively assuming that the question was directed to me, I answered with what I thought was reasonable authority. My companions were politely dismissive. 'No', said Jurek, 'that was last week. Yesterday it shifted.' They then went on to discuss fluctuations in the rates of the deutschmark and the yen in relation to the American dollar, current exchange rates set by the Polish government as opposed to those realizable on the black market, and the pros and cons of dollars versus deutschmarks as stable forms of investment. In this context, the pound was not mentioned even as an also-ran. I, realizing I was quite out of my depth, remained strategically silent. But it was a salutary lesson. These people were daily operating with monies, or at least the ideas of monies, in far more complex ways than I had assumed or imagined, and certainly than I, as a young and broke graduate student, was myself. At a time when the BBC World Service and Radio Free Europe, both of which might have been considered sources of information about Western currency, were systematically blocked, when possession of undeclared foreign currency was a criminal offence, and when most Westerners were automatically assumed to be spies, these villagers' information about types of money and informal and formal exchange rates was up-to-the-minute. Over the months and years to come those closest to me regularly expressed doubt about my ability to survive with any kind of competence in what they saw as, essentially, a dealers' world.

Throughout the 1970s, Gierek's government attempted to assuage Poland's growing economic crisis by taking on hard currency loans, primarily from the Americans. As the national debt grew, the government increasingly turned a blind eye to foreign currency dealings in the informal economy, dealings which were largely although not exclusively conducted through the medium of American dollars. By the late 1970s it was impossible for a Western European or North American to walk down the street in a small town, let alone in Krakow or Warsaw, without hearing a buzz of furtive whispers from the shadows: 'Change money? Change money?' In the village in which I worked, nearly every house had access to dollars through some avenue, very few of which were legal but almost all of which were socially approved and valued in local terms.

As my fieldwork progressed I became more and more interested in the importance the villagers attached to money not only, obviously, in their economic transactions – and these were by no means straightforward – but also socially and symbolically. With the exception of the very old and the very young, all residents of the village in the 1970s and 1980s operated their lives using the medium of money, and very few confined these transactions to the Polish złoty. American dollars were in certain contexts at least as important as złotys, and in some contexts even more so, and other currencies, primarily the deutschmark and to a lesser extent the rouble, were also used in the informal economy. Different currencies had different social value, were used in different situations, and above all carried different symbolic meanings (i.e., deutschmarks and roubles were politically loaded in a negative way, dollars in a positive one). Secondly, the use of money was subject to various unspoken but commonly understood restrictions. There were situations in which it would have been inappropriate to use money at all, or in which if money did change hands the transaction was masked, and its direct nature disguised. Or, there were certain sorts of exchanges, usually between unequal parties, in which it was acceptable for money to flow in one direction but not in the other. What I want to explore in this chapter is the ways that Górale (literally 'highlanders'/'mountain people') used money during the socialist period, some of the meanings which attached to the different usages and finally, ways that these appeared to change in the early postsocialist years. Although the different uses of money during the socialist period in some ways fit models of spheres of exchange, and of general- versus specific-purpose money, these concepts are too limited to portray the complex and nuanced nature of the social meanings Górale attached to money, some of which were tied to local ideologies of kinship, belonging and community, the value of labour and perhaps most obliquely political relations with the state.

Anthropological writings have examined the relationship between the domestic, house- or kin-based economy, characterized by trust and morality (the moral economy proposed by Thompson (1971) and elaborated by Scott (1976) is an obvious forerunner here) and the external/state economy, based on commodified labour relations, and individual self-interest. Thus, Parry and Bloch discuss the co-existence of short-term and long-term cycles within the same culture, rather than what they refer to as the 'false history' which constructs around them a divide between cultures (1989: 29). Gudeman and Rivera (1990), writing about rural Colombia, propose a dialectical relationship between the house, which aims to maintain, and the corporation, the aim of which is to increase. Carsten (1989) describes the process by which Malaysian women transform the money earned by men in the competitive domain of commodified labour into the social food of kinship and the house. In a different context, Comaroff argues that the money earned through economic migration in southern Africa is seen as symbolizing rupture in the unified process of production, reproduction and consumption. By feeding the money back into the community in the course of Zionist Pentecostal ritual, she argues, people reunite what has been torn apart (1985).

All of these ideas can help us to make sense of Górale money dealings. However, as in each of these ethnographic examples, the particular complexities and range of meanings which attach to money, and the ways these change over time in response to specific historical and political circumstances, need to be understood. There is no doubt that Górale ideology places enormous moral legitimacy on the house, its production, consumption and ritual. It is through house membership more than anything else that full personhood is derived, that social relations emerge and develop, and that individual belonging and family relatedness are constructed and elaborated (Pine 1996b). Equally, Górale villagers tend to view the state, and any other outside force which exercises power over their beings and above all their mobility and their labour, with hostility and suspicion (Pine 1999). The house is the proper location for the consumption and display of money, while the outside – beyond the village, beyond the world of kinship reciprocity and exchange, beyond local and national borders – is the field from which money can legitimately be obtained, and almost any means of obtaining it is legitimate (Pine 1997, 1999). However, during the socialist period, and since 1989 in the postsocialist era, money constantly shifts its meaning according to context both within the house economy and outside. To reduce these shifts to a straightforward dichotomy between the moral economy of the house and the economy of the amoral, immoral or negative outside oversimplifies the nature of Górale economic and social life and ideology.

In the late 1970s there was a particular joke which villagers loved and often repeated.

Question: What is the difference between the dollar and the złoty?

Answer: There is no difference. In America the dollar buys everything and the złoty buys nothing. In Poland the złoty also buys nothing and the dollar also buys everything.

I want to suggest in this chapter that this juxtaposing of the dollar and the złoty was truer for Górale than for most other Poles during the socialist period, but that the sentiments of the joke also serve to obscure the complex roles played by both currencies during the years of crisis and shortage and, further, that these complexities to some extent only become clear in the light of the postsocialist economy. Contrasts between the local economy of the Podhale (literally 'under the high pastures'), the home of the Górale, and other parts of Poland interest me, but I am also struck by similarities between ideas about money in the Podhale in the late socialist period and in nineteenth- and early twentieth-century America (Zelizer 1994). To a great extent this chapter is rooted in the past, and that past, particularly the late socialist period but also before, is my point of departure.

Górale

Górale live in the Carpathian Mountains, in the foothills and high pasture reaches of the Tatra range which forms a natural border between Poland and Slovakia. Górale are renowned throughout Poland for being exotic, colourful, and rather wild. Men are depicted as hard-drinking even by Polish standards, as poised to fight and enter into blood feuds at the slightest provocation, and above all as autonomous – almost beyond the arm of the law. The women are seen as beautiful, strong, earthy and sensual, and as skilled and often flamboyant traders. Conversely, they may also be portrayed as primitive, often brutal and shifty or dishonest. In many ways these popular images of Górale are close to those many Poles hold of Roma – they are seen as dangerous, as uncannily 'knowing' in their pursuit of the ultimate deal, and as excessive in all things – numbers of children, size of houses, pursuit of visible signs of affluence and consumption always won by slightly dubious or shady means (or, when Górale themselves tell the stories, by the dramatic skills of the trickster) (Pine 1997, 1999). Unlike Roma, however, Górale are believed to be hard-working: men from other parts of Poland are said to seek Górale wives, for their labour and their fertility. Górale themselves consciously and often whimsically play on these images, partly I think because they serve to differentiate them from other Polish peasants but also because they provide a protective boundary which outsiders are reluctant to cross. For the present purposes the important points here are the distinction, internally and externally imposed, between Górale and other Poles, and Górale propensity for dealing and economic juggling.

Originally Vlach shepherds, the forebears of the present-day Górale migrated north-west along the mountain ridges, eventually becoming sedentary farmers although often, by necessity, continuing to herd and do other things as well. The village in which I work was first settled in the early seventeenth century, on land belonging to the Polish king and awarded to minor gentry as reward for service. Villagers held their lands in usufruct, and owed the local lord labour and payment in kind. In the mid-nineteenth century they were emancipated under Austrian law, and since that time have held title to their own lands.

In the past 500 years the Podhale has been part of the Polish Kingdom, the Austro-Hungarian Empire, the Polish Republic, Nazi-occupied Poland, the Polish People's Republic, and now the postsocialist republic of Poland. The politico-geographical space which the Podhale occupies has tended to place its inhabitants in ambiguous positions. On the one hand, the remoteness and inaccessibility of the mountains historically reinforced villagers' exclusion from political and economic centres, but on the other hand, trade and other traffic crossed the mountains, giving rise to market towns on the trade routes which provided villagers with venues for selling surplus and crafts. Less legitimate trade also grew, as the borders between nation states allowed local people to use their knowledge of the rather daunting landscape to develop networks for smuggling and dealing in contraband. From quite early in their history, therefore, Górale were simultaneously excluded from or marginal to the states in which they were politically situated, and actively involved in a transnational trading circuit.

From the mid-nineteenth century until the 1950s, while there can be no doubt that most villagers lived in quite abject poverty, the existence of the nearby market town afforded them opportunities not only for buying and selling but also for forging links with outsiders which could lead to further deals or to temporary economic migration. Through these practices they gained access to knowledge and information networks extending far beyond the Podhale itself: this paradoxical exclusion from the centre and participation in the wider outside economy remains a feature of Górale economy and culture.

In the late nineteenth century, outbreaks of plague and famine, combined with the dwarfing and fragmentation of peasant holdings which arose from partible inheritance, drove scores of villagers to leave their mountain home for the United States '*za chlebem*' (in search of bread). Most of the emigrants maintained ties with their natal villages, sending back money and care parcels, and often either returning themselves in their old age or sending their children back to marry. Many also provided the means for close kin to join them, at least temporarily, in Chicago. Thus, from relatively early on, villagers were familiar with and had unusual access to American dollars and to at least a second-hand version, if not first-hand experience, of American culture. Unusually for the eastern Bloc countries, this pattern of emigration to and contact with America was maintained throughout the socialist period, and particularly became of great significance during the Gierek period (the 1970s) and the years of crisis and martial law which followed.

The Socialist Period

The socialist regime in Poland, established in 1947 after the German occupation and the short but brutal and divisive civil war which followed it, precipitated substantial change in even remote rural areas like the Podhale. In the 1950s, the Stalinist industrialization drive swept through the countryside, generating the building of factories and the recruitment of both women and men into industrial production; the policy of full employment meant that for the first time in Górale history, regular waged labour and regular interaction with the state monetary economy became a normal rather than an exceptional pattern. (It is important to remember here that Poland, alone of all the Comecon countries, never succeeded in collectivizing more than a very small percentage of its agriculture, and in the Podhale all farms remained in private ownership.) In the village where I did research, people worked in the nearby shoe and ski factories, in the state-run dairy, in shops and government offices in the market town, and in the service sector. State employees were entitled to free or subsidized child care, medical and dental treatment, and to sickness and maternity benefits and pensions. Always downplaying their admittedly low wages, villagers would often state that they worked solely in order to avail themselves of these benefits and other more shady perks, such as moonlighting with state vehicles or machines, or access to goods and commodities which were in short supply. Within the farming economy, most villagers were contracted to deliver milk, and some meat, to the state cooperative. Only in rare cases did such sales provide the house with enough income to meet its needs, and the money these sales generated was usually portrayed in negative terms, as yet another example of the state's exploitation of farmers. On the other hand, in comparison to waged labour and agricultural production for the state, subsistence agriculture (working the land for the house) and home-based craft production were represented as the central and most important occupation of most villagers. Work for the state was, I would argue, viewed as an encroachment on both individual autonomy and the integrity of the house economy. People took holiday or sick leave, or simply failed to show up at the workplace, during planting, haymaking and harvest. Whenever possible, they transformed their waged labour into entrepreneurial activity: thus, the factory, shop or office was represented as the place where they went to earn złotys, but also as the place from which to go shopping on someone else's time, to make deals and arrangements and, at times, to smuggle out material or goods which could be used in production or for trade in the second economy. For instance, Maria worked for a weaving cooperative. From time to time, she would smuggle out scarce high-quality wool, with which she would knit and weave at home. She would sell the products on the market, or sometimes sell the raw wool to other village women. She did not earn a great deal from these ventures, but she saw them as a legitimate extension of her poorly paid waged labour.[1] Similarly, Marek, an ambulance driver, would 'borrow' the ambulance from time to time to make private deliveries or do haulage.

Such pilfering had its antecedents in the pre-war period, when poor villagers scavenged firewood and vegetables, by moonlight, from the forests and fields of the landed estates. Significantly, there was no context, in the reciprocal economy of house and community, that such pilfering was ever viewed as legitimate or moral: it was activity firmly located in relations of inequality between the village house and the outside.

As well as working in farming and in the state sector, many villagers continued during the socialist period in older patterns of marketing, trade, craft production and private manual labour. Most women sold produce and crafts in the local market from time to time. A small number became highly successful entrepreneurs: women dealing in smoked cheeses, tooled-leather slippers, hand-knitted woollen garments, and occasionally gold and foreign currency travelled as far afield as Warsaw and Gdansk, and sometimes even Russia and Turkey. Men worked closer to home as carpenters, roofers and highly lucratively as sheepskin curers and craftsmen. Finally, most houses earned additional money by providing services for tourists.

Skilled entrepreneurs enjoyed very high local status, in marked contrast to the low status and negative value associated with working for the state. They channelled the money they earned into the house and farm, building large brick houses or buying tractors and other machinery. Rooms in a large house could be let out informally, to tourists; tractor drivers could hire out their labour. Thus, informal or second economy activities allowed money to grow. This created a pattern similar to that of earmarking described by Zelizer (1994) in *The Social Meaning of Money*. Zelizer argues that the same currency may have different social meanings in different contexts, and may be distinguished, or earmarked, for different purposes; for instance, an American housewife in the nineteenth century might put money aside in a jar for school clothes and books, and this was separate from, and not interchangeable with, money for day-to-day household expenses. Górale villagers also maintained such practices, but they judged different categories of złotys by the context in which they were earned. Złotys earned in the state sector were systematically undervalued, while those earned through entrepreneurial activity, individual skill or house enterprise were highly valued. Sometimes the actual notes and coins were kept separately, state earning crumpled up in a pocket, wallet or drawer, going into the house 'pot' usually managed by the senior woman, and second-economy earning kept separately, in a cupboard in the best room, or traded for dollars. Sometimes these earnings actually came in the form of dollars, when the transactions involved very scarce goods or were made with foreigners or outsiders. This money was spent only after consultation among the adult members of the house, and usually went toward some major expenditure such as machinery, building or a ticket to the United States. In some households, very successful entrepreneurs or young unmarried dealers handed their state wages over to the 'pot' but kept their private earnings for themselves. In this case, however, it was expected that while some money might be used for personal consumption and display – buying drinks in the bar, expensive foreign clothes in the market – most would eventually be put toward the general well-being and growth of the house. A negative example makes this clear. In the late 1970s there was an old woman in the village who was reviled by most of her neighbours, because she was seen as being lazy and self indulgent. She refused to do farm work, they said, and instead spent her time reading books – to such an extent that she neglected her children, letting them run wild and hungry and poorly clothed. When it rained and the roof leaked, she let her children get wet, they claimed, simply putting up an umbrella for herself and continuing to read. Her daughter, with support from other village women, managed to become a successful market woman, establishing a trade route into Czechoslovakia, and made large sums of money. She put this aside for her dowry, usually the responsibility of the parents, and refused to give her mother money even when she needed it desperately. This was the antithesis of proper child-parent behaviour, but villagers were unanimous in approving of it. Her mother, they maintained, had failed to nurture and nourish her children, and they had no obligation to her. The daughter's only hope was to provide herself with a good dowry so she could marry, escape, and set up her own house. This story was often told to children, I think to instruct them in the proper role which money plays in the hierarchy of kinship and generations: within the domestic economy, the younger generation was expected to give most of what they earned to their parents, and unless highly successful kept back only 'pin money' or 'pocket money' for their own pleasure. Equally, however, parents were expected to provide for the young, and to work hard in order to do so.

Not only the earning of złotys, but also the spending of them, was socially nuanced. By the late 1970s, the state distribution system was at best arbitrary and at worst chaotic, corrupt and virtually non-functional (Wedel 1992). It became progressively more difficult to buy even the most basic goods in regular state shops for złotys. Far from being the impersonal, individuating medium of exchange described by Simmel and others, złotys as the putative general-purpose money in fact only 'worked' in restricted ways, in many contexts only with the mediation of wider social relations. Kin took turns queuing; queues were gendered, men standing in line for vodka and machinery, women for everything else, including food, clothes, toiletries, etc. Grandmothers held the family's place in a queue for hours at a time, and sometimes non-kin were paid a small sum to queue for others. Close networks of kin and *znajomy* (acquaintances) developed within which people exchanged favours and traded off any scarce resource to which they had access. Buying things for złotys was rarely a straightforward process. Rather, if people wanted a radio or washing machine, or vodka for a wedding, or even a place for their child at university, they approached someone in their network who worked in the relevant area, or who knew someone who did. Gifts and favours were exchanged, often over several ostensibly purely social meetings, before the złoty transaction was completed. The person buying normally paid the correct shop price, had the desired object been available in a shop. However, the entire process, including the final exchange of the item for the money, would take place outside the shop, in private houses or in bars or restaurants. It is significant, I think, that both in the socialist context and the current postsocialist economy, such extended social dealings were not (and are not) regarded as bribery (Wedel 1992; Ledeneva 1998). This is similar to the Russian practice of *blat*, which Ledeneva defines as 'ways of obtaining or arranging things using connections' (1998: 12). *Blat* is different from bribery, she suggests, because it takes place within a 'circle (of friends and acquaintances), involves long-term rather than immediate reciprocity, and implies ordinary people using their contacts, which may be justified by urgent need and by their aims if they do not exceed modest norms of personal consumption, while bribery implies a bribe-taker using their public office and their power for their own material gain, which is reprehensible' (1998: 39–40).

If złotys were multifaceted at this time, dollars were even more so.[2] Within the economy of shortage, nationally the dollar-based second economy flourished. Dollars became the currency with which it was possible, legally, semi-legally or illegally, to buy almost anything. At the national level, the dollar represented a multitude of social transactions, and had different values in different contexts. Officially, dollars had to be exchanged through state channels for złotys, at a rate far lower than that of the black market – i.e., while the official exchange rate was 30 złotys to the dollar in the late 1970s and early 1980s, the street value of the dollar rose from 100 złotys to 150 and higher. In hard-currency state shops called Pewexes, Western clothes, foods and consumer durables ranging from electric razors to IUDs (at a time when birth-control devices were essentially unavailable to the public), and foreign and Polish alcohol were available to anyone who was able to pay with Western currency. Change was often given in small paper notes called *bony*, reminiscent in size and colour of Monopoly money, which were issued by the government in denominations parallel to American coins – one, five, ten and twenty-five cents. If the change required was an irregular sum, or if the Pewex was short of *bony*, change might be given instead in sticks of American gum or candy bars. *Bony* could be used for purchases in the Pewex, and were also incorporated, as was genuine American currency, into both first- and second-economy dealings. Although buying and selling real foreign currency was illegal except in state banks, the government permitted a market in *bony*. Small personal ads regularly appeared in the newspapers, declaring 'I am buying (or selling) *bony*'. Like real dollars, they were also sold as commodities for złotys on the black market. I would argue that the existence of these peculiarly fake but official notes symbolically reinforced the perception of second-economy dealings as a competitive, individualist game with quite different rules from those of the state economy.

The dollar was also a means for legitimate queue-jumping: during this period those paying złotys for a car had to wait for delivery for two years and often more; those able to pay with hard currency received their vehicle in a matter of weeks or even days. In the second economy, consumer goods were bought and sold for dollars, palms were greased with foreign coins, taxi drivers in some city areas only took fares who would pay in dollars.

In the village, as well as fulfilling the functions outlined above, dollars played even more important and varied roles. Dollars came into the village in the hands of economic migrants returning from Chicago, as remittances sent home by kin abroad, and through informal transactions and black-market dealings. If the złotys earned as state wages were disparaged, and złotys earned through entrepreneurial activities valued, dollars were the most prestigious symbols of all. As in the rest of Poland, they were used in economic transactions, both legal and informal, such as I have described above. They were also an integral part of ritual and conspicuous display, both for what they bought and in themselves. Thus, dollars were accumulated and saved to pay for wedding vodka, because it was substantially cheaper in the Pewex than in state złoty stores; they were used to jump queues and buy tractors, cars and other large goods; on the informal market they were used to buy building materials and other scarce goods. They also demonstrated individual and house status. Returning migrants would ostentatiously place a five- or ten-dollar bill in the collection plate at Mass, and they and members of their family would keep a dollar bill prominently displayed at the front of their wallets. Identical goods were differentiated by their means of payment: Jurek's small Fiat was referred to in the normal way as a '*taksowka*', but his neighbour's identical vehicle was always 'the *taksowka* that Andrzej bought with dollars from America'. If large sums of entrepreneurial złotys were treated differently from wage złotys, dollars received the most care and attention, kept in a locked cupboard in the best room, taken out and counted from time to time, doled out within the house with almost ceremonial solemnity. Złoty earnings were used to keep the house going and to provide for basic needs which could not be met through farming. Dollars were used in the expansion of the house and farm, in contracting good marriages, and in conspicuous consumption and display. In other words, they were the source of both wealth and prestige.

Money and Ritual

Throughout the late socialist period, money played an important role in rituals of the house. After a child had been christened, there was a celebration in the house and the new member was presented to the community for the first time. Kin and neighbours were shown the baby, dressed in all its christening finery with its head resting on a white linen pillow. On the pillow was a sprig of greenery, the symbol for growth and fertility. Visitors would admire the child and slip money under the pillow. The sums were quite large, the equivalent of a week's wage or more or, even better, five or ten dollars. At weddings, guests would dance with the bride and slip an envelope of money into her hand – this was the equivalent of a month's earnings or, again, dollars – a substantial enough sum that people often tried to avoid going to weddings, claiming to be in mourning, or arranging to be away from the village for the weekend. These payments can be seen as presents, and as the community feeding into the individual house and nourishing its growth, fertility and member-ship. They were part of long-term reciprocity cycles in the sense that although people claimed not to account such sums, they usually gave similar amounts to those which had been given them at their own weddings and christenings, or they gave in the expectation that they would receive in return when they had children or when their daughters married. However, it was incumbent upon the celebrating house to provide lavish food and drink and, at weddings, entertainment. A poorly catered christening or wedding was spoken of disparagingly, while a lavish one was praised. Preparations for the *wesele* (wedding party) involved accumulating food for weeks ahead of time, the labour of all of the women of the house and close female kin for days in baking and cooking, and the purchase of a litre of vodka per guest. Overall, with about one hundred guests and lasting two full days, the average *wesele* cost the equivalent of about a year's earnings. An equivalent amount was generally received by the bride in wedding money. Frugal *wesele* were viewed as a cheat, and the house scorned as *dziad*, or beggarly. Generous, even ostentatious, weddings were remembered and spoken of for years, and greatly added to the prestige of the house.

In weddings particularly, some of the different contexts in which it is appropriate to use money are revealed. There is a strong ideal of equivalence between the amount expended and the amount received. However, the money was always represented as a gift freely given, not as a payment and, of course, although the amounts involved were roughly equivalent, it would have been unthinkable for the wedding house to skip the festivities and give the guests money instead.

This brings us to the question of household exchange and labour. Ideally, money as payment, as opposed to money as ritual gift, is confined to dealings with the outside, and as such it is surrounded by ambivalence. Within the house economy and the wider village community, labour is represented in terms of long-term reciprocity between equals: 'we help each other because we are kin; because we are neighbours; because we are *kumotor* ' (co-godparents). However, when farm labour is being organized, accounting clearly does take place. If a man and a woman and their three teenagers help their neighbours with threshing, the same quality of labour should be returned when their own threshing takes place: if there are fewer people available to help, they must work for longer periods. If only a woman and child help their kin plant potatoes, only a woman and child will return to help them.[3]

The same kinds of calculation apply to weddings and christenings. Although the ideal of free and unaccounted kinship reciprocity masks a complexity of economic relations which remain largely unacknowledged, such exchanges between houses should not involve direct monetary payment. Eggs should be repaid with eggs, labour with labour, favours with favours, and wedding gifts with wedding gifts. Obviously, this implies long-term, open-ended reciprocity. Money as direct and explicit payment enters into intra-village labour arrangements in two different ways, as remuneration for general help or for specialist skills. In the former case, poor villagers with little or no land work for day wages for their wealthier neighbours. Such work is undertaken because of pressing economic need, but it implies an uneasy mixing of categories. Farm labour should be done on one's own fields or reciprocally on the fields of other houses; the overriding principle is one of intra-village and inter-house equality. Payment in cash for labour implies inequality. To introduce a direct money transaction into the process threatens the village ideal of kin-cooperation and equality, not only showing the day labourer to be lacking because she or he must work for others for pay, but also indicating that the villager who has to hire help is unable to command enough labour on the basis of long-term reciprocity. The following example illustrates the ambiguity which arises when money enters explicitly into arrangements for farm labour.

Seeing Josek and Anka, who had little land and were known to be hard up, working in the fields of their wealthier neighbour Wladek, I stopped to chat to them. Rather embarrassed, Josek volunteered that they were working in Wladek's fields because they were kin, their mothers being cousins. Wladek, he said, often helped them with the loan of his tractor, also because they were kin. Later on, meeting Wladek, I mentioned having met Josek and Anka in his fields. 'Yes', he said, 'I hire them'. Somewhat taken aback, I said I thought they were kin. 'Oh no', he said. 'Well, perhaps a long time ago, but not really. They work for me, and I pay them cash. Or they use my tractor, and pay it off with labour.'

Here Wladek, in denying kinship reciprocity and claiming to pay cash for labour, was essentially dissociating himself from people he saw as *dziad* and asserting instead his own superior status. Josek, on the other hand, through claiming kinship and labour reciprocity, was both defending his own status and conforming to the ideal of equality. In such relations and exchanges, money takes on a negative connotation. Even more negative, however, is the absence of money which is clearly not based on reciprocity. The poorest villagers may be paid in kind rather than cash, which places them in the position not of separate, independent adults but one more like that of dependent children in the house. Zelizer (1994) has discussed the way in which charity bodies in the early twentieth-century United States reflected inequality, denying the poor their adult personhood by providing them with food, clothes or special tokens rather than allowing them to take control of their own spending. A similar process is taking place here. If reciprocal, long-term exchange indicates equality and autonomy, and cash payments indicate inequality, payments in kind confuse categories, treating non-house members as junior house members with none of the advantages such a position entails and thus implicitly denying them their adult autonomy. I shall return to this at the end of the chapter, when I discuss the way similar ideas are being reproduced on a quite different level in the postsocialist economy in relation to Western business, development organizations and 'know-how'.

Direct cash payment is made unambiguously within the village for expert services: a trained butcher may be hired to slaughter a pig and supervise the sausage-smoking; a skilled baker may be paid to plan and co-ordinate the cooking for a wedding; market women buy wool and sweaters from their neighbours to sell in the market; specialist cheese-makers sell their smoked cheeses within the village or to market women and so on. All of these transactions are to some extent masked as social rather than purely economic processes. House members work side-by-side with the paid specialist, and the fact of payment is somewhat modified by commensality and often by an emphasis, in reference and address, on any kinship tie. Market women who come to buy wool or neighbours who purchase cheeses embed their transactions in social visiting behaviour, sitting down in the kitchen to drink tea, coffee or vodka, and exchanging news and gossip before the purpose of the visit is raised. In this way, they disguise the monetary transaction as a social one. Money is socialized and the transactions distinguished from those which take place with outsiders, or between employer and employee.

Money and Morality

This brings us back to the morality of money, exchange and reciprocity. Górale distinguish between different types of labour and different kinds of money and types of exchange. However, these distinctions are not as clear as a dichotomy between the external economy, waged labour and 'anti-social money' on the one hand and house economy, reciprocal labour, and sharing and commensality on the other. Carsten (1989), for instance, describes the way money earned by men in the Malay fishing economy is seen as anti-social and implicated in relations of hierarchy which are antithetical to kinship equality. Thus, women 'cook' money, transforming it through consumption, commensality and sharing, to fit the morality of kinship. There are obviously some parallels between the Malay case and that of the Górale, particularly in terms of the ideology of kinship equality and the process of feeding individual earnings into the house economy. For the Górale, however, these are not gendered processes, and neither is there a sense in which women are associated primarily with the morality of the house and kinship or men with the anti-social external economy. All Górale adults, women and men, are expected to perform all sorts of work, both within the house and outside it; indeed, it is often women who are long-distance traders and economic migrants, and knowing how to deal and make money are highly valued aspects of womanhood and an essential part of good motherhood. Neither is there a sense in which money per se is viewed negatively by Górale. To the contrary, on the whole money is seen as a very good thing, and the more one can get of it, the better. Rather, where the question of morality, and of negative and positive ascriptions attached to labour and money, enters is in the context in which money is earned or used.

I would argue that, rather ironically, złotys provided masked or disguised support for the house economy during the late socialist period, while dollars were visible and marked for display. Similarly, waged labour for the state in fact provided steady and indispensable, although low, income for nearly every village house, but was constantly downplayed. Earnings from entrepreneurial practices or from economic migration were displayed proudly and overemphasized but actually provided in most cases only sporadic windfalls. I think that what is reflected here is a very complex set of ideas about individual autonomy and entrepreneurial skill, house solidarity and kinship equality, and waged labour, dependency and inequality. For a plethora of reasons, historical and contemporary, Górale were and are extremely hostile to the state. The socialist state was viewed as threatening the things which villagers most valued and which underpin what it means to be Górale: the government was suspected of planning to collectivize agriculture (never in fact a realistic option in the mountains), which in turn had the potential to threaten the centrality of the house and farm economy. The government attempted to regulate the movements of villagers, making children go to school; and not work in the fields during harvest and planting, expecting adults to go to work in the state sector, preventing free movement across borders, and so on. The government was hostile to the Church; the government attempted to control Górale dealing and trading, limiting the degree of private enterprise possible, always apparently on the verge of rounding up and arresting market women and traders, always monitoring agriculture and private sales, withholding passports from people who wanted to go to Chicago. Waged labour regularly and specifically made visible the state's control over individual Górale, and hence was devalued. Villagers may well have done the same work or worse in the United States, but it resulted in a totally different degree of pay, and held a different meaning. The United States was imagined as a place of great freedom of movement, a source of riches and consumer commodities. Yet some of the migrants who returned told stories of the appalling conditions in which they lived, of discrimination directed against them and of harsh treatment they endured, of more general racism, poverty and pollution. However, they also brought back enough dollars to transform the house and by extension the village. The money and goods were displayed and consumed far away from the place of exploitation and humiliation, the limitations to individual autonomy took place not only 'outside' but invisibly, over there. The individual price paid for the money was extreme but so were the rewards gained in terms of both earnings and status. If the main tension in Górale ideology lies in the opposition between collective morality of the house and community, and individual autonomy and individualism (see Pine 1999), this has a parallel in the contrast between capitalism and communism. Capitalism generally, and American capitalism in particular, appeared to be the pinnacle of successful entrepreneurialism, while communism stressed a far wider and more inclusive collectivity than did Górale kinship and house ideology. In practice both 'outside' economies propped up the village economy and subsidized farming, which continued to be represented as the real core of Górale society.

Postsocialism

All of these ideas were challenged in the first years after 1989. With the collapse of socialism came changes in the nature of waged labour, its availability, and the 'perks' associated with it. Regulated private trading in dollars became a legitimate activity, and the disparity between legal and black-market prices rapidly diminished. Capitalism, rather than being located outside, over there, in places the villagers could go away to, itself came to the mountains in the form of Western '*biznes*' men looking for cheap labour, cheap holiday resorts to promote package holidays, and so on. Western goods and commodities, which for years had been, like dollars, the basis of status, display and conspicuous consumption, flooded the new private shops. There was a period in the early 1990s when everything seemed to be out of focus, in reverse or slightly wrong. Unemployment rose dramatically and very quickly in the region, as state factories were closed or production drastically cut back. Polish goods, always scarce, became increasingly unavailable, while Western goods, often of poor quality, were available in abundance but at prices most could not afford. With the opening of international borders, new opportunities arose for economic migration within Europe. Gradually, economic practice changed, and with it local ideas about money, both foreign and Polish, changed as well.

In the first years after the fall of communism, the extent to which the village economy had in fact been dependent on state income became painfully clear. For many villagers, unemployment meant loss of their steady income, and increased costs of living in the form of new healthcare and childcare costs, insurance and taxes. Those who remained formally employed in state enterprises often went for weeks without being called into work, or months without being paid for the periods they did work. Low prices for agricultural produce and competition from Western produce dumped on local markets placed extraordinary pressure on the farms, and one by one families decided to cut down their production for sale, or stop it altogether and produce for house subsistence only. With rising feed costs, animals were slaughtered and not replaced, for people could not afford the costs of over-winter feeding. The real fragility of farming was no longer possible to disguise.

A new category of goods and labour emerged, which I have described elsewhere (Pine 1996a, 1998). People began to do things at home which they had previously paid others to do, such as sewing, hairdressing, and extensive canning and preserving. These activities and products were referred to as things '*domowie*' (domestic, or of the house), with a combination of pride and conscious irony. Paying money for outside goods and services on a day-to-day basis was increasingly rejected; the goods were too expensive, people said, and they could make better things themselves.

By the mid-1990s, however, old economic practices were re-emerging in slightly changed form, and were creating economic opportunity and occasionally a basis for new affluence for at least some villagers. Economic migration to Italy, Greece, France and Germany by then represented the major source of income for many houses. In 1996, one in four village houses stood empty, their owners away working in other parts of Europe. In the summer of 2000, when I was last in the village, my impression was that this European migration had become even more widespread. The new migration tends to be shorter-term but more frequent than emigration to the United States under socialism. Young villagers go to work seasonally as farm labourers in France and Germany, and occasionally Great Britain. They work as nannies, au pairs, house-keepers, cleaners and builders in Italy and Greece. They bring or send back money and return with their cars full of goods and foodstuffs, for home use and to sell. Money earned tends to be used in housebuilding, which feeds into the growing international tourist trade. None of this is new – it was all going on during socialism and before that. What *is* new, I would argue, is the scale of these activities. For the successful migrants and traders, the rewards are extremely high. Pawel and Marta, for instance, went to work in France, leaving their children with Marta's sister and Pawel's mother. On their return they expanded their house, transform-ing it into a guest house with a swimming pool and an attached video-rental business. They now cater to tourists from all over Poland and from other parts of Europe, who often book by e-mail. Others have been less successful. Hanka worked in Italy as an au pair for five or six years, while her mother and her husband cared for her own children in the village. The money she sent home, combined with her mother's earning from selling knitted garments, her father's pension and her brother's disability allowance, supported the entire house of eight. However, her elder daughter experienced a troubled period in her mid-teens, and Hanka returned home permanently. The family now relies primarily on their own farm produce, and income from knitting and pensions: it is a hard and uncertain existence.

As the new economy takes shape, money becomes imbued with different social and political meanings. Foreign money is exchanged at the bank, or in licensed and regulated *waluty* (exchange outlets). There is little variation now in public and private exchange rates, and people often choose to use the bank, seeing this as a way of 'helping Poland'. It is no longer the Polish state, but Western business and governments which are viewed with hostility. While individual tourists with foreign currency to spend are still courted, the West as a category is regarded as using its money to buy up Poland.[4] In that sense, foreign money is now regarded as oppressive rather than liberating. Money earned abroad still has high status, but primarily in its capacity for conversion into prestige consumer items. An offer to pay in dollars, which would previously have been welcomed and usually actively solicited, is now more likely to be shrugged off indifferently, or even met with an expressed preference for złotys.[5] At weddings and christenings recently, expensive presents – bought in Poland or brought back by returning economic migrants – have come to replace money as the main gift. The emphasis which was placed on the farming aspect of the house economy in the socialist years appears to be being replaced by an emphasis on the house itself, as a building and as a site of consumption, a display case for 'modern' goods, furnishings and style. Money has become more generally a means to an end, and in this process the gap between the poor and the new rich is growing.

This raises various questions about the contexts in which money is used as a medium for a multitude of social purposes, and about the circumstances in which it may come to be regarded as dangerous or destructive. Foreign money which villagers go and get themselves continues to be highly regarded, but foreign money brought in to them, by strangers and outsiders, is certainly construed as potentially destructive. By converting money into things, people are building new systems of prestige and are to some extent making money itself less personal. Money becomes in this sense a path to commodities, which are seen as epitomizing what is modern. However, as discussed above, commodities, and the very process of consumption itself, are also viewed politically. The negative associations growing around foreign money, and the stated preference for Polish money, connect to ideas about local and national autonomy, and fears about encroachment, both economic and cultural, from the West (Pine 1996a; see also Humphrey 1995). In these contexts, people are vocal about their choice of the złoty, rather than the dollar or deutschmark, and of Polish goods, rather than foreign imports.

By the mid-1990s what seemed to be a new popular discourse on money, development and aid was becoming apparent. People spoke of foreigners or city Poles with foreign currency from dubious sources coming in and buying up local resources and property. These people, referred to as *'obcy ludzie'* (outsiders or strangers), were depicted as uncouth and uncivilized, endangering local children by driving too fast on narrow village roads, drinking excessively and causing trouble, engaging in clandestine deals with definite mafia overtones, and polluting the mountain environment (Pine 1997). Much discussion also centred around Western aid and development agencies. Foreign experts were portrayed as sitting in expensive hotels in Warsaw, earning $500 a day for telling people in the countryside how to develop local enterprises and how to farm. Villagers' reactions to such expert advice are clear and succinct. 'We know how to deal and produce; we know how to farm. We need money to get things going, but they spend the money in the city and send aid to the countryside as a package of advice we don't need.' This is highly reminiscent of Zelizer's discussion of charity in the United States, to which I have already referred. At issue appear to be perceptions of control by and dependency on outsiders, both anathema to Górale ideals of autonomy and independence. I suspect that these attitudes may go some way in explaining the rejection and negative appraisal of Western money in certain social contexts, and the new perception of money not only as a source of growth and independence but also as a dangerous element out of control.

Górale at the moment seem to be caught between worlds. Part of their social and economic practice is reminiscent of the years of intense migration in the nineteenth century, which also occurred as the old empires declined and also generated dramatic changes in farming practice and local economy. At another level, however, they seem to be shooting out of Soviet modernism into a new world of global capitalism and consumption. These are ambiguous positions, and the ambiguity is reflected in the uneasy ambivalence and tension currently expressed about types of money, commodities and consumption.

Acknowledgements

The original research on which this chapter is based was carried out in 1977–79, sporadically during 1980–84, and in 1988–90, 1991–95, and sporadically again during 1996–2000. I am grateful to the (then) SSRC for research funding 1978–80, and to the ESRC for funding in 1988–1990 (R0002314) and 1991–95 (R000233019) and to the British Council, which also supported the early research. I would also like to thank Ruth Mandel and Landon Mackenzie for suggestions, help and general input to this chapter.

Notes

1. Such practices were not exclusive to Górale, but widespread throughout Poland. See Pawlik (1992) and Firlik and Chlopecki (1992).
2. Most foreign currency was highly regarded. From the Eastern Bloc, Czech crowns, Hungarian florints and German marks were most respected. Roubles were valuable but were also associated negatively with Russia. All Western currency was coveted, but American dollars were the most common: people were more familiar with them than with any others, and they had the added value of being associated with the United States which was viewed as the height of all things Western.
3. This is flexible, however; in times of illness, or hardship, kin and neighbours willingly give far more than they expect to receive. However, if the imbalance continues for a long time, over several seasons, help begins to be cut back.
4. Again, this is by no means an attitude confined to the mountains. I heard the same discussions, frequently in exactly the same words, in rural central Poland.
5. I think it is important to distinguish here between expressions of politicized sentiment and actual practice. While many people choose Polish currency and goods, others speak about doing so, but in fact continue to buy, and show off, Western ones.

References

Carsten, J. (1989), 'Cooking money: gender and the symbolic transformation of means of exchange in a Malay fishing community', in J. Parry and M. Bloch (eds), *Money and the Morality of Exchange*, Cambridge: Cambridge University Press.

Comaroff, J. (1985), *Body of Power, Spirit of Resistance*, Chicago: University of Chicago Press.

Firlik, E. and Chlopecki, J. (1992), 'When Theft is not Theft', in J. Wedel (ed.), *The Unplanned Society: Poland During and After Communism*, New York: Columbia University Press.

Gudeman, S. and Rivera, A. (1990), *Conversations in Colombia: the Domestic Economy in Life and Text*, Cambridge: Cambridge University Press.

Humphrey, C. (1995), 'Creating a Culture of Disillusionment: Consumption in Moscow, a Chronicle of Changing Times', in D. Miller (ed.), *Worlds Apart: Modernity Through the Prism of the Local*, London: Routledge.

Ledeneva, A. (1998), *Russia's Economy of Favours: Blat, Networking and Informal Exchange*, Cambridge: Cambridge University Press.

Parry, J. and Bloch, M. (1989), 'Introduction', in J. Parry and M. Bloch (eds), *Money and the Morality of Exchange*, Cambridge: Cambridge University Press.

Pawlik, W. (1992), 'Intimate Commerce', in J. Wedel (ed.), *The Unplanned Society: Poland during and after Communism*, New York: Columbia University Press.

Pine, F. (1996a), 'Redefining women's work in rural Poland', in R. Abrahams (ed.), *After Socialism: Land Reform and Social Change in Eastern Europe*, Oxford: Berghahn.

—— (1996b), 'Naming the house and naming the land: kinship and social groups in the Polish highlands', *Journal of the Royal Anthropological Institute*, 2(2), 443–59.

—— (1997), 'Pilfering Culture: Górale identity in post-socialist Poland', *Paragraph*, 20(1), 59–74.

—— (1998), 'Dealing with fragmentation: the consequences of privatisation for rural women in central and southern Poland', in S. Bridger and F. Pine (eds), *Surviving post-Socialism: Local Strategies and Regional Responses in Eastern Europe and the Former Soviet Union*, London: Routledge.

—— (1999), 'Incorporation and Exclusion in the Podhale', in S. Day, E. Papataxiarchis and M. Stewart, *Lilies of the Field: Marginal People who Live for the Moment*, Boulder, Co.: Westview Press.

Scott, J. (1976), *The Moral Economy of the Peasant: Subsistence and Rebellion in Southeast Asia*, New Haven: Yale University Press.

Thompson, E.P. (1971), 'The moral economy of the English crowd in the 18th century', *Past and Present*, 50, 76–136.

Wedel, J. (ed.) (1992), *The Unplanned Society: Poland during and after Communism*, New York: Columbia University Press.

Yurchak, A. (1997), 'The Cynical Reason of Late Socialism: power, pretence and the anekdoti', *Public Culture*, 9, 161–88

Zelizer, V. (1994), *The Social Meaning of Money: Pin Money, Paychecks, Poor Relief and Other Currencies*, Princeton: Princeton University Press.

Part II
Consumption and Modernities

– 6 –

Chasing Moths: Cleanliness, Intimacy
and Progress in Romania

Adam Drazin

Through the Spring of 1997, I found myself regularly running around my apartment in Suceava, a town in north-east Romania, pursuing the seemingly endless threat of moths with my landlord, Mr Bendea (all names have been changed for reasons of confidentiality). We dragged chairs about, investigating the top corners of the rooms for them. I knew how moths are a danger to clothes and woollens, but the hunt was nonetheless accompanied by his bemusing explanations and the details of their life cycle. His insistence could take me aback. On one occasion, dissatisfied with my help or my enthusiasm, he solicited the assistance of our neighbour, Mr Rusu, who obligingly came over to hunt the moths with us. Mr Rusu concluded that the moths weren't eating away at the flat, they were eating away at my landlord's head. The two neighbours had been friends since the 1960s when the block was first built; they often took a close interest in one another's homes, accompanied by jokes and cajoling. At times such as this, Mrs Rusu developed a tendency to threaten me with a carpet-beater unless I did my bit in keeping the place tidy.

I shared the flat on and off with my landlord, who was retired and aged just over seventy, while I researched domestic material culture in Suceava. The living room contained an array of his ornaments and life-long souvenirs, and a profusion of rugs, mats, covers and cloths. The heavy sofa was also a bed, if the lower part was dragged out; a compartment behind the back-rest contained the bedding. In Suceava apartments, living rooms commonly double as bedrooms, and sofas (*fotoliu* or *pat*) share a denominator with beds (*pat*). A woollen throw hid the age of this sofa. More cloths and rugs, which were vulnerable to moths, covered other surfaces. The worn beech parquet floor showed around the edges of a large carpet, which was regularly beaten or switched with the spare, standing rolled-up beside a wardrobe. Inside the old 1960s-style display cabinet were the obligatory holiday souvenirs, books and crockery, all set out on hand-made crochet mats. The burnished blue cups and saucers were distinctively arranged, lying at right-angles on each saucer, and one visitor commented that they must have been set out by the hand of a Romanian woman. My landlord had recently been widowed, and spent more time with relatives than in his own flat; but presumably still arranged the ornaments as they had been arranged during his marriage.

The apartment in many ways reflects what might be seen as a typical style for the older generation in Suceava. Younger guests, aged in their twenties, seemed very awkward. Although I hadn't anticipated it, they were sensitive to the apartment; everything about the place spoke to them of the older generation. The older style in Suceava tends to involve a big central table for guests, while since the 1980s, living rooms increasingly have a low coffee table beside the sofa instead. Younger Suceavans can be disconcerted to find themselves in a circle at a table, not reclining facing the TV and displayed ornaments. The arrangement of carpets and rugs, cups and saucers, tables and sofas, can speak volumes, even though the material world can be so diverse and complicated that words alone cannot describe it adequately. My landlord's regular moth hunts show how taking care of the home and the objects in it is at once incomprehensibly personal and also inclusive of others. While some housework can be done by one person, such as wiping down surfaces or cooking, an older style of decor often means everyone, women and men, adults and children, must pitch in with the work of taking care of the place. In this chapter, I look especially at the carpets and rugs which are a feature of many homes in Suceava. These objects are a focus for cleaning work, which can be burdensome for everyone; but they can seem sometimes to annoy the younger generation just by being there. They thus provide for feelings both of domestic reinvigoration and of historical stultification.

This chapter investigates some particular ways in which dirtiness and cleanliness relate to a sense of progress in Suceava, a progress which elides the passing of historical events and the passing of the generations. Some studies link a sense of clutter, or tidiness and untidiness, with the idea of postsocialism, because many elements of the socialist environment seem subject to a transformation into an inheritance of dust and dirt. Victor Pelevin writes in his novel *Babylon* of a pair shoes in a Moscow shop window which makes the hero of the story realize he must do something different with his life:

> The shoes were covered by a thick layer of dust: the new era obviously had no use for them . . . In front of that shop window his heart suddenly sank in the sudden realisation that the dust settling on him as he stood there beneath

the vault of the heavens was not the dust that covered a vessel containing precious wine, but the same dust as covered the shoes. (Pelevin 2000: 4–5)

Not everyone necessarily experiences a sudden realization like a story-book hero. Nonetheless, objects do come to be perceived as old or dirty. My fieldwork suggests that cleanliness and dirtiness in Suceava have been changing and transforming for many years, and that developments since 1989 are a part of longer-term processes, not a sudden shift.

I argue that the work of cleaning, establishing a *feeling* of cleanliness, amounts to a progressive and gradual reinterpretation of the past, through rejection of certain elements; and that this transformation of the material world of the home can then impact back upon the actors involved and their relationships. To expand on this argument: the investigation of cleanliness requires making a distinction between the cultural construction of cleanliness, and the means and practices employed to achieve it. As a cultural form, cleanliness in Suceava is a quality which is not necessarily measurable or self-evident, but must be demonstrated, for example through entertaining guests who become witnesses to cleanliness, or through the presence of particular material objects. The growth of the market has shifted attention on to soaps as signs of cleanliness, but traditionally a well-beaten rug might be a better one. Cleanliness as a form of labour in Suceava homes takes different forms as well. There are demonstrative, cathartic events which I call 'household clean-ups', involving many family members; and there is also ongoing daily tidying and caring which is more often done by the woman of the house and is less demonstrative. These conceptualizations and practices of cleanliness provide habitualized ways in which Suceava households fashion and change themselves, both during socialism and today. In changing the material world of the home, people in Suceava fashion a world which has an impact on how cleanliness is to be achieved in the future; that is, different objects require different ways of organizing labour to achieve the sensation of renewal and cleanliness. In particular, in households which have benefited from the market economy, certain new aesthetics of household cleanliness negate the idea of labour by discarding those objects which are associated with the 'household clean-up', such as carpets and rugs. This change could have significant implications for cross-generational and gender relationships.

Adam Drazin

Domestic Cleanliness, Order, and Progress

Douglas (1966) famously described dirt as 'matter out of place', making the point that dirt is something which occurs when we have an image of how the world *should* be organized. Thus dirt can be an indicator of cultural structuration. The rejection of dirt, cleaning, amounts to the activity of organizing, and giving meaning to, the world. Douglas' interpretation of dirt can be applied to the way that people in Suceava and across the postsocialist world were talking of socialism through much of the 1990s. The joke runs: 'What's the definition of socialism? The longest way from capitalism to capitalism.' Socialism is commonly referred to in Romania as a 'dead end', or as forty years 'out of history'. In phrases such as these, the socialist past is a form of dirt in the sense that it should not be there, and at some cultural level should be expunged.

I should like to highlight two contrasting ways of approaching cleanliness and progress (drawing on Linde-Laursen 1993), then indicate how they may be particularly pertinent in a postsocialist context such as Romania (drawing on Humphrey 1997), and suggest how an investigation of material culture (Buchli 1999; Miller 1987, 1994) may address the contradiction between these approaches. Linde-Laursen (1993) writes about his experience of the 'trivial' act of washing-up (in North American terms, 'doing the dishes') in Sweden and Denmark, and tries to explain how he, as a Dane, was told he was washing up the wrong way when staying with Swedish friends. According to previous historical studies (Schmidt and Kristensen 1986), both countries participated in the 'modern project' (Linde-Laursen 1993: 278) of hygiene, instituting programmes of research and mass education in the mid-twentieth century which included scrupulous attention to the best and most scientific way of doing the washing-up. Among the conclusions in Sweden was that one should rinse dishes after washing and then let them dry in the air; while in Denmark, the favoured efficient method was not necessarily to rinse after washing, but to dry with a cloth. When cleanliness is seen as a 'modern project', the reason why Danes and Swedes wash up differently is simply mass education in the past. Linde-Laursen, however, is critical of the 'mass education' approach. He suggests rather that 'trivial routines' (281), everyday practices and material culture may, over time, come to be perceived as distinctive signs of the national. It is more important for him that Danish and Swedish households have come to favour different kinds of sink: paired sinks for washing and rinsing in many Swedish homes, and a single sink in most Danish ones. It is these kinds of difference which Swedes and Danes come to perceive as fundamentals of cleanliness and of *being* Swedish or Danish.

Caroline Humphrey (1997) looks at material culture in the building of Russian homes, and notes some parallels in the postsocialist situation. In building new villas, people who are considered a part of the bourgeois up-and-coming New Russians attempt to mould the form and fittings of the house to fulfil their lifestyle aspirations, and yet rarely if ever make a successful match. The new house almost invariably emerges as a sort of Frankenstein's monster of a place, the jacuzzis and grand staircases resembling heaps of junk more than indicators of the wealthy and successful lifestyle which they desire. Among her many conclusions, Humphrey describes this phenomenon as a 'contradiction of myths' (86): 'between mytho-historical self-images (interpretation of one's material objects that provide a placement of self in the world) and what is said about these same objects when no such mythic work has been achieved' (85–6).

Anthropologists have examined these processes of cultural ordering and achieving cleanliness in different ways, and observed that not only do we order objects, but we are ordered by them. One approach looks at 'dust' rather than 'dirt' (see Amato 2000). Buchli (1999) examines the material world of a Moscow block of flats through socialism, and looks at how assorted efforts to structure the material world almost always resulted in 'bits' of meaning that were left over, and which he compares with the idea of dust. Pure ordered meaningfulness was never achieved: this was both because no ideology could actually ever achieve a pure, internally consistent state, and because the material world always defied explanation somehow. Banal elements such as small figurines or the partitioning of space could always be reinterpreted, however innocent or incongruous. From this perspective, the meaningfulness of the material world does not relate only to the imposition of order. Bits of it evade ordering, or are rendered inconspicuous, and this quality can be central to the development of meanings, not necessarily something to be eliminated in order to create cultural meaningfulness.

Miller (1987, 1994) takes on board these perspectives in looking at how the material qualities of the world relate to meaning:

When the phrase the 'meaning of things' is used in anthropology it tends to implicate something beyond the narrow questions of semanticity by which artefacts, like words, might have sense and reference. Rather, the notion of meaning tends to incorporate a sense of 'meaningful' closer to the term 'significance' . . . Artefacts are a means by which we give form to, and come to an understanding of, ourselves, others, or abstractions such as the nation or the modern. It is in this broad sense that their very materiality becomes problematic (Miller 1994: 397).

Miller suggests therefore that this dichotomy of people ordering things (e.g. cleanliness) while things also order people (e.g. dirt, dust) is seen as problematic in many cultural contexts. He suggests that one way we may deal with this situation is through the way the varied lifespans of objects may help the construction of coexistent senses of temporality. Some objects possess longevity, becoming ancestral, or elements of architecture or landscape which are difficult to change. To a certain extent, objects are long-lived because we permit them to be:

> All people initially experience the world as something given by history rather than something they create . . . Among the items encountered are those which children may be taught to treat with special respect because they are icons of identity, commonly tokens of the longevity of their culture and of cross-generational continuity (Miller 1994: 410).

Other objects evoke transience, particularly in societies of mass consumption, and shift with fashions. Thus, whereas some objects stand for cultural processes which are supposed to be slow-changing, others embody processes which stress continual change.

The material culture of the experience of transition in postsocialist countries is thus related to the social interactions around objects. This is especially so to the extent that people feel able to create longevity, stability, and transience around objects. I am engaged in a similar project to Linde-Laursen's, employing apparently trivial moments of cleanliness to comment on the mytho-historical viewpoint on cleanliness and civilization which is offered by the project of building a market in Romania. The conception of the market offers what Linde-Laursen (1993: 278) would call a 'modern project', and Humphrey (1997: 91) a 'grand myth'. The market represents an attempt to impose a particular kind of order and interpretation of cleanliness. Domestic cleanliness in Suceava also relates to attempts to order the world and reinterpret its meanings, which at the same time are an exercise in self-creation and self-discovery; but as I shall reveal, the mechanics of cleanliness are very different at a local level. When my friends came round to my apartment, and seemed dismayed at the dated surroundings, their distaste amounted to a rejection. On the one hand, they anticipated a domestic intimacy and homeliness which would be a rejection of the dirty outside world. On the other hand, they unexpectedly experienced a feeling of rejection of the older generation and the past which it represents. Rejection of the dirtiness of the present and of the past are intertwined in the material world.

This chapter continues by discussing the 'modern project' of the market among marketing executives, and how this project articulates cleanliness and progress around soaps and cleaners. Following this is a discussion of Suceava, its 'trivial routines' and material culture, which reveals a more complex picture of the linkage of cleanliness with progress. The nature of my data is essentially qualitative, not quantitative, and is not intended to make sweeping generalizations about cleanliness or life in Romania. Rather, I wish to unpack the experiences of a few households to demonstrate the ways in which these themes of gender, labour and generation can interact.

The Meaning of Cleanliness in the Market

The glib usage of the word 'market' in relation to postsocialist countries has been criticized as oversimple, since it may imply that these societies are in the process of a 'transition' from socialism to capitalism, involving democracy and a market economy. In fact, it is difficult or impossible to define what a market economy actually is (see Hann 1994; Burawoy and Verdery 1999). I consider the market here as a representation which different groups may use for their own purposes with wholly different meanings. In spite of criticisms, the image persists locally that Romania is in the process of transition (commonly referred to as *schimbarea* – the change) to a market economy. People may make the distinction between the market economy (*economia de piata*) which Romania has now, and the 'real' market economy (*economia de piata adevarata*) which exists in Western Europe, and which Romania may have at some future time. The market therefore expresses a sense of future progress and is closely intertwined with the idea of the modern.

These various themes of the market in Romania can be very clearly seen among marketing executives of care and cleaning products, with whom I conducted a series of conversations in 1997–98. These business-people comprise a small but influential group of Romanians who are actively engaged in the building of a 'real' market. While many people at home in Suceava in 1997–98 were extremely pessimistic about economic prospects, people involved with marketing were extremely optimistic. Over the next few years, sales of soaps and cleaners were broadly expected to expand and expand. Marketing executives display a very developed and subtle knowledge of life in Romania, in different places and generations, and the significance of different activities; and they repetitively inscribe this knowledge in marketing language. The concept of the market clearly provides for them a particular lens through which to perceive the situation. Products and brands meanwhile are a medium to represent Romania, the market, and the people ('consumers'). One market research director explained to me how a market develops, with reference to domestic cleaning products:

> So, before '89 and even several years after that, let's take one category like – I don't know – detergents. They were used to clean all the house, yes. And I am talking about laundry detergents . . . But what I wanted to say is that the market was developed and a lot of internationals came on the market, and in time the consumer was educated. Certain activities in the house, you had to use certain types of product – so it was certain categories of product. So, for dishwashing you will use dishwashing detergents and dishwashing liquid, yeah? For household, you will use household cleaning products. So more or less, let's say, the internationals have educated the consumer, and the consumer first went to cheap products, but then they realized that with probably the same amount of money they could buy quality products, and they would be more satisfied by them.

For this director, the mass-education project of the market involves an individualized Romanian consumer who thinks, learns and acts to clean and order the material world about them. One way in which this ordering process works is by efficiently segmenting all of the labour involved in the home into separate activities, and corresponding categories of object. The nature of cleanliness in the home becomes embedded in particular objects for marketing executives. The kind of object which is seen as embodying cleanliness is soap or detergent, a relatively transient object. In a household where everything (clothes, surfaces, floors, shoes, etc.) is cleaned using one kind of detergent (such as the long-standing brand *Dero*), there is also seen to be a lack of knowledge about cleanliness. The increasing use of specialized cleaners is seen to involve more knowledge about what cleanliness *means*.

Various different authors have considered the relationship between cleanliness and progress in this vein, and pointed out how the market can be one of the projects which drives this link. Burke (1996) discusses the development of an 'African Market' in apartheid Zimbabwe through the categorization and recategorization of body-care products. Other considerations take class into account (e.g., Frykman and Löfgren 1996

[1979], 1980). Forty (1995 [1986]) discusses ideas of cleanliness and hygiene with reference to the history of furnishings. First-class railway carriages in Victorian Britain had to reflect the class distinctions of the period, and made use of conspicuous heavy brocade, plush seating and fittings. However, the middle class began to assert ideas of hygiene and cleanliness, increasingly vocally, partly in order to distinguish themselves from the working class. The plush first-class fittings became seen over time as harbouring germs and dust, difficult to clean. New carriages had sleeker, more hygienic lines, and were more likely to reflect distinction in modernist lines than in plushness. Thus, over time, the object world and cultural conceptions ordered one another.

The grand narrative of the market economy is evidently inscribed in some people's homes in Suceava, notably of those with money to achieve a new aesthetic. Some families are able to set out their home in a style which closely resembles the surprisingly shining and sparse interiors featured in the proliferating Romanian media. The type of home interior featured in a magazine such as *Casa de Lux, Camina,* or one of the many women's magazines, is well-lit and spacious, with very few cloths, coverings or chintz. Successful families who buy new flats in Suceava are able to design their new apartments in this style, which makes success evident because, among other things, a more open, lighter style self-evidently requires less work to maintain. There are fewer places where dirt can accumulate, more smooth surfaces, especially of wood, which can be swept or wiped, and fewer carpets to beat. Cleanliness is achieved through purchasing cleaners, which require money, and so this new, modern aesthetic is linked both to new interpretations of cleanliness and to economic success and new economic formulations. The new style contains the message that you do not have to do so much physical cleaning work because you can afford products which lighten the load.

Housework (whether we are considering Romania, other postsocialist countries, or in fact any country) is generally seen to be feminized. Socialism is often considered to have exacerbated women's burden, by making them participate in work and political life without providing any help at home (Funk and Mueller 1993; Wolchik and Meyer 1985; Gal and Kligman 2000). This is especially true in Romania, where the brutalising impact of the State's pro-natal policies created so much despair among women. Different writers remind us of how the socialist regime did nothing to encourage men to participate in work in the home (Fischer 1985, Verdery 1996, Kligman 1998). Nowadays, women's magazines lament on the same theme (e.g., Constantin 1998).

However, talking of housework can disguise the variety of work involved. Baban (2000: 242) reports the findings of a 1994 poll across Romania: 50 per cent of respondents reported that women cleaned the house, compared with 75 per cent who considered cooking was women's work, and 78 per cent who said women did the washing and ironing. Cleaning the house is less gendered in Romania than other housework, although women are likely to be in overall charge of the business.

While the general thrust of assertions that housework is gendered must be acknowledged, I would argue that the grouping together of domestic activities under the term 'housework' tends to obscure the variation within these activities, and consequently to avoid having to deal with the actual meaningfulness and effect of different activities, objects and styles within the home. Cleaning can express the relatedness between household members (Carsten 2000). Harris (1981) makes the point that the household is often represented in social science as a 'natural' domain, but this may hide its rich internal variety, especially inequalities between the genders. Generalizing about 'housework' or 'the household' may exacerbate the difficulties of talking about society in postsocialist countries. That is, it represents the members of households, especially women, as shaped by the past but having very little choice in the shaping of their future.

The market's interpretation of cleanliness, as we shall see, is not only important in marketing circles; its principles are expressed in many Suceava homes by women wishing to express (among other things) their liberation from household drudgery. However, I consider it a limited interpretation. Cleanliness for marketers is expressed in certain commodities, notably certain kinds of soaps and cleaners. In Suceava, cleanliness is also expressed in an event I call a 'household clean-up', in which the experience of labour has more significance in creating a clean home. The kinds of labour which marketing executives consider are largely 'wet' labour: wiping, washing and polishing for example. In Suceava, the labour which may express deep cleanliness best is the one which is most tiring and most exhilarating: carpet-beating. Seeing cleanliness in soap-based commodities is also to ignore the way many families have limited cash incomes, even those who have large amounts of other forms of capital. The market-linked modern project of cleanliness is manifested locally in new domestic forms of decor establishing a sudden break with the past. In the following section I show, however, that there has been a gradual year-by-year evolution in most Suceava homes, continually reinterpreting cleanliness and the labour which goes into it. Lastly, the market's representation of cleanliness suggests more liberation for women through reduced labour. One possible effect of this is to reduce a woman's ability to appeal to the assistance of other family members' labour to help clean, such that ironically the burden on her own shoulders could be increased by efforts to reduce it.

Cleanliness and Material Culture in Suceava

The most literal word for 'clean' in Romanian is *curat*. Sometimes, one hears *ingrijit* (cared for), or in a more general sense *frumos* (beautiful). *Frumos* is so ubiquitous a term that it can be used to describe almost any situation or thing, like the word 'nice'. Tidying up an apartment for visitors is making the place *frumos*; smartening oneself up, or putting on make-up, is making oneself *frumos* (or *frumoasa* for women); a good atmosphere at a party or concert is *frumos*. The work of making people and places *frumos* can be described in different ways: housework is commonly referred to as *curatenia* in Suceava; another term might be *ingrijire* (caring), which may refer to taking care of the family, or of the home, or of one's own person. While these terms for 'clean' and 'caring' are often used to describe the home, the domain outside the front door is more often described as *murdar* (dirty). Streets are said to be more dirty in Romania than in the West, however often the people in orange uniforms come along sweeping up. Romanian business and politics are commonly described as dirty too, evoking repugnance and implying again the cleanliness of public institutions in the West.

In Suceava, the signs of keeping the home clean and tidy are unmistakable, partly because of the obvious work required by the assortment of woollens and fabrics in the home; and cleanliness is not measured by how much soap the shops sell. One of the loudest sounds in the town is the beating of carpets on purpose-built iron frames, which rebounds around the blocks from an early hour of the morning. Sometimes they will just be shaken from a balcony, with the recognizable thud of the dangling carpet hitting the parapet. Windows and balconies also commonly display arrays of drying washing. Although the socialist architects built laundry rooms, most women would not leave clothes to dry there in case of theft; so when the weather is fine, the big, grey block faces sport colourful arrays of laundry.

The home should be thoroughly cleaned both before and after receiving guests, and also at particular times of year (especially before festivals when guests may be expected). Before Easter is the time for a Spring clean, during the Lenten fasting period, when many purify themselves with a strictly vegan diet. Not only are families supposed to beat carpets and clean surfaces, but also should renovate the home. Furniture should be mended and utilities put in working order. This is also the time to furnish anew, or redecorate – although not as much as in the countryside, where whole rooms may be repainted annually. The home should also be clean for Christmas entertaining, which similarly is preceded by a fasting period. At this time, rather than use the frames, people may lay their carpets out on the surface of the snow to beat them.

In practice, however, any time of the year appears to be a good time for a clean-up. The arrival of summer brings cleaning for the summer, and autumn brings cleaning for autumn. Any day of the week might be a good day for a weekly clean. Cleaning the home can be a quite cathartic group event, exhausting both physically and emotionally. The labour involved in beating a carpet is too much for one person: moving heavy pieces of furniture back; rolling up carpets and mats; transporting these heavy tubes down the narrow, turning staircase of the block; hauling them over a high iron frame; repeatedly beating the surface, perhaps covering eyes from the dust, for as prolonged a period as possible; and then reversing the whole process. Since the space of a typical flat is limited, cleaning and renovations should ideally be quick, because the space is needed to live in, and you often have to move the furniture around. For a major clean-up, everyone in the home, of all ages, may be drafted in, and perhaps relatives from the country, godparents (*nasi*) or godparents' families (*cumatri*). The work is customarily accompanied by sharp interchanges, jibes and jokes which seem to both needle everyone into sweaty irritation, and at the same time keep spirits lively and get the job done. Some friends of mine, the Tileas, decided in March to redecorate a room while they did their spring clean. Mrs Tilea's mother came from the country to help. When I myself (naively) came around to offer to help, I discovered them all, red-faced, fighting to move the immense *biblioteca* (a bookcase/display case perhaps four metres long) and arguing bitingly. Past grievances and personal issues were being aired, peppered with exhortations to lift, put down, move back, move forward, do it this way or don't do it that way. It seemed as though, if they hadn't been fighting with the *biblioteca*, the three of them would have been fighting with one another. The end result, however, was a living room wonderfully repapered in a smart ivory colour and new ensconced light fittings.

If a family somehow fails to carry out these household tasks, their failure may become evident when entertaining. In one family who invited me around for a meal, an unusually awkward atmosphere was compounded by collapsing furniture. Struts from my chair fell to the carpet.

Chasing Moths: Cleanliness in Romania

After we retrieved a photo album from a cupboard, the cupboard door slowly, serenely leaned outwards and hit the floor. Little disasters like these can reflect badly on a hostess, but are actually the job of the man of the house to repair. He set about repairing these things, swearing under his breath. In Britain, such minor disasters would seem normal to me; but in Romania, where entertaining is more of a ritual, even an art form, these unexpected events may be interpreted as signs. They are not supposed to happen, and may be read as indicating unmentioned household difficulties.

This experience of cleaning and cleanliness in Suceava is the culmination of a long history and a changing material environment. At the beginning of the twentieth century, Suceava had a population of around 17,000 people, many of whom were ethnically Jewish or German. At that time, it was a border town of the Austro-Hungarian Empire. Alongside the traditional Moldavian-style compounded farmsteads, there were also more monumental forms of architecture. Several old churches and monasteries dated back to the sixteenth century, when Suceava was for a time the site of the Royal Court of Moldavia. In the centre stood streets of shops overlooked by balconies. After the First World War, with the dissolution of the Austro-Hungarian Empire, the town became a part of Romania. Then, after the advent of socialism, its landscape was reshaped entirely. Most older houses were progressively demolished, and blocks built. Factories were established in the valley, and in-migration encouraged to provide a labour force. Villages became suburbs, and their farmsteads and gardens became blocks. By 1989, the population of Suceava stood at around 120,000. Very few of these families lived in Suceava before socialism, and it is very likely that a person was born in a village or that their parents were. Their grandparents almost certainly live in a village, especially since many pensioners move to the country to farm their land. Even native-born Suceavans are likely to have been raised in the village by their grandparents until they started school. Thus, from early years people are familiar with and socialized into both the architecture of the village house and the urban apartment.

Village homes are seen to be more authentically Romanian than the concrete blocks of the town (see Kligman 1988). In the towns, although the apartments are in many ways explicitly modern, and seen as the antithesis of traditional life with their plumbing and cable TV, nonetheless tradition persists like an echo in certain objects. The assortment of cloths and drapes are one of these. Traditionally, these linens form the main part of dowries, and towels and embroidered cloths are significant in wedding and funeral rituals (ibid.). Woven mats sit on tables, crochet vine-leaves hang from the handles of cupboards, and these are generally the handiwork of the woman of the house. Many women learned to crochet by making little vine-leaves when they were teenagers in the country. Three different women I knew each spent her first pregnancy making a table-cloth, which was still on view. In kitchens, bathrooms and balconies, the floor is often covered with rough rag rugs, woven in country homes. They are very different from the smart carpets of the bedroom and living areas, but must also regularly be taken out and beaten. Most householders prefer self-contained square or rectangular carpets (*covor*) to fitted carpets (*mocheta*), according to a newspaper article about the carpet market (Vaschi 1998).

Space in the apartments is often limited, and mediates the sense of intimacy among the inhabitants. Several people in Suceava asserted how Romanian families are closer than in Britain, for example: people cook for one another more, or share bedrooms more, because it is more *Romanian* to do so. Other people complained of lack of space, the rabbit-hutchlike quality of their homes: teenagers sleeping in the living room, or young couples without a place of their own. Suceava households are intimate, through either choice or force. They are intimate both through physical proximity and the emotional rubbing-shoulders which this entails.

Over time, the style of apartments changed. I have described above how my landlord's living room was laid out. The central table with chairs around it, a tablecloth or vase of flowers at its centre, gives a central focus to the room. The table is always set out as if ready for guests, and so is an appropriate expression of rural traditions of hospitality. During socialism, such hospitality had no competition from, for example, television; of two hours television each night, one was generally about the Ceausescus. This arrangement began to develop variations over the decades, for a number of reasons. The design of furniture changed. The layout of the flats came to be less central, appropriate to a more relaxed form of entertaining, involving cups of coffee balanced on the knee rather than a meal at a table. A sofa, perhaps a corner sofa, is set alongside a low coffee table. *Biblioteci* (bookcases or display cases) lost their legs and grew until in the 1970s they came to dominate one wall of the living room. The books, personal ornaments, and perhaps the TV, on its shelves are probably visible from the sofa across the room. Wooden floors are also revealed as carpets shrink, and wealthier families install new parquet, such as in opulent oak (see Drazin 2001). The transformation of the home might be sudden or progressive. The Tilea family, whom I discussed above, furnished in a modern style when they first obtained their flat from the town hall in the early 1980s. Another family, who set up home in the

1970s, reported how they first shifted the table slightly off-centre; then later moved it fully up against the wall, which meant disposing of a chair or two; and then finally dismantled it altogether. A young couple who moved into town from a village in 1989 got themselves a central table when they married, but soon dismantled it and stored it in a corner, with the six chairs stacked on top of one another. They did not have the money to buy a small coffee table, but had the option of putting the big table back together if required.

Many different anthropologists remark on equivalent processes in different social and historical contexts, and note connections between ideas of scientific progress, hygiene, a growing middle class and education. Buchli (1999) relates how in the USSR the modernist attack on unhygienic chintz in the 1920s was replaced under Stalin by ideas of domestic comfort (*uiut*) which used many traditional cloths and coverings, which in turn was attacked by modernist ideas under Khrushchev. While modernist ideologues justified their version of home decor through hygiene, by contrast many ordinary people considered such reforms as being adverse to housework and cleaning, and hence dirty (Buchli 1999: 178). In Romania, the home was not subject to quite the same level of co-ordinated approach (see Sampson 1984). By the 1980s, visions of home favoured by the Party were unlikely to be a part of any kind of co-ordinated 'ideology', as much as being subject to the whims of the Ceausescus or the vicissitudes of local functionaries (see Shafir 1985: 39–40).

Since 1989, a number of trends have influenced how cleanliness is objectified. The media have proliferated, offering many more aspirational images of homes on cable TV and in magazines such as *Camina* and *Casa de Lux*. There has also been a massive multiplication of available soaps and cleaners. Previously, there would be periodic gluts of the same kind of cleaner at a fairly affordable price. The main detergent *Dero* (a brand now owned by Unilever) might be used for clothes and for household cleaning. In 1997–98 however, there were many cleaners of all kinds, prices, qualities, and standing. Searching for familiar good-quality cleaners is potentially one of the skills which accompanies cleanliness in the home, involving knowledge and money. One direction to which people have turned are the direct-selling organizations. These firms vary, but generally comprise a network of distributors who both sell goods and, in some cases, recruit more distributors (see Drazin and Cimpoes 1999). Some marketing executives consider these firms the vanguard of market expansion (although their overall merit is hotly debated), able to explain new product concepts face to face.

In general, how cleanliness works in Suceava has more to do with trivial routines than the modern project of marketing firms. Traditionally in Suceava, manifesting cleanliness means periodic clean-ups in which everyone can participate. The physical exhaustion is exasperating but means you *feel* you have cleaned and reinvigorated the home. Everyday household work, which falls primarily to women, may not give the same sense of achievement, but is just plain exasperating. For many years, progressive household clean-ups have created more open (*mai deschis*) and lighter (also *mai deschis*) decor. Since 1990, with a wealthier entrepreneurial group, the new domestic aesthetics have become altogether different signs of success and labour efficiency. Soaps and cleaners acquire renewed significance in the quest for cleanliness.

The history of Suceava therefore involves the development of a range of objects which may embody and express cleanliness. Suceava homes are not uniform however. In a home, there can be severe fault-lines along gender and generational lines, which cleanliness and progress reveal; and three different families provide illustration. The Ghicas represent a more typical family, the Dorus one in which the generational tensions are more evident, while the Petrus are a more wealthy family. While at first sight the Petrus have developed a different aesthetic of domesticity and cleanliness, all of these families continually renovate their homes as a part of demonstrative clean-ups, and materialize a sense of progress.

The Ghica Family

The Ghica family live in one of the older 1950s blocks in Suceava. Their apartment has fairly restricted floor space, but delightfully higher ceilings than most. Mrs Ghica does clerical work at one of the unions, while Mr Ghica used to be an engineer at one of the factories but has retired. Their only son Dragos was born in 1966 and is a doctor, a job renowned in Romania for the low official salary. Dragos was dissatisfied with his position in 1998, saying he did not get a job as good as his training merited because he could not pay the requisit bribe. Consequently, he had high hopes to emigrate to Canada through some contacts there.

The living room in 1998 had a matching set of pale furniture (a *biblioteca*, table and chairs), and also honey-coloured armchairs. This set had replaced the original 1960s dark-wood set fashionable when they got married, and gave a lighter (*mai deschis*) feel to the room. They kept the central dining table surrounded by chairs, even though this room doubled as Mr and Mrs Ghicas' bedroom. Dragos had the back room, where he piled up all sorts of furnishings in preparation for when he married and got his own place. On the wardrobe, bedding and pillows were heaped. A rolled-up carpet stood on end in a corner. On the floor of Dragos's room and the kitchen were rag rugs (*tol*), made by Mrs Ghica's mother in the country.

My second visit to the Ghicas's home was on a Saturday, when they were engaged in cleaning the house, the three of them. Mrs Ghica was wiping down the kitchen, while Dragos had been outside shaking (*scutura*) the mats and carpets. They cleaned the home like this weekly, every Saturday. Because of his plans to emigrate, Dragos said he was trying to ensure that his parents' home was fully functional and well-appointed before he left. He paid for a new wooden front door, and was considering changing the furniture, and perhaps having the kitchen tiled. When I asked whether his mother didn't prefer it as it was, he responded that actually it was a lot of work to keep the floor clean. It was a grey, grainy concrete-colour surface, and the rag rugs were a lot of work. Tiles would be less work (although I suspected that even with tiles, at least one rug would have remained).

The transformation of the Ghicas's home is progressing normally, which is to say gradually and with little reference to any radical new set of ideas, but for comfort. Work is central to their ethics of cleanliness, and this relates to an apparent integration between older and younger generations. Dragos made a point of declaring their weekly clean. On the other hand, they are making small renovations to reduce the work, and he still wishes to emigrate.

The Doru Family

The Doru family is extensive. When I talked with them, nine were living under one roof, while three others had married and moved out. They lived in a four-room apartment at the time, so in addition to the living room, there was a bedroom for Mr and Mrs Doru, one for the three brothers, and one for the four sisters. Each bedroom was about large enough for one or two sofa-beds, so at nights inevitably late-comers might sleep on the floor, or spill over into the living room.

There were hardly any surfaces in the Dorus's home which were not covered by some sort of rug, mat, or cloth. In the living room, the sofa had a thick woollen covering (*husa*) on it. A large carpet (*covor*) covered the floor except for a couple of feet at the edges, but was impinged on by all the furniture. A rag rug covered the exposed floor by the door to protect it. The three chairs had crochet covers, while the table had a colourful tablecloth (*fata de masa*) which stretched down to the ground, and a sheet of glass to protect the cloth from food. A stool beside the table had a cloth over it. A fridge stood in one corner (there was not room in the kitchen), with a traditionally embroidered cloth on top. In other rooms, similarly, every sofa-bed, chair, or shelf sported some kind of covering. These diverse coverings and mats clearly protected the surfaces of the home, especially the wooden ones, keeping them clean and undamaged.

Whenever I visited the household, Mrs Doru was always very careful to never be seen idle and made a virtue of work. She embroidered or she ironed while we talked. As the assorted children arrived home from school one by one, she directed each girl to a task: one the garbage; another cleaning the bathroom. The boys meanwhile escaped these tasks. Mrs Doru was clearly head of the household, but needed particular organizational skills since her husband was alcoholic and contributed nothing to the home. I would meet him around that part of town, always staggering drunk and incomprehensible. His day was one long quest for drink, which his wife forbade at home, punctuated by trips back to eat or sleep.

It can be expensive to keep a large family in Romania. The Dorus had two old-age pensions, and they received some food from country relatives. The older boys each began to work before they left school to bring in some more. In 1997–98, most of the family became keenly involved in the direct-selling organization Amway with the hope of eventually bringing in some extra money. Amway representatives distribute products and also try (often avidly) to get others to join the network by subscription. Amway is known most of all for its home-care, and some body-care, products: when it launched officially in Romania in November 1997, its four key products were multi-purpose Liquid Organic Cleaner (LOC), Glister toothpaste, Honey and Glycerine soap, and Dish Drops for the washing up. The Doru family would organize events to tell people about the business, invite them to join, and perhaps demonstrate products. They also had an Amway Carpet Shampoo Applicator, and bottle of shampoo (which were not officially available in Romania then, but came from Amway Hungary). They would offer to clean people's carpets with this device, perhaps for money, but largely as a demonstration to try to recruit people.

On one occasion, when Mr Doru had been escorted to bed to keep him quiet, I found myself in the living room with two of the boys, and we discovered a couple of moths flying around the room up against the ceiling. They made rather a drama out of the pursuit, as young men might. One bounced across the sofa after one moth, another climbed on a chair to catch the other. After a couple of minutes we found ourselves breathless but invigorated, having trapped them at last.

In spite of some enjoyable moments like that, the atmosphere in the Doru home was however generally difficult. Even though the family cooperated, organizing seminars, dealing with household chores, and getting through daily life, Mr Doru's condition cast an abusive shadow over them. The older boys verbalized their feelings of oppression most. They all would have liked their own room. Amway encourages its distributors to 'visualize their dreams' for motivation, and the boys visualized the freedom of future homes toward which Amway would help them work. One brother also said that his older siblings had married purely as a strategy to get their own breathing-space elsewhere. As in the Ghica household, the Dorus organize cleaning in a complicated fashion, but make the labour very visible. Laundry and daily cleaning of surfaces are more feminized. They are all (except Mr Doru), however, socialized into caring for the many carpets, mats and covers around the place, which are much easier to beat with the kind of large labour force the Dorus can mobilize. Unlike the Ghicas, mutual cooperation among the Dorus happens in spite of severe tensions and the desire of younger members to move out as soon as possible.

The Petrus

Mr and Mrs Petru, who insist on being called Paul and Maria, met while at university in the late 1980s, and had only just married when the events of 1989 occurred. At that time, they were living with their baby daughter, Brindusa, in a one-bedroom flat. However, Paul was lucky enough to get a job in a prominent local firm which was on the lookout for young, open-minded managers in the early 1990s, and found his income rose fast, benefiting from particular investments in Suceava. Maria maintained a clerical job to a certain extent, but her heart is really at home. They obtained a spacious four-room apartment in a desirable block, and she set about decorating. The flat was completely overhauled twice in as many years, with scrupulous attention to detail. She mixed the living room paint herself to an exact shade of blue, when the workman's efforts failed to please. It took over a year to find a fitted carpet which exactly matched this shade, and she had it cut so as to leave a couple of feet of floor showing around the walls. She had no mats or cloths on the shelves and tables; yet somehow crochet vine leaves, made by her mother, still found their way on to the handles of all the cupboards. Fittings such as the tops of the curtains she had made specially in local workshops, as well as many of the cupboards and kitchen fittings. A couple of years after redecorating the flat this way, Maria decided to repeat the process, which involved knocking through the wall of the corridor to create a much more open, lighter space from the living room and corridor combined. The walls were repainted in a pale yellow. The previous light blue shade had been, she said, a little too dark.

Unlike many other families, the Petrus gave few hints that any work might be involved in maintaining their home, and the decor reinforced this. The living room carpet did not require beating, Maria told me; although she did have an Amway carpet shampoo in the bathroom. When entertaining, they use disposable packaged foods, which are expensive and unheard-of in most homes.

The distinctive fittings were Maria's own idea, although she used a German catalogue for inspiration. Brindusa, who was nine, promptly produced the catalogue, dog-eared from use, and showed me what kinds of furniture she herself preferred in it. The tastes seemed to be transmitting from mother to daughter, and Brindusa also instinctively knew some ways to care for the home. One time while I talked to her parents, she lifted herself up on the settee and snatched at the air. When we looked at her, she looked back with solemn eyes and pronounced "moth" (*flutur*) by way of explanation. She also acquired other kinds of aspiration. When her uncle, Maria's younger brother, emigrated improbably in a shipping crate, Brindusa said seriously that she wanted to go abroad too. She risked upsetting her mother at a time when their whole family was distraught that they might not see uncle Stefan again for many long years. He had spent some time formulating his escape, complaining all the while of corruption and dirt in Romania, and perhaps Brindusa had taken in some of his idealistic portrayals of the West.

The Petrus are similar to the bourgeois New Russians. They are seeking to embody a new, relaxed and prosperous lifestyle which involves minimal housework. Yet successfully achieving the right style for a successful household can evade them, and seems to mean frequent decorating, knocking through walls, and conspicuous consumption of disposable objects which express transience. Cleanliness is still central to this home, but cleanliness of a kind which is expressly separated from labour. Practically every household in the town has been modernizing somehow, bit by bit, often as a group, but Maria has made a more radical break with the past, by aiming at a new aesthetic. The objects which are a prime focus and motivation of group labour, in periodic clean-ups, are largely lacking. In reducing the visibility of the compulsion to work, Maria has also taken upon herself the responsibility to clean the place. There are still, however, some unavoidable, unobtrusive elements which creep into the home, such as crochet vine leaves and moths, and which are a part of the socialization of children. At a young age, Brindusa has already participated in some form of moth hunt to protect the woollens in the home against invasion from outside.

Conclusions

Suceava is full of variety and contradiction. In this chapter I began investigating cleanliness and progress through the ambivalent sets of reactions to the layout of a room. People do not want to be associated with clutter and dust, because they would feel dirty themselves. But when one person's tidiness is another person's clutter, complications arise. Dirt does not only happen because of activity, but can occur through inactivity. If one leaves the home as it is, then over time certain objects may be seen as 'matter out of place'. A particular carpet or cloth which was once smart becomes dated, and is transformed into clutter, or what Buchli (1999) might compare to dust.

I see several levels of analysis to explain the particular examples of cleanliness and progress which I have described. First, there is the modern project of cleanliness favoured by people who see themselves as engaged in building a market. This project envisages a radical break from the past, and individualized, compartmentalized labour practices around soaps and cleaners. In families such as the Petrus, new forms of decor attempt to materialize these principles of labour, reducing women's work. Cleaning is often presumed to be women's work, and to be oppressive and backward because it constitutes a form of drudgery and labour. In this way, a family may escape the oppressive weight of the past and move on to a new life.

Secondly, however, at the level of trivial routines, a different picture is revealed. Cleanliness and progress are often examined as aspirational discourses, and thus necessarily divorced from the experience of most people. By contrast, it is possible to see them as potentially creative activities whose meaning may lie in the hands of people themselves. Cleanliness and progress lie at the heart of relationships in Suceavan homes of all kinds, and have done so for many years, as part of the exercise of reordering the world through organic more than abrupt development. The wealthy younger generation of the year 2000 may have been developing a home different from those of their parents, but the young couples of the 1970s had also been developing homes different from those of their parents in the country. The periodic physical activity of renovating and cleaning the home can involve a social or personal renovation as well. Garvey (2001) looks at the apparently insignificant activity of shoving furniture around in Norway, experimenting with new alignments as a response to, and way to address, an individual's inner state of mind. In similar fashion, the institution of the household in Romania is subjected to regular cleaning, and the relationships in it to regular scrutiny. The younger generation may feel oppressed by the closeness of the household, and the way they are drawn into having to beat old carpets and rugs. The older generation meanwhile may perceive households which seek to reduce this regular, thorough clean-up as problematic, because cleaning is linked to a sense of reinvigoration and progress and the work is morally good. The epitomy of household clean-ups is the exhausting beating of carpets. This beating generally involves no cleaners or soaps of any kind (although carpet shampoos are beginning to appear), and so is largely ignored by private firms engaged in marketing. The feeling of having beaten the carpets, aching down one side, is one way in which men and women know that they have really cleaned their home, having literally beaten the dirt out of it.

Older styles of decor thus enable the mobilization of the whole household, even normally intransigent men and children, to lend a hand and work. Although I have discussed too few examples to generalize too broadly, it does seem that women who aim to liberate themselves with a 'reduced labour' home *may* be increasing their individual responsibilities, and subjecting themselves to new strictures and disciplines. They are sacrificing some of the objects which are their allies in obliging others to share some small degree of responsibility for creating cleanliness.

Lastly, there is a level of analysis of what I would call the materiality of the home. That is, not only people but the objects of the home can be seen as having agency (Gell 1998). People order objects, but then the objects can act back and order the people, for example by directing their labour. The physical presence of the limited space of the home obliges close cooperation by people in it. The carpets and coverings of the old style of home are versions of ancestral objects (as Miller 1994 might say). Carpets are particularly physical objects in Suceava. They possess qualities of relative longevity. In the small space of Suceava apartments, physically shared and physically intimate, taking up carpets generally involves everyone because there is no alternative. There is rarely other space to escape to. Even young children, who are very likely to rebel against their parents in the future, perhaps breaking their hearts or abandoning Suceava altogether, must participate in taking care of rugs and carpets. Unceasing vigilance against moths, an apparently trivial and occasional activity, I would suggest, one sign of the largely unseen power of the home.

In the longer term, cleanliness may prove significant in establishing the nature of 'transition' in a town such as Suceava. The hypothetical end-point of the experience of transition may involve a situation in which a form of cleanliness develops which is more taken for granted, and unproblematic, than currently exists. There is always some uncertainty in change. Objects will never do the work for themselves, nor necessarily transform habits. Children of both sexes will perhaps always be socialized knowing how to hunt moths, even in some hypothetical future of a home containing no woollens, rugs or woven ancestral handicrafts where they might feed or nest.

Acknowledgements

The research on which this paper is based was primarily conducted between January 1997 and April 1998 in Suceava. It comprised discussions with a range of households concerning a range of objects in their homes; discussions with local traders; and interviews with marketing executives in soap and toiletries companies in Bucharest. I wish to gratefully acknowledge the assistance of a grant from the Research Support Scheme of the Soros Foundation, which provided financial support during fieldwork.

References

Amato, J. (2000), *Dust: a History of the Small and the Invisible*, Berkeley: University of California Press.
Baban, A. (2000), 'Sexuality in Romania: a Psychological Approach', in S. Gal and G. Kligman (eds), *Reproducing Gender*, Princeton: Princeton University Press.
Buchli, V. (1999), *An Archaeology of Socialism*, Oxford: Berg.

Burawoy, M. and Verdery, K. (1999), *Uncertain Transition: Ethnographies of Change in the Postsocialist World*, Oxford: Rowman & Littlefield.

Burke, T. (1996), *Lifebuoy Men, Lux Women*, London: Leicester University Press.

Carsten, J. (2000), *Cultures of Relatedness*, Cambridge: Cambridge University Press.

Constantin, M. (1998), 'Familia si cariera nu fac casa buna', in *Stil de Viata*, supplement of *Capital* 2(3), 26 February.

Corbin, A. (1986 [1982]), *The Foul and the Fragrant: Odour and the Social Imagination*, London: Papermac.

Douglas, M. (1984 [1966]), *Purity and Danger*, London: Ark.

Drazin, A. (2001), '"Omul se va Mobila": Wood and Domesticity in Urban Romania', in D. Miller (ed.), *House Possessions: the Material Culture of the Home*, Oxford: Berg.

—— and Cimpoes, N. (1999), '"Toate Sapunuri sunt Jafuri" – "All soaps are rip-offs": Success, Domesticity and Material Culture in Urban Romania', in *Year Book of the Romanian Society of Cultural Anthropology 1999*, Bucharest: Editura Paideia.

Fischer, M. (1985), 'Women in Romanian Politics: Elena Ceausescu and the Promotion of Women', in S. Wolchik and A. Meyer (eds), *Women, State and Party in Eastern Europe*, Durham: Duke University Press.

Forty, A. (1995 [1986]), *Objects of Desire*, London: Thames and Hudson.

Frykman, J. and Löfgren, O. (1996 [1979]), *Culture Builders: a Historical Anthropology of Middle-Class Life*, trans. A. Crozier, New Brunswick, NJ: Rutgers University Press.

Funk, N. and Mueller, M. (eds) (1993), *Gender Politics and Post-Communism*, New York: Routledge.

Gal, S. and Kligman, G. (eds) (2000), *Reproducing Gender: Politics, Publics and Everyday Life After Socialism*, Princeton: Princeton University Press.

Garvey, P. (2001), 'Organized Disorder: Moving Furniture in Norwegian Homes', in D. Miller (ed.), *House Possessions: the Material Culture of the Home*, Oxford: Berg.

Gell, A. (1998), *Art and Agency: an Anthropological Theory*, Oxford: Clarendon.

Hann, C. (1994), 'After Communism: Reflections on East European Anthropology and the Transition', in European Association of Social Anthropologists, *Social Anthropology*, 2(3), 229–49.

Harris, O. (1981), 'Households as Natural Units', in K. Young, C. Wolkowitz and R. McCullagh (eds), *Of Marriage and the Market*, London: Routledge, 49–68.

Humphrey, C. (1997), 'The villas of the 'New Russians': a sketch of consumption and cultural identity in post-Soviet landscapes', in R. Staring, M. van der Land and H. Tak, *Globalization/Localization: Paradoxes of Cultural identity*, Focaal No. 30/31, 85–106.

Kligman, G. (1988), *The Wedding of the Dead*, London: University of California Press.

—— (1998), *The Politics of Duplicity*, London: Routledge.

Linde-Laursen, A. (1993), 'The Nationalisation of Trivialities', *Ethnos*, 58(3–4), 275–93.

Mihailescu, V. (1995), 'Le Bloc 311', *Ethnologie Française*, XXV(3).

Miller, D. (1987), *Material Culture and Mass Consumption*, Oxford: Basil Blackwell.

Miller, D. (1994), 'Artefacts and the Meaning of Things', in T. Ingold, (ed.), *Companion Encyclopedia of Anthropology: Humanity, Culture and Social Life*, London: Routledge, 396–419.

Pelevin, V. (2000), *Babylon*, London: Faber & Faber.

Prost, A. and Vincent, G. (eds) (1991), *A History of Private Life*, London: Harvard University Press.

Sampson, S. (1984), *National Integration through Socialist Planning: an Anthropological Study of a Romanian New Town*, Boulder: East European Monographs.

—— (1994), 'Money Without Culture, Culture Without Money: Eastern Europe's Nouveaux Riches', *Post-Communist Transition*, 3(1).

Schmidt, L-H. and Kristensen, J.E. (1986), *Lys, luft og renlighed: den moderne socialhygiejnes fødsel*, Copenhagen: Akademisk Forlag.

Shafir, M. (1985), *Romania: Politics, Economics and Society*, London: Frances Pinter.

Vaschi, M. (1998), 'Birocratii si bancherii calca in picioare hectare de mocheta', *Capital, no.*26, 2 July, 3.

Verdery, K. (1996), *What Was Socialism and What Comes Next?*, Princeton: Princeton University Press.

Wolchik, S. and Meyer, A. (1985), *Women, State and Party in Eastern Europe*, Durham: Duke University Press.

Re-constructing the 'Normal': Identity and the Consumption of Western Goods in Estonia

Sigrid Rausing

Introduction

This chapter,[1] which is based on fieldwork carried out on a former collective farm in Estonia, considers certain aspects of household consumption during the period of fieldwork, 1993–94. My argument will be that the transitional period of the collective farm was largely conceived of as a return to 'normality', and that consumption of expensive Western household products played an important part in that process. The consumption of Western products, I will argue, constituted a form of appropriation of Western-ness, whereby the whole village was moving from east to West, from what they believed to be a state of the 'not-normal' to the 'normal'. The intrinsic 'Western-ness' of the Estonians, as opposed to the 'easternness' of the Russians, represented Estonia's past in the form of the brief period of independence from Russia between the two World Wars, as well as a perceived cultural, ethnic and geographical proximity which represented the 'normal'. The consumption, therefore, of 'normal', i.e. Western, household products symbolized the collective return of the village, and the country, to 'normality', articulating a key feature of the present Estonian identity. The intrinsic 'normality' of these products had no relationship to affordability: the relative-to-income extremely expensive Western products were considered more 'normal' than the less expensive, and more familiar, Eastern European goods, which represented the 'not-normal' Soviet past. It is also perhaps no accident that the transition, which on the collective farm was experienced as often bewildering and sometimes frightening, should have been anchored to a term which denotes its structural opposite, i.e. the 'normal'.

Ethnography

The association between 'normality' and the West, which is relevant for Estonia as a country, was framed on my fieldsite with a particular connection with Sweden.

The former collective farm was located on an isolated peninsula on the north-west coast. Before the Second World War the population on the peninsula, then about 4,000 people, was just over 50 per cent Swedish-speaking. In all of Estonia there were about 8,000 people whose ethnicity was identified as Swedish, living mainly on the islands and coastlines of the north-west of the country. The majority of the Swedes escaped or were evacuated to Sweden during the war, and the area was partially resettled by the German army with Estonian refugees from the front. Despite some subsequent Soviet efforts to repopulate the area, the population today is still less than a quarter of what it was before the war. The central village, which before the war consisted of the manor house, a village school, and a small number of scattered farms, now also has a number of Soviet workshops, two shops, a defunct dairy, and nine apartment blocks, built between the early 1960s and the late 1980s. The village also housed the administrative office of the collective farm, and was still the centre for the local political administration. The population in 1993 was about 320 people, almost all of Estonian ethnic origin, the only village on the peninsula whose population had increased between 1934 and 1994.

My informants on the collective farm fell into three main categories; the farming families who had been present in the area before the war; the people who, tempted mainly by the availability of new flats, had moved to the area to work in the collective farm; and the teachers who had come to work at the school, a well-known state boarding school at the High School level. In addition to the post-war blocks of flats, there were two new private houses side by side (the mayor's and the builder's), and some old private houses on the road out of the village. The collective farm had never been wealthy, and hence there had been a relatively high degree of migration both to and from the collective. The inevitable decision to privatize had been taken in early 1993, and many people had, as a consequence, lost their jobs. At the same time, there was an extensive aid programme in the village, set up by a small Swedish town which had created an official link, a twin town agreement, to the area.

The poverty in the village was striking, particularly in the winter when the central coal-fired heating system broke down, bringing the previously sporadic heating to a complete halt, while outside temperatures plunged to -33 degrees Celsius. My survey of the central village showed that the total unemployment rate was about 17 per cent: this, however, concealed the fact that many women having lost their jobs now described themselves as 'housewives' rather than as 'unemployed'. Male unemployment was 23 per cent, and many, wary of the 'authorities', were reluctant to sign up for the meagre unemployment benefit. Nevertheless, people did still buy goods imported from the West. The question which I set out to explore in this chapter is why people were willing to buy, for example, Ariel washing powder at a cost equal to income from employment for six average working hours, when their old washing powder was available for 1/6th of the price – which in itself constituted a considerable increase since the Soviet times. Why did they buy Swedish margarine, when for a fraction of the price they could buy the – to my mind – much superior fresh Estonian butter? Why did they buy Swedish cream cheese in a tube when the much cheaper Estonian cream cheese was of the same quality or better?

The old shop and the new shop

On my first visit to the village, in spring 1993, the new, cooperative/ private shop had just been started up by a small group of villagers and farmers who saw a commercial opportunity in a new shop. Situated behind a wooden counter in a small space in the old workshops, it resembled a kiosk more than a shop. The day I came in it was stocked with cigarettes, coffee, alcohol, some dry and tinned food, and, incongruously, two live fish on a plastic tray. The old shop, at that time, was stocked mostly with Soviet-style cans and jars, as well as some household goods. By the time I moved to the community in August 1993, the new shop had moved to larger premises, and had expanded to include a small café. They sold dry foods and bread, along with some seasonal vegetables, meat products and cheese from a cold counter, household products, and, occasionally, shoes and clothes. The products were mainly from Eastern Europe, including many 'new' products from, for example, Poland or Bulgaria, mimicking the colourful packaging of the West. Some products, such as milk, still only available from a steel bucket under the counter, and vegetables, were local. Most people bought them privately from the farmers, storing apples and potatoes, and sometimes cabbages and root vegetables in the basements of the blocks of flats, much as these products had always been stored on the farms. Western products, mostly imported from Sweden and Finland, included coffee, cereal, washing powder, margarine, cream cheese and hard cheese, crisp bread, ketchup, biscuits, chocolate alcohol and cigarettes. These kinds of product were only rarely sold in the old shop, which was still mainly stocked with 'old' east European products.

The choice between the old and the new shop was complex, revealing some aspects of the process of transformation which the village was passing through. The new shop was more expensive, and generally more popular: the food products were said to be of a higher quality, and there was a greater degree of choice. In an obvious sense the old shop represented Soviet Estonia, while the new one represented the new system. The people most opposed to the old system, however, were also the people who were in many ways the least happy about the new one: they tended not to be happy with the way in which the progress of the new independent Estonia was increasingly framed by the development of capitalism, or in other words by what you could buy rather than by what you could say. Some of the teachers at the school, therefore, preferred the old shop because, in contrast to the new shop, it signified a degree of integrity and non-profit. At the same time, those people were more concerned with what was happening to Estonian culture than with what was happening in the village: the evident polarization between those who were getting by and those who were sinking down into real poverty was of less concern to them. Indeed, there was much contemptuous talk about the rough and alcoholic ways of the poor, and a strong sense of the disparity between the educated and the uneducated.

In addition, the two shops had come to constitute magnets for opposing ends of the village: the old shop was in the 'down-market' end, where the oldest and most primitive apartment blocks were situated, whereas the new one was in the 'better' area, near the old manor house, which was under renovation, and the most recent blocks of flats. In the crystallization of all the various processes in the village, then, a class element was emerging in the identification of the two shops. Again, however, it was a more complex process than it appeared to be: when the oldest blocks of flats were built in the 1950s, people counted themselves lucky if they gained access to a flat, but gradually, as the more modern blocks were built, their luck paled in comparison to the luck of the people going into the new flats, which were of a higher standard. In the time of my fieldwork, however, it was becoming apparent that the old flats were cheaper to run, both in terms of rent, which was still negligible, and, more importantly, in terms of heating and electricity, since they were still heated by wood stoves, and were not connected to the central heating system. For a short while, therefore, the people in the old flats began to count themselves lucky again. No doubt, when the buy-back process gets underway the luck will shift once more, since a certain number of work-years entitles the potential buyer to a certain number of square metres, whatever the standard of the flat, and in the long run a modern flat will be more valuable than an unmodernized one.

In addition to the old and the new shop, people also used the small supermarkets and other shops in the local town an hour's bus-ride away, as well as a cheap shop-on-wheels, a bus stocked with groceries which would arrive about once a week. In the local town, people still tended to use several different shops in one shopping expedition, now in search of good value rather than, as in the recent past, availability. Similarly, while the old shop was used by most people at some time, the new one was mainly used by people who were better off, or in other words people who still had paying jobs. Few people actually saw the need for two shops: although they used them, they were still, following the logic of the command economy, generally seen as 'unnecessary' for a village of this size.

Consumption and the concept of the 'Normal'

The relationship between consumption of Western goods and the concept of the 'normal' is associated with a second relationship between the notion of what qualities constitute Estonian-ness – i.e., thrift, order, quiet, stubbornness and individualism – and the conception of a set of opposite characteristics which are associated with the Russians and the Soviet Union – profligacy, disorder, emotionality, and a tendency towards collectivity and brutality. While my Estonian informants associated their own characteristics with restraint and order, they regarded the Russians as inherently excessive and disorderly. The logic of this relationship pivoted around the term 'not normal': the Soviet Union, represented in popular discourse by the Russian minority in Estonia, was often referred to as 'not normal', whereas the West, and particularly Finland and Sweden, were represented as 'normal'. The 'normal', then, tended to mean not what Estonia, or the collective farm, actually was, but what it should have been had the Soviet invasion not taken place. The 'norm', in other words, was not used in the meaning of what the norm *was*, but rather in the meaning of what it *should have been*: what 'normality' would have looked like had Estonia's development itself been 'normal', i.e., uninterrupted by the Soviet takeover.

While the notion of the 'normal' has anti-Soviet associations, it is also contextualized within the Soviet culture, or world-view. Present efforts and sacrifices were still sometimes referred to as 'building capitalism', and linked with national, rather than individual, aspirations. At the same time, the term derived from a critique of the Soviet system: the notion that the system was 'not normal' long pre-dates its current usage. Similarly, the notion that the Estonians culturally and geographically belong to the realm of the West rather than to Russia was always part of the identity of Soviet Estonians.[2]

The 'normal', then, as it was used on the collective farm, represented the imaginary good and ordinary: that which should have been 'normal' had Estonia not been incorporated into the Soviet Union. Since part of its force was derived from the Soviet ideology, and habit, of normativity, it tended to articulate material and social ambitions in terms of the collective rather than of the individual. One of my informants, for example, complained about the fact that he had only one bathroom, stating that it was 'not normal' to have only one. The fact that there was not a single flat in the blocks with more than one bathroom, and that the blocks themselves were standardized replicas of a ubiquitous model, was not relevant: his statement implied that the entire settlement, and, by implication, Soviet Estonia, was 'not normal' in comparison to his imagined construction of the 'normal'.

Another informant, discussing the new advertising on television, told me that she likes it as long as it's 'normal'. Thus she didn't like the Sheba cat food advertising, because it's not 'normal' to decorate a cat's dish with a sprig of parsley, but she liked the straightforward Kite-Kat commercial message, in which a normal-looking cat is fed in a normal way. Also, the cat in the Sheba advertisement was arguably less 'normal' than the Kite-Kat cat: with its long silky hair, it certainly looked more expensive than the ordinary and robust Kite-Kat cat, creating a slightly decadent image of luxury. The 'normal', then, was not luxury as opposed to the present poverty – that was associated with the 'New Estonians', i.e. the newly rich, who in their own way also lacked 'normality'. Instead, the 'normal' was associated with the solid ordinary comforts of northern Europe, which in the context of the former collective farm were actually anything but ordinary.

Furthermore, the act of placing a sprig of parsley on a cat's dish is not only decadent (and hence not 'normal') but it is also deceptive: advertising was acceptable, though wearing, when it was giving straightforward information to the consumers, but not when it was trying to trick them. The 'not normal' in this case was therefore also associated with *obman*, the Russian term translated by Humphrey as the 'gigantic deception of the Soviet regime' (Humphrey 1995: 43). Whimsical skits, such as the

Sheba advertising, therefore, were regarded by my informant as a form of deception, subverting what she thought ought to be the 'real', informative, function of the commercial message.

It should be emphasized again that the 'normality' of the advertisement bore no relationship to what was actually normal on the collective farm: all the dubbed advertisement looked odd, but the ones for pet-food looked particularly out-of-place in the village where the semi-wild dogs and cats fed at night from the rusty rubbish bins by the flood-lit generator.

Usually, however, the 'abnormality', or new-ness, of the 'normal' was only gradually revealed to me. One informant suddenly told me how helpless they – the villagers – felt when the first coffee-makers arrived in the village with incomprehensible instructions. Later she told me about when the first buses came from Finland three years ago, how the children were running around, whispering, telling everybody that the buses had toilets, and trays for food, and how struck she was by how well the foreigners looked. Then the aid shipments of second-hand clothes started to arrive, and within weeks the look of the community had changed radically.

The concept of the 'normal', then, was used as a deliberate differentiation from the Soviet, often derogatively referred as 'not normal', as well as a differentiation between acceptable degrees of Western economic practices. There were, however, also other meanings of the term which were more specific to the collective farm, and which were connected to notions of the rural. Elsewhere (Rausing 1998) I have looked at the concept of the land from a particularly Estonian point of view, where the relationship to the land is regarded as constitutive of the national characteristics of the Estonians. The original Soviet view of the land, however, which had had a certain influence on the collective farm, was quite different, and had much more in common with the pre-revolutionary notion of the backwardness, poverty and ennui of the remote peasant villages in Russia. One of the intentions of the forced collectivization was to transform what was regarded as an intrinsically reactionary class into a class of agricultural workers with a revolutionary consciousness. With their quasi-urban nature, the collective farms' urban architecture, cultural programmes, and general emphasis on the industrial and the modern were constructed as a deliberate antidote to the backwardness of the countryside which had been thought to be the main impediment to revolutionary development in Russia.

The sense of boredom on the collective farm, therefore, was also infused by a certain amount of anxiety, stemming from the fear that the village was moving from being the centre of a sizeable collective farm to becoming a dead-end place where people just got by from job to job; the cultural programme was more or less closed, and people were leaving. Without the cultural programme, then, people were not only bored, but also anxious that the village was becoming de-cultured, passing into a state of passivity and alcoholism, which was both 'not-normal', i.e. not-good, and to be expected: it represented the Soviet notion of the default state of the peasantry, as it were, which the collective farm had counter-acted. The connections with Sweden and Finnish Swedish communities which were building up in the area were generally regarded as an antidote to this development. They were still, however, considered to be piecemeal and fragile, not coherent or co-opting enough to be seen as a viable replacement of Soviet practices.

Soviet Normativity and the 'Normal'

In 1983 the collective farm produced a brochure in order to attract more people to the area. Amid photographs of the young director and the newest blocks of flats, there was also a characteristic text about *Kolhoosi parim lüpsja*, the best milker of the collective farm, who in 1983 got on average 4071 kg of milk from each cow. The brochure also stated that the farm planned a new school for 1985, and a new block of flats, which would include an old people's home. There were at that time two restaurants, three shops, and a service centre. The brochure is in itself a representation of the model on which the collective farms were built. They all had shops, dining-rooms, kindergartens, schools, a doctor and a nurse, a vet, an agricultural expert and a cultural expert. The spatial layout was functional and normative. The *kulturnik* ran a cultural programme in the culture house, which included films, Soviet or foreign, twice a week, dances once a week, and other events such as performances by visiting theatre groups or choirs. The dining rooms served the same food, the shops stocked the same products, and the cultural programmes were more or less identical.

Soviet – and by extension Estonian – culture tended generally to be expressed within certain set formulas. This was true for most areas of life, including work, food, dress, home decoration, entertainment, and even to some extent speech. If one wanted to build a private house, for example, there were a few set models to choose from, all limited to the maximum 60 square metres. The three-storey blocks of the collective farm where I worked were replicated in collective farms all over the country. Practically every flat in the blocks had the same sets of furniture, arranged in the same way, with the same colour schemes on the walls and floors. At the time of my fieldwork, in 1993–94, only the few people who were very well connected in the West deviated from these formulas, which effectively marked their 'Western-ness'.

Caroline Humphrey writes about the exact similarity of propaganda images of homes in Soviet Russia and people's actual homes, arguing that the limited range of products enforced an 'involuntary homogeneity' (Humphrey 1994: 15). This homogeneity was partly a matter of economics and partly a matter of ideology, or in other words partly an unintended and partly an intended effect. The Soviet economic system of course inevitably led to a degree of uniformity of production. The political organization of the economy provided no incentive for innovation or variation in the realm of industrial production and the orientation toward mass production to cover identified needs led to a sameness in the realm of material culture which is striking in relation to Western cultures.

The lack of experimentation in the area of material culture, however, was arguably also a more complex expression of Soviet culture, which was connected with the Stalinist suppression of the movement of Russian modernism and, with it, the concept of experimental living (Benjamin 1986, Golomstock 1990). Experimentation came to be associated with deviation and bourgeois individualist decadence, where it lingered in the post-Stalin era. The uniformity, in that sense, was political as well as economic, producing a culture of normativity as much as a normative economy of staples. The notion of staples is an appropriate concept for an economy and cultural/political programme based on the concept of 'need' rather than 'want'. There was a staple diet of furniture, architecture, clothing, schooling, cultural events, books and slogans, as well as of food. The only significant variation in interior decoration I saw on the collective farm was a display of a collection of beer cans. This seemed like the exception to the rule of normativity until I came across a virtually identical collection in another flat, displayed in exactly the same way – beer cans, like the little porcelain figures or empty bottles of Western shampoo, had become identified as collectable, and there was a taken-for-granted cultural knowledge of exactly how to display collected items. This is significantly different from the individual variation in London council flats described, for example, by Daniel Miller who argues that the diversity of house decoration – and, in a wider sense, consumption – functioned to express the individual's sense of belonging, origin, and self (Miller 1987). On the collective farm there was virtually no sense of the expression of individuality through house decoration, which, like cooking, was essentially traditional, or normative, rather than inventive.

There was, then, a general tendency toward normativity in Soviet culture which went beyond the question of production and the absence of the process of individual – but class-based – 'distinction' described by Bourdieu (1986). There is obviously a relationship between the Soviet history of normativity and the current emphasis on Western things and culture as the 'normal', as we shall see below.

Status and Distinction

The Western products represented the imaginary 'normal' which expressed the inner core of 'normality' of the Estonians themselves. Clearly there was also a certain amount of status attached to the consumption of Western products. It would be a mistake, however, as I argued above, to regard the consumption of Western goods as wholly, or even mainly, motivated by Bourdieu's process of distinction and status-seeking (Bourdieu 1986). Material success, entangled in notions of connections and corruption, was still regarded with a considerable degree of ambivalence on the collective farm. Consequently, just as the imaginary good was described as 'normal', individuals felt a powerful need to act as though the imported goods really *were* normal, despite the fact that they paid astronomical prices for them. Margarine, for example, would be offered much as it would be in Sweden, the plastic tub casually placed on the table. Western biscuits would be offered on a plate at a coffee session, looking so deceptively 'normal' to the outside eye that it would be easy to miss the economic reality and symbolic nature of the gesture.

Moreover, the goods consumed were themselves resolutely 'normal': this was a question of products such as shampoo, cornflakes, and Heinz ketchup. They were things for which a perceived and everyday need already existed, rather than the extravagant and decadent goods which the New Estonians were suspected of indulging in. On the collective farm 'luxuries', or perhaps rather products which marked festive occasions, remained what they were in the Soviet times: champagne from Georgia and Estonian chocolates. These products were not items which were previously unknown, for instance Parmesan cheese, peanuts, or olive oil, which have become 'normal' in Scandinavia, but would have been novelties on the collective farm. The consumption of 'normal' products was not intended to enhance the status of the individual consumer: competitive consumption was perceived as a feature of being a New Estonian, and was regarded as suspect, and based on the consumption of exclusive, esoteric, and hence decadent, Western goods. In contrast, the 'normal' Western products consumed on the collective farms resembled pre-existing Estonian products. My argument in this chapter is that the consumption of these products helped to establish the natural and inherent 'normality' of all Estonians, the community of the village and of the nation, rather than the superior status of the individual consumer.

Identity and Change

About halfway through my fieldwork, at a coffee party given by one of my informants, I was told two jokes: the first one was about a man visiting a prostitute, who, when he was about to leave and the prostitute mentioned payment, drew himself up and announced that he was a politician, and could not accept any money. The second joke was about a man telling his doctor he thought he was a Lesbian. When the doctor asked why, he answered that there were all these attractive men around and yet he found himself being drawn to the women. Both of those jokes have a meaning pertaining to the conception of the changes. The world had (yet again) turned upside down, and imaginary reversals and structural opposites abounded.

Those changes were a dominating topic of conversation to most of my informants, particularly when talking to me. At times my informants self-consciously set out to inform me, the ethnographer, of what they thought I was interested in, i.e. the state of Estonia as a nation. Choosing the state rather than themselves as subjects was a statement about their own identity: unlike the remaining Estonian Swedes on the old farms, the people in the blocks of flats on the collective farm did not see themselves as ethnographically interesting. In settings such as a coffee party, which demanded a certain formality, my informants tended to fall into a recognizable pattern, regarding themselves as representatives of Estonia, and myself as the representative of a university and also, ultimately, of two nations, England and Sweden. To interpret the jokes, therefore, as jokes about the state of Estonia is not a deviation from the kind of interpretation which my informants would themselves express – following Sperber, there would be little loss of faithfulness to the original material (Sperber 1995 [1974]: 168). The jokes, then, were about structural opposites; the transformation of a (male) politician into a (female) prostitute, and the transformation of a heterosexual man into a lesbian, reflecting the common perception on the collective farm that 'the changes' had involved a move from order to disorder – albeit a move from a forced order to freedom – and certainty to uncertainty.[3]

The process of cultural change which was part of the transformation of the collective farm was largely framed by the contemporary notions of what it meant to be 'Estonian', constructed, mainly, as the non-Soviet northern European. In terms of my fieldwork, the fact that I was a representative of the northern European culture which was represented as both 'normal' and normative turned the relationship between me and my informants from the general relationship between ethnographer as a representative of the 'global' and informants as representatives of the 'local' into a process which was both more urgent and more specific. For the Estonians, the northern European identity did not signify the 'other' into which, for better or for worse, they were merging, but rather was seen as a representation of their own inner core, which had been denied its natural expression and development during the Soviet rule.

Identity, however, is an essentially relative concept. The identity of the Estonians, geographically situated between East and West, is presently shifting: as the country moves from the edges of the East to the edges of the West, the identity of the people seems to be moving from that of being Westerners in the east to being Easterners in the West. While Russian observers during the Soviet times noticed superior roads and harder-working people, Western observers see pot-holed streets and inefficient work practices (e.g. Sakharov 1992; Young 1989; Wachtmeister 1992). One much-travelled informant in Tallinn told me about the satisfaction of being mistaken for a Westerner in Soviet Russia: of being better dressed and speaking a seemingly 'foreign' language, of strategically avoiding speaking Russian and hence momentarily escaping the Soviet identity by small acts of distinction. In a fitting illustration of the present changes, she later described her current efforts at trying to pass for Russian in Russia: the previously coveted foreign-ness which the new Estonian passports entails means that access to museums and other services are several times more expensive.

Access to the cultural knowledge which was needed to cement the identity of 'normal-ness', or Western-ness, was fraught with ambivalence. The perceived dangers of pretentiousness and individualism, in conjunc-tion with the Soviet policy of merging the concepts of ethnicity and nationality, meant that the affinity with the Nordic region tended to be described in terms of collective and ethnic, rather than individual, kinship. This particular fragment of cultural knowledge, therefore, came to be defined as 'normal', and was widely seen as the logical extension of a core, or an essence, of Estonian-ness, which itself belonged more to nature than to culture. Actual knowledge generally had to be gathered discreetly, although there were important generational distinctions on the collective farm between older people, who identified more with the Soviet system, and young people, whose interiorized Western-ness was already quite secure. The people in between, however, tended to vacillate between the two, uncertain of how to acquire the culture which their teenage sons and daughters seemed to absorb out of thin air.

One strategy was to interview me, orchestrating a reversal between the roles of observer and informant, whereby I was turned into an informant of the culture of desired 'normality'. I was questioned, for example, about drinks, ranging from tea to alcohol. There was still a solid belief in a hierarchy of quality of which Westerners have implicit, or interiorized, knowledge. The project of constructing 'normality', therefore, also involved the notion of objective taste, and a process whereby people would, eventually, be able to create a legible map of products and brand names from the chaotic profusion in the new shops.

Constantly observing, I often also found myself being observed. I and my informants both trying to discover the authentic, or taken-for-granted, cultural knowledge of the other. If I put milk in my coffee this was noted with interest by my landlady, who invariably, like everybody else, took her coffee black, unless she was at a coffee party, when cream was sometimes added. They were interested in what they saw as my unusual consumption of water, as I was interested in the fact that they drank virtually no liquid except for tea, coffee, and alcohol. It should be emphasized again that their interest in the subtle differences between East and West was not primarily motivated by curiosity, but rather by the desire for knowledge of a coherent Western habitus to which they had a particular, collective, or national relationship of affinity, but which was also tantalizingly subtle and difficult to grasp for the individual.

Conclusion

My informants, then, were not moving from the local to the global, or from modernity to post-modernity (Appadurai 1990; Harvey 1992: 111). As a nation, the Estonians thought that they knew exactly what they would have been like if the situation had been 'normal', and thus what they wanted to become. 'Western-ness' as represented by American-ness was, on the whole, regarded as culture-less; the structural opposite, but also in some sense the spiritual twin, of the Soviet Union. The Estonians, rather, were in a specific movement away from the Soviet (and Russian) and towards a particularly Swedish, Finnish and German cultural sphere.[4] In that sense their process of change differed from the

Russian contemporary process, in that they were moving not only from one system to another, but also from one geographical realm of belonging to another. The consumption of ordinary Western products in a 'normal' way could be seen as rituals of inauguration; signs of belonging in the West rather than the East, the 'normal' rather than the 'not-normal'. One of the effects of this is shown in the interesting difference between Humphrey's description of the temporary reluctance to accept foreign goods in Moscow in 1993, and the desire to incorporate, and 'normalize', Western products in the households on my field site (Humphrey 1995).

I have argued in this chapter that the term 'normal' revealed an important aspect of the process of transition. While it originated in the Soviet system, it was primarily used to disassociate the speaker from the remnants of the Soviet, and to create a link with the partially imagined, partially perceived culture of northern Europe. The construction of the 'normal' to encompass the imagined habitus of the West[5] constituted a form of appropriation of that habitus: an appropriation which also predated independence from the Soviet Union, and functioned as a means of distinction from the Soviet system. The 'normal', in other words, was not used in the meaning of what the current norm actually was, but rather in the meaning of what the norm should have been, and, specifically, what 'normality' would have looked like had Estonia's development itself been 'normal', i.e. uninterrupted by the Soviet takeover.

The consumption of Western goods represented an important part of the process of appropriating and 'normalizing' Western-ness: the consumption of ordinary products, used in an 'ordinary' way, tended to conceal the fact that these goods were, in fact, extremely expensive, and still relatively new to the consumers. This form of consumption, I have argued, functioned more to institute the notion of Estonia as a 'normal' Western country, like Finland or Sweden, than to display individual economic and social ambition, which was still regarded with a great deal of ambivalence in the community.

Notes

1. This chapter develops the arguments I presented in a 1998 paper, 'Signs of the New Nation: Gift exchange, consumption and aid on a former collective farm in north-west Estonia' (Miller (ed.) 1998). It

was given at a conference at SSE Riga 17–19 September 1998, and, in an extended version, at Emmanuel College, Cambridge on 26 February 1999.

2. Although this identification was perhaps also tempered by the notion of the Finno-Ugric origins of the Estonian people, which forms a distinction between the Estonians, Finns and Hungarians, as well as a number of other Finno-Ugric tribal peoples, and other Europeans, including the Russians and the Scandinavians. The language is not part of the Indo-European linguistic group, and there is a strong awareness of the 'other-ness' of the original Estonian culture, which is conceived of as largely constituted by an ancient and shamanistic relationship to the land.

3. It is, however, important to recognize that the local perception of the changes involves a number of factors, the most important ones being the liberation of Estonia from the Soviet empire, the end of the socialist system, and the end of the collective farm. While independence was predominantly welcomed, the end of socialism, and particularly the end of the collective farm, was viewed with a great deal of ambivalence.

4. There were of course important distinctions between the three: somewhat glibly one might say that the Finns were regarded as rough, the Germans as arrogant, and the Swedes as a mixture of both.

5. 'The West' is arguably our own code for the 'normal'. It was not a word which was commonly used on the collective farm.

References

Appadurai, A. (1990), 'Disjuncture and Difference in the Global Cultural Economy', *Theory, Culture, Society*, 7, 295–310.

Benjamin, W. (1986), in G. Smith (ed.), *Moscow Diary*, Cambridge, Mass.: Harvard University Press.

Bourdieu, P. (1986a [1970]), *Distinction: A Social Critique of the Judgement of Taste*, London and New York: Routledge & Kegan Paul.

—— (1986b [1977]), *Outline of a Theory of Practice*,
Cambrige: Cambridge University Press.

Golomstock, I. (1990), *Totalitarian Art in the Soviet Union, the Third Reich, Fascist Italy and the People's Republic of China*, London: Collins Harvill.

Harvey, D. (1992), *The Condition of Postmodernity*, Cambridge, Mass./ Oxford: Blackwells.

Humphrey, C. (1995), 'Creating a Culture of Disillusionment: Consumption in Moscow, a Chronicle of Changing Times', in D. Miller (ed.), *Worlds Apart: Modernity through the Prism of the Local*, ASA Decennial Conference Series, London: Routledge.

Miller, D. (1987), *Material Culture and Mass consumption*, Oxford: Basil Blackwell.

—— (ed.) (1998), *Material Cultures: Why Some Things Matter*, London: UCL Press.

Rausing, S. (1998), 'Signs of the New Nation: Gift exchange, consumption and aid on a former collective farm in north-west Estonia', in D. Miller (ed.), *Material Cultures: Why Some Things Matter*, London: UCL Press.

Rosengren, A. (1991), *Två Barn och Eget Hus*, Stockholm: Carlsson Bokförlag.

Ruutsoo, R. (1997), 'The Estonians: Identity of Small Nation in Past and Present', *Anthropological Journal on European Cultures*, 6(1).

Sakharov, A. (1992 [1992]), *Moscow and Beyond: 1986 to 1989*, New York: Vintage Books, Random House.

Sperber, D. (1995 [1974]), *Rethinking Symbolism*, Cambridge: Cambridge University Press.

Wachtmeister, A. (1992), *Estonia*, Wallåkra: Sweslo Housing AB.

Young, C. (1989), *Growing up in Moscow*, New York: Ticknor and Fields.

–8–

Manufacturing the New Consumerism: Fast-Food Restaurants in Postsocialist Hungary
André P. Czeglédy

Introduction

Both scholarly (Gellner 1994: 125, 198, 210; 1995: 90) and popular (Drakulic 1993: 18) writing attests to the 'triumph of the West'[1] over state socialism as having had more to do with the heady attractions of consumerism than with the elusive promises of liberal democracy. For this reason, it is both prudent and culturally illuminating to examine the impact of iconic consumer products on societies whose post-war experience was framed substantially by an anti-materialist ideological legacy which has since been undermined by geopolitical events since 1989.

To date, prominent anthropological analyses of food have focused much of their attention on non-industrial societies. This is so throughout the influential work of Levi-Strauss (1969, 1973, 1978) as it is in the cases of Richards (1932, 1939), Douglas (1975), Douglas & Isherwood (1979) and Goody (1982). As a result, our analytical gaze has frequently been turned away from the mass market, and from commercial variants of pre-prepared cuisine in complex societies. With the exception of Farb and Armelagos (1980), Belasco (1987) and Warde (1997), it has been left to business analysts (Bertram 1975), geographers (Carstensen 1995; Jackle 1995) or urban sociologists such as Whyte (1948), Finkelstein (1989) and, more recently, Leidner (1993) and Ditman (1996), to investigate the qualitative aspects of food production in industrial society. With these precedents in mind, it is appropriate that anthropologists begin to look closer to home in order to investigate the cultural ramifications of the procurement of food. After all, this is what Radcliffe-Brown once noted as being the single most important of social activities (1922: 227).

This chapter takes an anthropological perspective to contemporary forms of culinary enterprise in the ethnographic setting of a complex industrial society. It does so by way of examining fast-food restaurants in postsocialist Hungary and the Central Eastern Europe (CEE) region, focusing on the early 1990s – the very highpoint of social 'transition'. The discussion opens by giving some background to the range of local fast-food equivalents. Proceeding from this contextual preface, the introduction of Western fast-food restaurant chains into the Hungarian milieu is examined in general, and then in more specific, ethnographic terms. As the ethnography presented in the second half of the chapter demonstrates, the introduction of non-indigenous fast food to Hungary has been varied and complex, impacting upon the way Hungarians conceive of themselves in relation to food itself, as well as to the restaurant industry. Of considerable interest here is the impact of fast-food processes on cultural notions of the division of labour, including the articulation with traditional structures of trade expertise, gendered aptitude and professional entitlement. This linkage is intended to elaborate contextual connections that hitherto have been largely ignored in the literature on job design (Kelly and Clegg 1982: i).

The discussion is based on participant-observation research, interviews with industry participants and the supplementary examination of both internal corporate communications and external public-relations literature. The original field research was conducted throughout the period 1990 to 1992, at a time when the author possessed a dual profile of researcher and operational consultant to the headquarters (HQ) of Alamo Chicken,[2] the restaurant chain in question. More general follow-up research on a biannual basis since that time has provided complementary data and added a longer temporal perspective. The most recent research, targeted to relate to the issues discussed below, was conducted in January 2001.

Local Fast-Food Precedents

A range of quickly prepared yet traditional 'fast' foods can be made in the home as a response to the need for less complicated and labour-intensive sustenance. The modern commercial variant of such traditional 'convenience' food is dissimilar in several respects, being differentiated in terms of the scale of production, the existence of the employee-employer labour structure, the primacy of monetary profit at the heart of production, and other relations of commercial activity which are firmly entrenched in business culture, industrial society and its organization of the food cycle. In an analysis of British perspectives, Goodman and

Redclift (1991) have gone several steps further, tying the emergence of convenience/fast foods into the post-war entry of women into the labour force, the transformation of rural regions via agro-businesses, and recent ecological considerations at the popular level of demand. For the Hungarian context, the first two conditions seem to apply – although it would be unwise to postulate deep-rooted similarities given the differing historical and cultural specifics involved.

Commercial fast food can be loosely defined as simple food, quickly prepared for easy consumption, and then sold to the widest clientele. It is made up in batch quantities prior to its ordering by the customer, a production trait that has its sympathies with the Fordist assembly-line techniques of mass manufacture. In following Henry Ford's vision of manufacture, commercial fast food involves a standardized set of (often interchangeable) components and a restricted level of customer choice (allowing for maximal labour cost efficiencies). As in the case of all processed food, these dimensions focus attention on the quick provision of the product rather than on the absolute quality of its ingredients or the complexity of its presentation (see Fine and Leopold 1993: 164–5; Warde 1997: 134).

Fast food is not new to Hungary, where indigenous equivalents have a long tradition of urban acceptance. Institutional cafeterias provide a commercial genotype for the self-service dimension – but sell differing dishes. Traditional fast foods in Hungary tend to fall into the category of savoury dishes rather than sweets. They range from baked dough biscuits (*pogácsa*), stuffed pancakes (*palacsinta*) and *Debreceni* pork sausages to sugar-dusted dough patties (*fánk*) much like the American doughnut. With the advent of mechanized meat processing in the first half of the twentieth century, thin meat sausages (*virsli*) also become easily available in Hungary, especially after the mid-1950s (when meat production increased after years of post-war scarcity).

In the 1960s, a few lucky entrepreneurs were permitted by the socialist authorities to revive the pre-war practice of private catering and allowed to establish small street kiosks selling traditional fried dough patties (*lángos*). These patties remain one of the most favoured of native fast foods. They are consumed with a variety of toppings, most popularly brushed garlic sauce along with salt, sour cream and grated cheese. As such toppings suggest, the taste emphasis is on strong and distinct flavours, a culinary dimension which many Hungarians perceive as contrasting with the relative blandness of American-originated fast foods.

The sale of some of the most traditional of local fast foods has tended to be subject to the agricultural cycle, and forms a reminder of the change

André P. Czeglédy

of seasons in a way which is consonant with a country where the connection between urban and rural populations remains intact. From at least the inter-war period, the post-harvest late summer days of Budapest and the larger cities were regularly punctuated by the cries of street hawkers – many of them women – selling cooked corn-on-the-cob (*fött kukorica*) from large woven reed baskets insulated by layers of old scarves. Later in the year, during the colder autumn and winter months, there arrived the familiar figure of the chestnut-cooker (*gesztenyesütö*), a solitary vendor selling roast chestnuts from a portable grill-cart.

Traditional fast foods in Hungary have been, and still are, sold by solitary hawkers working from open-air stands and kiosk stalls, sometimes from sidewalk kitchen 'windows' run by one, two – but rarely more than three – persons. In the latter cases, the division of labour is invariably a flexible or indistinct one that reflects the lack of hierarchical pretension and division of labour of the premises. All such operations are located in the vicinity of major public transportation nodes and/or wherever there is a high degree of pedestrian traffic, such as in the large open-air produce markets of the capital. These food stands are small-scale, often making use of semi-permanent facilities cobbled together from a bewildering array of materials. They tend to be sparsely furnished and chaotically decorated. If there is a permanent premises, it is often grubby with use and lacking in seated tables.[3] More often than not, the patrons make use of one or two closely situated countertops on which they may consume their loosely packaged food. The packaging itself is generally no more than a single paper serviette or a sheet of thicker paper.

In the case of window premises, a small ledge at the glass aperture acts as both condiment counter and serving platform. There is no question but that the food is meant to be consumed on the street by a pedestrian clientele.[4] The same goes for any drink on offer. For the children there are fruit juices and carbonated water-syrup mixtures and – since the 1970s – internationally branded soda-pop. For the adults there is the strong *eszpresszó* coffee which Hungarians prefer and, quite often, local wine measured out by *deci* (decilitre).[5] Stronger spirits, such as fruit schnapps (*pálinka*) or the native 'medicinal' brandies (*Unicum, Hubertus,* etc.), are more rarely in evidence – although commonly found at those premises which cater to the hard-drinking employees of nearby factories.

There is no attempt to promote the culinary product of such local businesses as 'cuisine' in any formal understanding of the term; this fast food is not a question of 'high culture' in the Gellnerian (1983) framework of elevated social sophistication.[6] For that sort of repast, Hungarians consider the formal restaurant (*étterem*), less pretentious restaurant

– 146 –

(*vendéglő*) or even the family home to be the appropriate setting. Rather, traditional fast food is very much a part of ordinary life and commonplace consumption for people who are pressed by the demands of their working schedule. Compared to a full-scale traditional meal comprising several courses (which may be composed of several different food portions each), the discretely compartmentalized and 'integrated' fast-food helpings are relatively small and easy to digest at a brief sitting. In conjunction with the short time element involved in consumption, such fast food is thus often considered to be but a meal substitute holding back the pangs of hunger until such time as a proper (*rendes*) meal might be consumed.

It is only in the rarefied opinion of culinary elitists that traditional fast food in Hungary is disparagingly categorized as part of the realm of some sort of 'low' culture or, more specifically (using the Hungarian expression), the 'peasant life' (*paraszt élet*). The reluctance of the majority of the population to make such a condemnation is at least partially rooted in a society which, on the one hand, retains much of its agricultural roots through part-time agriculture (see Czeglédy 2002) and where, on the other hand, native fast foods are themselves often articulated through pervasive folk recipes of widespread standing enshrined in the national culinary canon. As a consequence, their cultural standing is romanticized as much as even the most sophisticated of festive recipes.

Not surprisingly, the traditional fast foods use locally produced and/ or commonly available cheap ingredients such as wheat flour, eggs, milk, cheese, pork, sugar, cocoa, poppy seed and a broad diversity of fruits and nuts (particularly chestnuts, walnuts and imported peanuts). As in the case of other Central and Eastern European (CEE) traditions of culinary preparation, the frequent use of saturated fats such as lard as the cooking agent in combination with deep-dish frying methods imparts a distinct flavour, 'weight' (*súly*) and texture to many of the indigenous fast foods. This gives them what Hungarians sometimes refer to as their 'filling' (*laktató*) quality – a dimension which is considered characteristic to regional (CEE) cuisine and lacking from its Western equivalents – including fast food.

Apart from the endless variety of personal nuances which may be imparted to any given dish, there are no 'trade secrets' involved in preparing these local foods. Everyone is well aware of the ingredients, procedures and general conditions required to make such cultural staples. Hungarian men – generally not known to be proficient in the kitchen – often learn to cook based on simple recipes for such fast foods. As a direct consequence, the appearance of indigenous fast food is nearly as ubiquitous on the family kitchen table as it is outside the home. The two basic supply dimensions of this food – ready local ingredients and culturally acknowledged base recipes – have ensured a popularity which remains in place despite the incursions of international fast-food chains into Hungary and the CEE.

Fast-Food Restauranting in Hungary: Alamo Chicken Comes to Town

The relatively recent, international expansion of fast food restaurant chains beyond North America and Western Europe has not always been an easy one. A combination of factors, which include the high costs of opening larger-than-normal centrally located restaurants in busy downtown areas, has been but partially offset by high sales volumes (see Oznian 1991). The result of this and other hurdles (such as having to develop a supplier network from scratch) has significantly raised the stakes of local competition in new regional markets such as Central Eastern Europe. Nonetheless, a large number of international companies have sought to take advantage of the iconic status of fast food in countries which are just now beginning to adjust to the full array of modern consumer choice. Alamo Chicken, a restaurant chain specializing in fast-food poultry products, is one of them.

Comprising over 400 licensed restaurants spread throughout North America and Western Europe, the wider Alamo Chicken chain of restaurants entered the Hungarian market in an oblique fashion. Alamo Chicken (Hungary) – the 'HQ' mentioned in the introduction – was established in 1989 as a joint venture company between two partner enterprises: the private licence-holder of the licence rights for Austria and a (state-owned) Hungarian conglomerate which sought to diversify some of its holdings prior to eventual privatization.

While still in the course of assembling a small central staff team, the joint venture company quickly moved into premises occupying the bottom floor of a villa situated in one of Budapest's most affluent residential neighbourhoods, a section of the city dominated by imposing turn-of-the-century and communist *nomenklatura* mansions. This exclusive location would later exacerbate frictions between the HQ (as the local licence-holder) and the individual restaurant licences, feeding into the latter's complaints regarding the lack of communication and constructive contact with HQ personnel. Criticized by many of the licensees as 'lounging around in a palace' (*palotában üldögélnek*), the HQ staff were increasingly seen as comfortably living off the hard-won proceeds of the struggling restaurants.

Manufacturing the New Consumerism

The first of the chain's local restaurants opened its doors in 1990 in a town some 50 kilometres outside of Budapest. Within a period of three years, 14 Alamo Chicken restaurants were in operation in six different cities in Hungary. Half of these operations were located in the capital, the rest in major towns and other urban conurbations. This quick initial growth made Alamo Chicken the country's largest foreign fast-food restaurant chain in the short run. The potential for continued growth remained high for several years – even in the face of protracted economic recession in the country. In fact, from the point of view of commercial opportunity, the high consumer status of fast-food products made recession conditions an ideal environment in which to promote fast food as an easy way for parents to appease status-conscious youngsters without spending money on higher- priced and more substantial consumer goods.

Unlike other fast-food chains where the exterior and interior decor is tightly controlled by a head office, the HQ left much of the layout design of the restaurant premises up to the respective licensees. This gave the licensees significant leeway in adjusting their investment to available capital resources – and resulted in Alamo Chicken developing a niche profile in attracting lower-financed entrepreneurs. As a direct consequence, the Alamo Chicken operations in Hungary have remained smaller affairs, lacking the large space and high seating capacity of much of the competition. Additionally, fewer of the restaurants have occupied the historic downtown locations that have since been thoroughly colonized by foreign fast-food restaurants in particular.

In spite of financial restrictions, all of the Alamo Chicken restaurants followed convention by furnishing their premises with glossy plastic, metal and tile decoration, including a range of mirrors to reflect the primary colours found within.[7] The restaurant layout ideally separated consumption and production areas within a single visible span, the two spaces being mediated by a customer-service counter combining cashier and food provision functions without aid of secondary (waitering) personnel. Along with the emphasis on elaborate product packaging and young staff in colourful co-ordinated uniforms, such visual features made it easy for customers to differentiate the new restaurants from traditional eateries. That is, in case they failed to notice the prominently featured product iconography of the chain displayed inside and out of each premises.

The early Hungarian customers of Alamo Chicken interpreted the restaurant surroundings completely differently from the low-prestige associations of the Euro-American imagination. In a country where commercial interior decoration had been underplayed as a 'capitalist

André P. Czeglédy

distraction', the new materials and designs of the fast-food businesses were initially considered a sign of foreign sophistication and cultural prestige. Only as time passed and more and more fast-food restaurants had taken root in the country did this perception begin to change in the minds of the general public.

The relatively high prices of the food at Alamo Chicken and its competitors served to double local perceptions of elite status. For example, a meal consisting of two chicken pieces, 'french fries', fried mushrooms and large 'soft' drink ran to a variable cost of 500 HUF[8] in 1990 – just above the *daily* average wage for the average Hungarian at the time. In the CEE as a consequence, fast-food restaurants such as Alamo Chicken initially developed a reputation as *luxury* establishments (in spite of their attempt to promote themselves as selling special but, nevertheless, convenience food appropriate for the entire population). As a middle-aged mother put it to me after purchasing a Saturday lunch for her three children:

> We only come here on special occasions like birthdays or name days; otherwise we cannot afford it – although both of us [parents] work hard to give the children what they want . . .

This comment brings under scrutiny the realities of socio-economic transformation in Eastern Europe, and the fact – as Chatwin's Georgian ethnography reminds us – that such changes have not necessarily opened the floodgates of agricultural abundance for everyone (1997: 75–6 and *passim*).

As supplied through the HQ, and reinforced by the authority of the licence contract, the official Alamo Chicken menu was composed of both *core* and *peripheral* products. The core product list in early 1990 included: (boned) pre-marinated chicken pieces, several types of 'chicken-burger', thick-cut breaded potatoes, and 'french fries' (*pommes frites*). By 1993, chicken 'nuggets' and several varieties of vegetable (cauliflower, mushrooms and broccoli) had been added to the list. These core products were all deep-fried in vegetable oil after being coated in a batter and breaded coating, a method of food preparation well-established in the Hungarian culinary lexicon.

The similarity of Alamo Chicken's special coating to the preparation of traditional Hungarian fried foods was an important selling point for older and traditionally minded customers. They appreciated the strong, slightly piquant flavour in contrast to the generally sweeter and blander-tasting food of competitors. The coating turned out to be a critical sales

dimension when, after some 40 years' absence, Alamo Chicken reintro-
duced broccoli to the wider Hungarian public in the summer of 1991.
Employees allayed customers' alarm at the verdant colour underneath the
breading by explaining the vegetable as a foreign (thus prestigious)
'green cauliflower' (*zöld karfiol*) and then referring to local traditions of
breading and frying vegetables as a form of final reassurance.

From the beginning, the nature of the Alamo Chicken batter and
breaded coating was of consequence within the chain, anchoring repeated
discussions regarding its specific ingredients. The coating consisted of a
special egg batter and a breading incorporating a secret blend of herbs
and spices (supplied via the Austrian partner of the HQ joint venture).
This 'secret' mix (designed, produced and imported from outside the
country) was more than just another example of proprietary rights
exercised across international borders. Its location at the heart of the
Alamo Chicken menu involved a radical realignment of the knowledge-
power relationships between people and food in local terms. Unlike the
established framework of public knowledge in the case of local cuisine,
the Alamo Chicken chain was introducing into the Hungarian milieu not
only a new product but also one whose make-up was substantially
dependent upon *foreign* manufacture, and whose taste was non-replicable
within the confines of the average household kitchen. Even the HQ staff
did not know what went into the mix. In fact, no one (in Hungary) was
able to fully access the Alamo Chicken products they sold or bought in
terms of the underlying knowledge of production.

For the independent-minded licensees in particular, this knowledge
dynamic was entirely unwelcome. It put them in a permanent state of
dependence vis-à-vis the HQ and its foreign connections. In addition, it
made things much more difficult for these individual operators to attempt
to replicate the breading mix on the sly – and thereby evade (if not avoid)
the high purchase cost of supplies imposed by the HQ. As one of them
confided in me:

> I can more or less do the [chicken] marinating myself – I've worked that
> [hurdle] out already – but that fucking breading mix is an entirely different
> matter.

Of course, his next question to me was:

> Now András, just between you and me, what *is* in the breading mix? I'm just
> curious, you know.

For these licensees, as well as for their employees and customers, the Alamo Chicken products served to highlight not simply the technological gap between Hungarians and 'foreigners' (*külföldiek*), but also the primary relationship of their postsocialist world: the ever increasing economic dependence on 'the West' for products, technology and commercial opportunity.

In contrast to the core menu, the peripheral products of Alamo Chicken played a low profile in every restaurant. These products included: another breaded vegetable (local squash), lettuce salad and pre-packaged ice cream treats in addition to a variety of drinks (soda-pop, fruit juice, coffee, 'hot chocolate') which were idiosyncratic to each operation. Going against conventional industry wisdom – but entirely consonant with locally established cultural strategies of product diversification ‾ nearly every licensee sought to rotate several of these peripheral products (and others) as a strategy in attracting more customers.[9] Such manoeuvring resulted in the dilution of the wider corporate image on the whole, and – in spite of HQ objections – the incongruous sale of chewing gum, baby shoes, cigarettes and non-'family-oriented' beverages (beer, wine, spirits) alongside the food in one restaurant or another. Crucially, the sale of alcoholic drinks was disparaged by no one outside of the HQ staff, a response by both customers and restaurant employees which can be traced to Hungarian traditions of encouraging familiarity with such beverages at the everyday family table.[10]

The use of poultry as the mainstay of its overall menu brought Alamo Chicken both positive and negative reactions from the local population. On the one hand, this dimension differentiated the chain from the other foreign fast-food operators who relied on beef as the main meat component. It also attracted (in Budapest) a growing sub-clientele of Arab students whose preference for non-pork products pushed them into avoiding the competing fast-food restaurants – which sold finely 'ground' (and thus difficult to ascertain) meats.[11] Unfortunately for two Alamo Chicken restaurants in particular, these much-valued customers attracted the attention of local skinhead groups whose racist violence spilled over into the restaurant premises themselves.[12] These events put further financial pressure on several struggling licensees who were required to incorporate added security measures into the running costs of their operations. Unfortunately for them, the HQ was not in a monetary position to underwrite these unanticipated requirements.

From the beginning, Alamo Chicken (Hungary) was substantially operating on its own resources and initiative. It possessed only limited financial, training and promotional backing through the two joint venture parent companies, a situation which severely restricted all corporate initiatives, including otherwise vital advertising campaigns. These background circumstances led to escalating organizational crises – especially when the HQ did not have the financial or technical resources to meet some of the obligations which were stipulated in the (standardized) licence contracts.

The paucity of HQ support encouraged a level of licensee autonomy that would otherwise be considered anathema in the conservative reaches of the fast-food industry. In truth, this dynamic fitted in extremely well with the entrepreneurial backgrounds and independent bents of the various licensees, all of whom had made their initial small fortunes under state socialism through working around the system as much as within it. This state of things was seriously challenged only once. During a crisis meeting of Alamo Chicken participants in 1990, the HQ was unable to bring to heel the most noteworthy transgressors of the licence contract – largely because its leadership was forced to admit to parallel failings which were contrary to the legal agreement, and then, also shown to have little control over its own (wholesale) pricing structure.

From the anthropological perspective, such a loose relationship between licence-holder and licensees presented unique opportunities to witness the meeting between conventional wisdoms of fast-food restaurant operation as originated outside the country and indigenous models of commercial organization, authority and reward. These issues are addressed in the following section.

Divisions of Labour and Patterns of Profession

As Whyte pointed out in his seminal analysis of *Human Relations in the Restaurant Industry*, all restaurants possess a unique position in society, in that they are

> ... a combination production and service unit; thus [the restaurant] differs from the factory, which is solely a production unit, and from the retail store, which is solely a service unit. (1948: 17)

This duality is one which often places opposing demands upon employees caught up in the conflict between performing their jobs *efficiently* (in a purely productive sense) on the one hand, and performing them *professionally* and *courteously* (in cultural terms) on the other. In spite of the fast-food industry's objections to the contrary, profit-driven motivations generally emphasize the former when push comes to shove.

Recognizing that this contest echoes a more pervasive principle of commercial production in general – that of economic over social values – is part way to understanding some of the primary realities of the fast-food industry as an international commercial phenomenon. More importantly (from the distinct ethnographic perspective), this insight gives us a clear line of approach for accepting fast-food restaurants as a unique focus of conjunctive and disjunctive forces in contemporary Hungarian society situated over and above the established discourses of de-skilling (Braverman (1974) and routinization (Leidner 1993).

When Alamo Chicken first entered the Hungarian market, the HQ placed great emphasis on the sort of procedural efficiency mentioned above, a clear indication of its reliance on the orthodoxy of fast-food industry knowledge. This reliance was engendered not by advice given by the foreign partner (who already operated several restaurants in Austria), but through the exhortations of Ferenc Matvölgyi, Alamo Chicken's Operations Director. Matvölgyi was a forceful 38-year-old Hungarian who had worked and trained as a manager in the McDonald's licence system, even attending its chief training centre (the so-called 'Hamburger University') in the United States. He was hired not only to bring some of the professional cachet of the McDonald's name to the HQ's central staff, but also to take the managerial lead in introducing the correct operational procedures to the individual licensed restaurants.

Matvölgyi immediately tried to organize each restaurant on an essentially 'organic' basis, a structural-functionalist paradigm that infuses the entirety of the international fast-food industry. This is one where each employee is seen as an interlocked organ of the total restaurant organism, always in motion and constantly striving to match production with an (ideal) queue of enthusiastic customers. Although a clocked system of production was never employed, the individual licensees were encouraged to conceptualize their operations as broken down into a regular set of specialized and integrated employee responsibilities. In general terms, these comprised the following 'stations' of duty:

1. General food preparation
2. Cooking (french fries & burgers)
3. Cooking (chicken & vegetable dishes)
4. Counter service
5. Cash register (if separate from 4).

Such specialization fits well with earlier traditional Hungarian notions of craft professionalism in the hostelry and catering trade. These have since been reinforced by the essentially guild nature of vocational training and employment prevalent under state socialism throughout the CEE.[13] Irrespective of the reality of their subordinated position vis-à-vis the totality of the food production system or the demands of the customer, the sense of craft – of being a part of the established Catering and Hostelry Trade (*vendéglátóipar*) – provided Alamo Chicken employees with an important sense of self-esteem which was culturally reinforced by the high social prestige of fast food as a phenomenon representative of capitalist commercial achievement. This positive dimension to employee status is completely missing from comparative accounts of the restaurant industry in the United States, where Whyte (1948: 283) found restaurant service workers (such as waiters and waitresses) commonly perceived – and self-perceived – as *unskilled*. More recently, Leidner has noted for the United States that the combination of youth, low pay and the character of the work, 'apparently led some customers to believe that anyone working at McDonald's must be an idiot undeserving of consideration' (1993: 132).

In spite of the relatively positive cultural background in Hungary, the division of labor at Alamo Chicken restaurants produced considerable strain among the employees (especially those at the work-stations removed from customer interaction and thus unable to socially mitigate the flow of their work). The relentless pace of customer orders, coupled with omnipresent standardization in the production and customer-service processes, generated strong countercurrents in employees' sense of expertise and achievement. Many of these feelings they privately contrasted with idealized perceptions of job satisfaction in the West. Similar to the case of Whyte's (1948: 28–9) restaurant chefs forced to adjust to menu standardization and a lack of creative control over the production process, most Alamo Chicken employees felt robbed of the dignity of their work after the first few days on the job.

In several of the restaurants, the shreds of this dignity were seen to be further assaulted through employees being asked to share in general cleaning duties during and after the course of their shift. Although this request did not seem to bother older workers (who were generally resigned to the hardships of wage labour in general) – younger employees felt sorely abused. In this belief, their opinions seemed to reflect a reactionary conservatism, set off by the traditional custom that the cleaner role is historically both a *separate* and exceptionally *low-status* role in the Hungarian workplace. For the affronted employees, this sort of task was simply below their status as either 'cooking' (*szakács*) or 'service' (*felszolgáló*) personnel, in a way which highlights the familiar anthropological division between polluted versus non-polluted work (see Douglas 1972).

Many Alamo Chicken employees also resented the way in which the regimentation of the fast-food restaurant constricted – even removed – their ability to make substantive decisions in the course of work. Péter Geller, a young sub-manager who had recently finished a catering education and was well aware of the cultural emphasis put on individual incentive and development in 'Amerika',[14] was one of them. He had this to say about his disappointment:

> After 6 years of middle school geared to the Hostelry & Catering industry; [after] learning about international foodstuffs, preparation and presentation; and [then] all the stuff we hear about the importance of independent thinking in Western business; here we are and I am not allowed to do anything differently during [the course of] the entire day. So I ask you: what is the difference between this new capitalism and the stupid, iron rules [of] Communism?!

In order to alleviate the boredom of work specialization, Matvölgyi encouraged the restaurant owners and managers to arrange rotationary work schedules which promoted job flexibility – an important dimension in case any given employee were to call in sick or be otherwise unable to work his or her expected shift. This idea was generally accepted by most of the licensees, but also butted heads against traditional notions of gender-specific work: both licensees and their employees were not entirely ready to relinquish certain ideas regarding the appropriateness of labour linked to cultural conceptions of gendered aptitude. This situation requires a slight ethnographic digression.

As in the case of other fast-food chain operations, the various employee responsibilities at each Alamo Chicken restaurant were grouped around either (i) the production or (ii) the serving of the various food products. This general differentiation – between 'back-of-house' kitchen section and 'front-of-house' counter section – is an elementary one that Leidner suggests both reinforces and constructs gender assumptions and expectations in the workplace. Men dominate the back areas and women the front; the former linked with 'technical' expertise and the latter with social interaction skills (1993: 62, 207). I saw the same sort of differentiation played out in restaurant after restaurant in Hungary, the only exception being found among those employees working the night shifts in the two 'non-stop' 24-hour operations in the chain. In both cases, the restaurant owners decided to staff the counters with men at night in order to respond to what they (correctly) perceived as a more rumbunctious clientele.

At Alamo Chicken restaurants in Hungary, the 'girls' (*lányok*) felt that the 'boys' (*fiúk*) lacked the social skills necessary to politely handle a rush of demanding customers, while the boys thought that only they were really capable of physically keeping up to the relentless demands of producing the food. Generally, each agreed with the other – except when an argument arose over who was the *most* flexible in the workplace. At this stage (in two separate restaurants), the employees asked the supervising manager to put their claims to the test – with the result that all of the gender prejudices were proved substantially false. This outcome did not, however, significantly alter the established opinions of any of the parties, and each manager (whether male or female) returned the division of labour to the accustomed pattern of job responsibility immediately after the brief trial was over.

In terms of cultural norms, an important convention in several of the Alamo Chicken restaurants was that of allowing tipping by customers – a custom otherwise prohibited in the orthodox doctrine of the fast-food industry. Thought to discourage the patronage of savings-conscious families on the one hand, and to lead to graft on the other, tipping has remained a controversial policy issue wherever fast-food restaurants have taken root outside of North America. In Hungary, however, the tradition of tipping is considered an essential prerogative of the service professions, particularly the hostelry and catering trade which envelopes the fast-food industry. In the four Alamo Chicken restaurants where the owners/managers allowed counter staff to accept tips from the customers, employees saw the practice in the light of professional entitlement. In the restaurants where tipping was prohibited, employees felt their labour to be demeaned. After all, noted 21-year-old Veronika Papúcs:

> If the customer chooses to reward one for the [quality of] service, why shouldn't we be able to accept it [the money]? It would be ungracious [to do] otherwise.

Like many of her colleagues at the Alamo Chicken restaurant in the southern city of Vesztér, Veronika had recently finished her secondary education and was just trying to make ends meet. She considered the idea of not receiving tips from two perspectives, one financial and the other cultural. First, it would mean a loss of personal revenue, however small. Secondly, and perhaps more importantly, such a prohibition constituted a professional affront predicated upon foreign notions of workplace behaviour. These notions of behaviour, she (and others) pointed out to me, were completely alien to Hungarian understandings of commercial exchange. In Hungary, an implicit understanding exists between service personnel and customers such that the rendering of a service *correctly* (rather than exceptionally) is generally considered to justify a (monetary or other) token of appreciation.

Norms of the fast-food industry such as the 'no tipping' policy and shared cleaning duties – but also the mandatory wearing of uniforms, an emphasis on non-social communication, etc. – encouraged the development of labour dimensions considered characteristic of the international fast-food industry as a whole, particularly the problems of employee motivation and high labour turnover.[15] While the Alamo Chicken restaurants were never able to fully come to grips with the former issue, they succeeded in confronting the latter through establishing traditionally paternalistic structures of authority of the type found throughout Hungarian society. They accomplished this through several strategies, the first of which involved a refusal to shift the costs of uneven demand on employees through jigging flexible work schedules subject to sudden variation – as in the case of other fast-food restaurant chains (see Leidner 1993: 83). Another successful tactic involved playing a familiar wages game contra the taxman: paying employees more than they earned officially so as to increase wage packets – while keeping in check social security expenses (which are deducted at source in Hungary).[16]

Many of the licensees attempted to reinforce the employment relationship by way of adding a moral dimension on top of the labour contract. Most were willing to lend their employees money in times of financial crisis. One restaurant owner even offered to lend the tuition money to any employee wishing to enrol in an accredited catering management course. In at least 6 (43 per cent) of the restaurants, however, the licensees went one step further: they sought to staff their operations with family members and/or close friends, thereby leaping over the questions of trust and community in the workplace through consanguineal and affineal ties. In spite of such measures, every restaurant (but one) had its share of 'strangers' (*idegenek*).[17] Why such employees choose to work at a fast-food restaurant in particular is the subject of the next and final section.

Foreign-ness, Employment and Status

Why work at a fast-food restaurant? The easy answer is that of employment, the need to earn an income in the classic terms of Marx's 'cash nexus'. This has always been the primary reason why employees at Alamo Chicken restaurants go to work day in and day out. Some of them toil through exhausting rotationary 12-hour shifts (as in the case of one 24-hour 'non-stop' Alamo Chicken restaurant in downtown Budapest). Others work on a part-time basis, filling in time after school or on weekends in order to earn some pocket money. This latter type of employee is, however, rarely found in the Alamo Chicken chain for two reasons. First, there is the pressure of high unemployment among the young in Hungary, especially those who do not possess post-secondary (educational) qualifications. Secondly, and more specifically, Alamo Chicken licensees and their managers have always preferred to hire full-time workers who, they believe, can be depended upon to see the workplace as a personal priority rather than an occasional addendum to one's social or educational life. As one licensee put it:

> Yes, it means that I have to pay higher wages than if I just tried to hire part-timers. But, this way I get to know my people over a long[er] time. The ones who really stay . . . it's like a family, you know.

The last sentence revisits the surround of traditional labour practices noted above, the sort of non-commercial dimensions which Alamo Chicken licensees clearly favoured in attempting to structure the employer-employee relationships of the workplace. Nevertheless, many employees admit to other – and just as potent – attractions to working in a fast food restaurant.

Chief among the non-pecuniary attractions mentioned by employees was the reflected prestige that accrues to the foreign fast-food industry. As a whole, the industry is considered by many Hungarians to be emblematic of the general success of the West as an idealized economic, political and social panacea. In succinct terms, it is a business that is seen as international, popular and profitable (in contrast to the more limited dimensions of indigenous enterprise). This is so irrespective of the familiar refrain in Hungary (and elsewhere) which rails against the industry's inherent spirit of cultural dilution and homogenization.[18]

In more specific terms, we can apply two other major directions of approach to understanding the prestige of fast-food employment in the CEE. The first of these directions points to perceptions of food which transcend its nutritional value (Finkelstein 1989: 156) and lead to the iconic status of foreign fast-food products as objects of 'conspicuous consumption' in the classical terms of Veblen (1970). Not surprisingly, the new fast-food restaurants serve a fare which is quite unlike traditional foods, presenting dishes which speak in a new language of the monied and status-conscious. This is a language that is understood as much *outside* Hungary's borders as within. What we eat is essentially symbolic of ourselves to others (Mintz 1985: 173), especially in terms of competition (*pace* Goody 1982: 141). In case the message is not clear enough, the food is carefully enveloped and then enclosed by a variety of emblazoned materials, each layer neater and more promotionally distinct than the preceding. The same is evident in the Japanese context, where 'the general value of wrapping [is placed] over and above its functional element' (Hendry 1993: 40).

In such terms, the consumption of non-traditional fast food in Hungary is (by very virtue of its foreign nature alone) a declaration of status by association, both to fellow Hungarians (involving income and, possibly, class dimensions) and non-Hungarians alike. Often, it is a declaration that is edged by wish-fulfilment. For example, Alamo Chicken employees repeatedly noted to me that the fast food which they served represented an 'Amerika' which had never lived through the trauma of the Second World War, had never experienced the confines of Communism, and where – it was remarked (in acknowledged exaggeration) – 'there is a millionaire on nearly every street-corner' (*ahol majdnem minden sarkon van egy milliomos*).[19]

It is as if the tidy bundles of Alamo Chicken servings reflect the confidence and placidity of some Avalonean history, while the messiness of traditional fast foods and their paltry packaging mirrors a more complicated past full of doubts and redoubts, roadblocks filled with their share of highwaymen. By such general logic, instead of pointing inward (toward the native cultural heritage), the foreign fast-food products direct Hungarians' gaze outward – toward the international arena of shared culture anchored by an omnipresent America in one of its own iconic guises. The Big Mac, Whopper and Fillet O' Fish are subsequently magnified in importance because the purchase of these products provides an avenue to (momentarily) forget the indigenous past and emphasize a positive future through comparative extrapolation.

The second direction from which we can understand the contemporary appeal of fast-food employment pertains to the operation of fast-food restaurants as commercial models and loci of more general social activity. This involves the sort of hierarchical inversion of substance and container which Hendry's (1993) ethnography reminds us takes place in the case of high-status goods (especially foods). To borrow her extended relation of culturally significant containment, the existential 'wrappings' of the fast-food restaurant itself (as a commercial vehicle for production and consumption) must be considered as seriously as the very products which such a restaurant sells.

As expressed in the comments of the more reflective Alamo Chicken employees, fast-food restaurants are perceived in Hungary as a stark contrast to the legacy of the past as much as a window onto the future. So much so that many of them have become the new urban landmarks, imbued with a geographical importance which 'everyday' conversation shores up on a daily, cultural basis. Their prominently located, well-appointed environments are a contrast to the dingy surroundings of the traditional eateries that were forced by the socialist state into the narrow crevices of petty entrepreneurialism. Not only are these entirely new and spacious premises furnished with the most 'modern' of materials and kept spotlessly clean, they seem – at an untutored glance – to be the very models of capitalist intensity. In relative terms, it would not be misleading to observe that they *are* (such models). Said one employee:

> People who come into the store (*bolt*) see us working like the devil and . . . really, we are working like the devil! You would never see that [sort of activity] in the communist era.

Indeed, to many Hungarians – both Alamo Chicken employees and their clientele included – the international fast-food chain restaurants are the very epitome of capitalist efficiency and consumer choice. These institutions remain powerful icons of modern wealth as well as symbols of social progress – irrespective of the frailties that may surround their local presence. As a case in point, the opening of a McDonald's restaurant on Moscow's Red Square in the early 1980s was seen in the Soviet press as a status marker of social achievement rather than as one more consumerist initiation.[20] As Ditman has observed, it was then considered one of the great successes of Mikhail Gorbachev's *perestroika* and *glasnost* campaigns (Ditman 1996: 133).

To add to the sense of difference, the new foreign fast-food restaurants are staffed by (professionally) cheerful employees who personally greet the customer – a far cry from the sullen attitudes that many Hungarians associate with customer service under state socialism. Most of these employees are young men and women in their late teens and early 20s whose energy seems to act as a veritable symbolic accompaniment to the freshness of their industry. Their age mirrors that of the main body of clientele, in a way which not only leads to customers often becoming employees but also to restaurants becoming the anchors of social engagement: friends meeting friends on either side of the counter. This curious dynamic might be said to be a feature of the wider catering industry in general, were it not for the way in which fast-food restaurants act as a special locus of social congregation for school-age children and young adults in particular (Finkelstein 1989: 26). In the Hungarian context, this role is doubled due to the local circumstances of multi-generational accommodation.

By assembling at the fast-food restaurant, the young leave behind the claustrophobic space of the family apartment in which so many urban Hungarians live. In so doing they assert their individuality in an interstitial environment existing halfway between the informal private surroundings of home and the formal public restaurants of traditional society. This activity thereby involves the repudiation of both the physical and the social walls of their rooted collective identity, giving them the opportunity to refashion social selves independent of traditional associations. Such conceptual dimensions echo Burgoyne and Clarke's general observation that it is not simply (symbolically) important *what* we eat, but also *how* and *by whom* food is eaten (1983: 162). 'Here', as one 17-year-old Alamo Chicken customer put it, 'anyone is served anytime', without reference to dietary custom or etiquette.

In so many ways, the new fast-food restaurants provide exactly that dimension of change suggested by the above-mentioned customer. They are so very different from the traditional models, producing food in a new fashion, packaging it in novel ways, selling it in a new environment, and encouraging its consumption on an entirely different basis stripped of cultural trappings. For Hungarians, this parallel multiplicity represents not only a new culinary phenomenon, but also an entirely new era of socio-economic structure.

Acknowledgements

The author thanks the managers and employees of Alamo Chicken (Hungary) for their support of the research. Further thanks go to Caroline Humphrey, Frances Pine, Deema Kaneff and the late Ernest Gellner for their comments on ideas expressed in an earlier version of this chapter.

Notes

1. See Fukuyama (1992) for the most celebrated example of such a tendency.

2. This is a pseudonym. For reasons of confidentiality, names and some descriptors have been changed in this chapter.
3. The majority of traditional fast-food stands do not have the available room to install seating. Furthermore, Hungarian zoning law requires a tabled eatery to provide toilets for its patrons.
4. The phenomenon of 'eating on-the-go' is sometimes referred to as 'grazing' (Whitehead 1994: 119), although this term also applies to patterns of eating which de-emphasize regular and substantial meals in favour of constant and restricted food intake.
5. In the post-war era (and especially in the last two decades of the twentieth century), beer became popular among Hungarians, largely because of its high volume-to-price ratio in comparison to that of wine. Lack of storage space often precludes its sale from traditional fast-food stands in Hungary.
6. This point is made while keeping in mind that not all cultures share the high/low cuisine distinction. Goody has written at length on how the distinction applies to European and Asian societies, but not to the African context (1982).
7. This garish convention is particular to the fast-food industry where providing 'spectacle' has been traditionally important (Belasco 1987: 21). Such materials provide relatively durable, fade-resistant components which are easy to clean and replace.
8. HUF = Hungarian forints: the national currency.
9. This practice of diversification originated in a post-war history of limited commercial marketing in Hungary and, hence, the important role of opportunistic sales for many small-scale entrepreneurs.
10. This practice is completely against American conceptions of operational viability (see Love 1986: 13ff).
11. Alamo Chicken's 'chicken burger' patty is composed of poultry meat shreddings. In the case of one of the Budapest restaurants, Muslim customer suspicions were cast aside by the company's hiring of an Iraqi student who personally vouchsafed the products.
12. Confrontations between Arab students and Budapest skinheads received considerable public attention in the period 1992–1994.
13. Rueschemeyer notes that professional associations have a hand in maintaining and developing their most important resource, which is the knowledge upon which their professional power is founded. By establishing the rarefaction of that knowledge and limiting access to it, they make a commodity of knowledge while discouraging 'unqualified' competitors (1986: 111). During the state socialist era, the general division of labour was magnified and interprofessional

movement restricted via statutory qualification procedures and distinct occupation grades.

14. Geller's line of thinking can be found in Whyte's analysis of the restaurant industry (1948: 213–14).

15. Jackle notes that the annual labour turnover rate can be as high as 300 per cent for the industry (1995: 107). The McDonald's operations in Hungary at the time of research were said to be half that. Alamo Chicken restaurants succeeded in reducing turnover to variable averages of between 50 per cent and 100 per cent per annum – figures that were supported by an avoidance of part-time labour.

16. This traditional employment tactic also possesses an exploitative dimension, since such 'under the table' (*asztal alatt*) manoeuvring effectively robs employees of important pension contribution benefits.

17. The exception was an operation run by six members of an extended family, the fiancée of one of them, and a family friend.

18. For a discussion highlighting these traits in the fast-food context, see Belasco (1987).

19. The association of modern fast food with the United States is not localized within the CEE. Favier cites the way his French students reminded him of the direct *equation* in their minds (1996: 119–20).

20. The April 1988 opening of the first McDonald's in Hungary was similarly greeted by Budapesters, who stood patiently in long queues in order to have a taste of the West.

References

Belasco, W.J. (1987), 'Ethnic Fast Foods: The Corporate Melting Pot', *Food and Foodways*, 2, 1–30.

Bertram, P. (1975), *Fast Food Operations*, London: Barrie & Jenkins.

Burgoyne, J. and Clarke, D. (1983), 'You are what you eat: Food and family reconstitution', in A. Murcott (ed.), *The Sociology of Food and Eating*, Croft: Gower, 152–63.

Braverman, H. (1974), *Labor and Monopoly Capital: The Degradation of Work in the 20th Century*, New York: Review Books.

Carstensen, L.W. (1995), 'Burger King: The Growth and Diffusion of McDonald's Restaurants in the United States, 1955–1978', in G.O. Carney (ed.), *Fast Food, Stock Cars and Rock 'n' Roll: Place and Space in American Pop Culture*, London: Rowman & Littlefield, 119–128.

Chatwin, M.A. (1997), *Socio-cultural Transformation and Foodways in the Republic of Georgia*, Cormack, NY: Nova Science.

Czeglédy, A. (2002), 'Urban Peasants in a Post-Socialist World: Small-scale Agriculturalists in Hungary', in P. Leonard. & D. Kaneff (eds) *Post-Socialist Peasant?: Rural and Urban Constructions of Identity in Eastern Europe, East Asia and the former Soviet Union*, Houndmills, Basingstoke: Palgrave, 200–220.

Ditman, L. (1996), 'Wash Your Hands with Coca-Cola: Coca-Cola's European Tribulations', in J. Dean and J-P. Gabilliet, *European Readings of American Popular Culture*, Westport, CT and London: Greenwood Press, 127–36.

Douglas, M. (1972), *Purity and Danger: An analysis of the Concepts of Pollution and Taboo*, London: Routledge & Kegan Paul.

—— (1975), 'Deciphering a Meal', in M. Douglas (ed.), *Implicit Meanings: Essays in Anthropology*, London: Routledge & Kegan Paul, 249–75.

—— and Isherwood, B. (1979), *The World of Goods: Towards an Anthropology of Consumption*, New York: Basic Books.

Drakulic, S. (1993 [1987]), *How We Survived Communism and Even Laughed*, London: Vintage.

Farb, P. and Armelagos, G. (1980), *Consuming Passions: An Anthropology of Eating*, Boston: Houghton Mifflin.

Favier, M. (1996), 'Pride and Prejudice: American Cuisine, the French, and Godliness', in J. Dean and J-P. Gabilliet (eds), *European Readings of American Popular Culture*, Westport, CT and London: Greenwood Press, 119–25.

Fine, B. and Leopold, E. (1993), *The World of Consumption*, London and New York: Routledge.

Finkelstein, J. (1989), *Dining Out: A Sociology of Table Manners*, Cambridge: Polity.

Fukuyama, F. (1992), *The End of History and the Last Man*, New York: Free Press.

Gellner, E.A. (1983), *Nations and Nationalism*, Oxford: Blackwell.

—— (1994), *Conditions of Liberty: Civil Society and Its Rivals*, London: Hamish Hamilton.

—— (1995), 'Freud's "Social Contract"', in E.A. Gellner, *Anthropology and Politics: Revolutions in the Sacred Grove*, Oxford: Basil Blackwell, 62–93.

Goodman, D. and Redclift, M. (1991), *Refashioning Nature, Food, Ecology and Culture*, London: Routledge.

Goody, J. (1982), *Cooking Cuisine and Class: A Study in Comparative Sociology*, Cambridge: Cambridge University Press.

Hendry, J. (1993), *Wrapping Culture: Politeness, Presentation, and Power in Japan and Other Societies*, Oxford: Oxford University Press.

Jackle, J.A. (1995), 'Roadside Restaurants and Place-Product-Packaging', in G.O. Carney (ed.), *Fast Food, Stock Cars and Rock 'n' Roll: Place and space in American Popular Culture*, London: Rowman & Littlefield, 97–117.

Kelly, J.E. and Clegg, C.W. (1982), *Autonomy and Control in the Workplace: Contexts for Job Redesign*, London: Croom Helm.

Leidner, R. (1993), *Fast Food, Fast Talk: Service Work and the Routinization of Everyday Life*, Berkeley, CA.: University of California Press.

Levi-Stauss, C. (1969 [1964]), *The Raw and the Cooked (Mythologiques I)*, London: Cape.

—— (1973 [1967]), *From Honey to Ashes [Mythologiques II)*, London: Cape.

—— (1978 [1968]), *The Origin of Table Manners (Mythologiques III)*, London: Cape.

Love, J. F. 1986 *McDonald's's Behind the Golden Arches* London: Bantam

Mintz, S. (1985), *Sweetness and Power: The Place of Sugar in Modern History*, New York: Viking.

Oznian, M.K. (1991), 'Golden No More: Why McDonald's has hit a midlife crisis', *Financial World*, 159(17), August 21, 30–3.

Radcliffe-Brown, A.R. (1922), *The Andaman Islanders*, Cambridge: Cambridge University Press.

Richards, A. (1932), *Hunger and Work in a Savage Tribe: A Functional Study of Nutrition among the Southern Bantu*, London: G. Routledge & Sons.

—— (1939), *Land, Labour and Diet in Northern Rhodesia: An Economic Study of the Bemba Tribe*, Oxford: Oxford University Press.

Rueschemeyer, D. (1986), *Power and the Division of Labour*, Cambridge: Polity.

Veblen, T. (1970), *The Theory of the Leisure Class*, London: George Allen & Unwin.

Warde, A. (1997), *Consumption, Food and Taste: Culinary Antimonies and Commodity Culture*, London: Sage.

Whitehead, A. (1994), 'Food Symbolism, Gender Power and the Family', in B. Harriss-White and R. Hoffenberg, *Food: Multidisciplinary Perspectives*, Oxford: Blackwell, 116–27.

Whyte, W.F. (1948), *Human Relations in the Restaurant Industry*, New York: McGraw-Hill.

Part III
Rural and Institutional Transformations

–9–

Coping with the Market in Rural Ukraine
Louise Perrotta

This chapter examines the effects of the various political and economic changes of the post Soviet period on the living standards of the rural population in Ukraine. The data is derived from a number of studies undertaken by the author between 1997 and 2000, on behalf of the World Bank, the United States Agency for International Development (USAID), and the UK Department for International Development (DFID). This information is complemented by the author's experience of advising the major aid agencies on the social aspects of change in post-Soviet rural Ukraine between 1995 and 2001.

The World Bank/USAID study was conducted between October 1998 and March 1999, and resulted in the production of various reports, including Perrotta 1998, 1999a, 1999b and Lerman and Csaki 2000. The purpose of this study was to determine the effects of privatization, land reform, and enterprise restructuring on:

- The size and structure of household incomes
- Access to services in rural areas
- The economics of subsistence agriculture.

The study was conducted in rural areas of five oblasts[1] of Ukraine, including Donetsk, Lviv, Odessa, Poltava and Zhitomir. In each oblast, research was undertaken in two raions (administrative district, smaller than a county), one relatively close to the oblast centre and one more distant, in order to determine the effects of proximity to markets. In each raion, research was undertaken in two rural locations, one of which was associated with an agricultural enterprise which had undertaken substantial restructuring, and one of which was associated with an enterprise which had undertaken only superficial 'change of name' restructuring, or none at all. The definition of 'substantial' versus 'superficial' restructuring was not predetermined by researchers, who left the distinction to the discretion of local raion-level advisors from the Department of Agriculture, or occasionally from another department of the Raion Administration. In each raion, the researchers explained the rationale for selecting one of each, and researchers were satisfied that the difference between 'substantial' and 'superficial' degrees of restructuring was adequately understood by these advisors. In each rural community, one-to-one interviews were conducted with between 20 and 40 individuals, usually at places of work or in the offices of the Village Soviet[2] or in the farm administration office. A total of 705 interviews were conducted in the five oblasts. One to three focus-group discussions were also undertaken with groups of between ten and twenty participants in each location. The purpose of these informal discussions was to enable participants to elucidate their concerns, to prioritize their problems and to elicit their ideas as to possible solutions.[3]

The DFID studies were undertaken in the oblasts of Donetsk and Odessa between June and October 2000. These were specifically aimed at assessing the impact of DFID-assisted interventions in the rural/agricultural sector, by comparing the well-being of populations in villages which have been participants in DFID-assisted projects with the well-being of populations in control villages. These impact assessments collected data on:

- The size and structure of household incomes and expenditures
- Access to services and whatever is necessary to a good quality of life.

In Donetsk, research was undertaken in ten pilot villages and in two control villages in four raions. In all 471 individuals were interviewed representing a population of 1523.[4]

In Odessa, research was conducted in eleven pilot villages and in three control villages. A total of 360 people participated in the survey, representing 1154 individuals. Rapid Participatory Rural Appraisal was conducted with at least one group in each village.[5] This chapter also includes occasional references to baseline information collected in Odessa in 1997 and 1998.[6]

Each study consisted of a questionnaire survey of respondents, which was conducted during the course of one-to-one interviews. Respondents were assured of confidentiality. Most were eager to participate in the survey, as an opportunity to express their problems in the hope that evidence of their increasing poverty might result in positive action. It should be acknowledged, however, that there are considerable methodological difficulties associated with the collection of information on household incomes. Reasons include the following.

Uncertainty and irregularity of incomes: the rural population suffers as much from the uncertainties and irregularities of income streams as it does from the very low level of cash incomes. Income from sales of goods from household plots[7] are seasonal and prone to unforeseeable changes as prices change and markets become inaccessible for a variety of 'unofficial' reasons. Many depend increasingly on sales to intermediaries and traders who control prices. Wages are often paid late, or annually in kind, or not at all. Although researchers were directed to instruct respondents to report their 'best estimate' of income from all sources, the irregularity of incomes makes this a difficult question to answer with any certainty.

Reluctance to reveal unofficial sources of income: the uncertainty associated with incomes is compounded by the not uncommon reluctance to reveal the quantity and source of unofficial incomes, be these from sales of products from their household plots, from unofficial trading activities or from unofficial employment. Fear of tax liabilities are well-founded and universal in Ukraine, which also contributes to the fear of revealing unofficial incomes, no matter how small.

Tendency to exaggerate expenses relative to income: many respondents take the opportunity of a survey to express their desperation and discontent, exaggerating expenditures (what they ought to spend rather than what they actually spend), and reducing incomes to regular or 'official' sources only, understandably disregarding irregular earnings. Although this is a common aspect of conducting survey work among the poorest sectors of the population, it should not be interpreted to mean that they are exaggerating their poverty. The poverty is real enough, and respondents are simply ensuring that the figures represent the desperation of their situation. Spot checks of the questionnaires indicate that respondents provided considerable detail about their household economies. Analysts have expressed confidence that the figures represent a reasonably true picture.

The difficulties of collecting household income data are acknowledged, and figures given should therefore be treated with caution. Comparative analysis of the data, between geographical locations, between pilot and control villages or over time does, however, yield important insights. If we cannot state with certainty that average household incomes are X UAH/mo. in village 'A', we can assert that average household incomes in village 'A' are higher or lower than average household incomes in village 'B', or higher or lower than average household incomes in village 'A' two years previously. For this reason, the 1998–1999 World Bank/USAID study compared populations on 'restructured' and 'unrestructured' farms. The impact assessments in the 2000 Donetsk and Odessa studies compare living standards in participating and in non-participating (control) villages. The more important comparisons will be those made over time. As noted above, there is some data available for comparative analysis of rural household incomes in Odessa between 1997 and 2000. It should, however, be noted that these studies do not necessarily include the same villages, as the focus and geographical locations of DFID project activities has shifted over time. Comparative analysis of household incomes over time is given here, but should be treated with caution. Similarly the 1998–1999 World Bank/ USAID study included some, but not all, of the same populations as the DFID 2000 studies, and did not include information on household expenditures. If the data from these various studies is not directly comparable, the information does provide a basis for measuring changes in living standards over time. Further impact assessments are planned for Odessa and Donetsk later in 2001.

These studies of household incomes did not take into account the value of food produced by households on their household plots. Incomes therefore include cash incomes from all sources, and the cash equivalent of payments received in kind. Where respondents sell a proportion of the produce from their household plots, the value of these sales was included in their income. The value of food produced was not included for the following reasons:

- The value of food produced on household plots is not 'pure income' as it does not include the costs of production (inputs). Part of the World Bank/USAID study examined the economics of household plot production, valuing inputs, produce and sales in cash equivalents. This data was then analysed separately (Perrotta 1999a).
- Rural populations in Ukraine are not claiming to have insufficient food to eat (except in an extreme minority of cases). The majority of the population is concerned with the absence of opportunity for acquiring cash incomes, in order to acquire all of the goods and services which can only be paid for in cash, including medical treatment, fuel (for heat, light and cooking), clothes, books and equipment for schoolchildren, etc. Official Ukrainian surveys often include the value of food production, without taking the costs of production into account and conclude that rural populations are therefore 'not very poor'.

The size and structure of household and per capita incomes

Household incomes were acquired by adding together incomes from all sources for all family members. Per capita incomes were calculated by dividing this total household income by the number of persons normally resident in the household. All of the studies show that the per capita incomes of the majority of the rural population fall below minimum standards set by the Supreme Rada of Ukraine, and are lower than the UN level for extreme poverty. Table 9.1 shows monthly household and per capita incomes in UAH[8] for 632 respondents in the World Bank/ USAID study in 1998.

Table 9.1 Household incomes in five rural areas of Ukraine in 1998

	Household income UAH/month (USD/month)	Per capita income UAH/month (USD/month)
Minimum	3.00 (0.85)	0.50 (0.14)
Maximum	874.00 (250.00)	306.00 (87.00)
Average	151.00 (43.00)	46.00 (13.00)
Median	118.00 (34.00)	36.00 (10.00)

- UAH – standard abbreviation for Ukrainian hryvna
- October/November 1998: 1 USD = 3.5 UAH; 30 USD = 105 UAH
- 1998 poverty level in Ukraine set at 73 UAH/month. Of households in sample, 62 per cent had per capita cash income less than 50 UAH/month.
- 1998 per capita income of over 98 per cent of families lower than UN level for extreme poverty (1 USD/day; 105 UAH/month)

The DFID studies in 2000 revealed the household and per capita incomes shown in Table 9.2.

Table 9.2 Household and per capita incomes in Donetsk 2000

	Household income UAH/month (USD/month)	Per capita income UAH/month (USD/month)
Minimum	28.50 (5.00)	9.00 (1.66)
Maximum	4650.00 (861.00)	2063.00 (382.00)
Average		111.00 (21.00)

- Donetsk 2000: 75 per cent of 471 households surveyed have per capita income below Supreme Rada of Ukraine's minimum subsistence level (118 UAH/month or 22 USD/ month), and 85 per cent below UN level for extreme poverty (1 USD/day, or 162 UAH/ month)

Table 9.3 shows monthly household and per capita incomes in Odessa (no. = 353) in 2000.

Table 9.3 Household and per capita incomes in Odessa 2000

	Household income UAH/month (USD/month)	Per capita income UAH/month (USD/month)
Minimum	13.00 (2.40)	4.00 (0.74)
Maximum	895.00 (166.00)	895.00 (166.00)
Average	N/A	83.00 (15.00)

- July/August 2000: 1 USD = 5.4 UAH
- three households claimed no cash incomes whatsoever; 13.00 UAH refers to lowest household cash income per month.
- analysis shows 80 per cent of households with per capita income below 118 UAH/ month: minimum income level necessary for subsistence set by Supreme Rada of Ukraine in 1999 unchanged at time of study in summer 2000), and 89 per cent of households with per capita income below UN measure for extreme poverty of 1 USD/ day (162 UAH/month) [1 USD = 5.4 UAH; 30 USD = 162 UAH].

If average per capita incomes have increased from 13 USD in 1998 to 15 USD (Odessa) and to 21 USD (Donetsk) in 2000, analysis of the difference between household incomes and expenditures in the latter surveys reveals that this apparent increase in incomes coexists with a high percentage of household budget deficits.

The DFID studies in 2000 also collected information on household expenditure. Subtracting household expenditure from household income in Odessa (Table 9.4) and Donetsk (Table 9.5) reveals a high percentage of household budget deficits in both oblasts.

In Donetsk in 2000, data was also collected on household debts, in order to ascertain the nature of these household budget deficits. This information is displayed in Figure 9.1.

There is, however, a critical difference between these two types of debt. Where the former (money owed *by* respondents) are 'real debts', which will be pursued by creditors and may result in cessation of electricity, gas or telephone services, the latter (money owed *to* respondents) are for the most part unlikely to ever be paid. The banks which 'lost' savings do not pretend to have any intention of ever making restitution. Similarly, wage debts are due to the inability of the employing enterprise to pay debts, usually due to insolvency. The continued operation of these enterprises, and their employment of large numbers of workers is wholly unsustainable. Over 80 per cent of agricultural enterprises are technically bankrupt, and will never recover. In a market economy, these enterprises

Table 9.4 *Income minus Expenditure, Odessa 2000*

Raion	Village	Average household income minus household expenditure UAH/month*	% of households with household budget deficits
Ovidiopol	A	−101.00	58%
	B	−103.00	82%
Velikamikhailovka	C	−85.00	79%
	D	+5.00	69%
	E	−56.00	45%
	F	−79.00	63%
Reni	G	−82.00	76%
	H	+102.00	13%
	I	−241.00	90%
Bolgrad	J	+98.00	13%
Krasno Oknyansky	K	−43.00	79%
	L	−168.00	89%
Komintern	M	−90.00	67%

* calculated by subtracting expenditure from income for each household, and then calculating the average of these balances.

Table 9.5 Income minus expenditure, Donetsk 2000

Raion	Village	Average household income minus expenditure UAH/month	% of households with budget deficits
Krasnoarmeisky	N	−85.00	59%
	O	−181.00	82%
	P	−20.00	56%
	Q	−60.00	40%
	R	−175.00	67%
	S	−100.00	79%
Starobeshevsky	T	−315.00	84%
	U	−14.00	53%
	V	−138.00	63%
Shaktersky	W	+163.00	70%
	X	−250.00	83%
Slavyansky	Y	−250.00	82%

would go through bankruptcy procedures, and the real levels of rural unemployment would become evident. As the Ukrainian government has seen fit to forbid the bankruptcy of agricultural enterprises, they continue to operate, at a loss, employing large numbers of people whom they cannot pay. However these theoretical debts enable poor rural households to feel that they are owed real money, and to claim to be willing to pay

---

Structure of debts owed *by* respondents

49% (no. = 233) of respondents owe money to creditors; this includes

- 40% (94) who owe money to electricity suppliers
- 36% (85) who owe money to individuals
- 7% (17) who owe money to gas suppliers
- 3% (7) who owe tax (mostly land tax)
- 3% (7) who owe money for the formalization of their land ownership
- 3% (7) who owe money for the telephone
- 7% (16) who owe money to other creditors

Structure of debts owed *to* respondents

49% (no. = 233) of respondents are owed money by debitors; this includes

- 62% (145) who are owed wages
- 19% (45) who are owed money by the national bank which 'lost' their savings
- 9% (21) who are owed money by individuals
- 7% (17) who are owed money for the lease of their land share
- 2% (5) who are owed money by other debitors

Figure 9.1

their creditors as soon as their debitors (employers) pay them. Hence the evidence of household budget deficits.

Of respondents (no. = 451) to the 1998 World Bank/USAID survey, 64 per cent also reported wage debts.

The data from these studies clearly demonstrate that populations in rural Ukraine are struggling. In all of the focus-group discussions held in 1998 and in all of the Participatory Appraisal sessions held in 2000, participants identified 'lack of cash' as the major problem facing rural

Table 9.6 Length of time wages unpaid in five rural oblasts 1998

Number of months wages unpaid	% of 451 respondents reporting wage debts
< 6 months	52%
6-12 months	20%
> 12 and <24 months	15%
> 24 months	13%

families. This issue was causally linked to other problems including most commonly:

- Inability to pay for medical treatment (medicine or hospital in-patient care)
- Inability to pay for fuel for light, heat and cooking
- Inability to pay for children's clothes, or the other costs associated with schooling.

The most critical of the effects of being cash-poor is the inability to pay for medicine or for medical treatment. Although some health workers are willing and able to provide diagnoses and prescriptions for free, these are useless in the absence of potential to pay for treatment. When asked if they had any suggestions as to how this situation might be resolved, most groups thought that 'only the government can help'. In the absence of government help, most felt that the only solution was 'to cross our arms over our chests, lie down and die'.

The main reason for the impoverishment of the rural population has been alluded to above: farm insolvency. There are a number of reasons for enterprise insolvency.

First, farm insolvency is due to the uneven effects of price liberalization which has resulted in a rapid increase in the price of agricultural inputs while the price for agricultural produce has risen much more slowly. This 'price disparity' is partly due to 'market forces', including most importantly, rises in the price of fuel, most of which is imported. It is, however, also due in part to price distortions, which are caused by a small number of monopsony buyers of agricultural produce, for example the 'Private State-owned Enterprise Khleb Ukraina'. This organization controls most of the grain market, and controls prices as well as charging inordinately high fees for collection, cleaning and storage of grain. Some enterprises claim that over 60 per cent of the price of grain sold is withheld against charges for these services. Similar monopsony practices operate in many other sectors of the agricultural economy.

Secondly, the main traditional purchasers of unprocessed livestock products (cattle for slaughter and raw milk) are the large formerly state-owned agri-processors. If almost all of these have been technically privatized, the majority are in similar financial difficulties to the primary producers. Most are not working to full capacity, are in dire need of modernization and investment and operate with many of the inefficiencies of the past. Those that continue to operate often fail to pay agreed prices for primary produce, or pay late or 'in kind'. Raw milk sold to a processor may be paid for in butter or other processed product, often at a rate which is extremely unbeneficial to the producer. Farms then either have to find a market for the butter or, more frequently, pass the butter on to the workforce in lieu of wages. As many households produce their own butter, many then try to sell the butter on in local markets.

Thirdly, farms have virtually no access to 'rationally distributed' credit for working capital. Banks distrust farms, and recognize that few are likely to be able to repay loans. In the absence of the bankruptcy option, banks are understandably unwilling to risk lending to farms, many of which have other large debts, some of which enjoy a statutory priority over commercial debts.[9] This means that enterprises rely on a variety of other sources of credit for working capital, most commonly the purchasers of grain and other broad-acre crops. Farms are then obliged to sell their products to these credit providers, at prices which reflect the farms' impotence and dependence. The Department of Agriculture is often involved in these arrangements, further reducing farms' ability to make economically sensible decisions. Departments of Agriculture are still de facto responsible for maintaining production levels, and interfere in farms' production plans in order to boost the quantity of production, without regard to the costs to the farms. Farms therefore pay a high price for access to working capital (or for direct access to inputs such as fuel), further reducing their efficiency.

Fourth, although the tax regime for agricultural enterprises was belatedly rationalized with the introduction of the single unified land tax, most enterprises still carry huge tax debts accumulated over a number of years as well as large debts to the Pension Fund. Non-payment of tax and Pension Fund contributions carries substantial penalties and fines for nonpayment. These debts further contribute to enterprise insolvency.

Fifth, one of the most problematic causes of enterprise insolvency is their continued official employment of large workforces. If some of the smaller farms employ a 'modest' 100 workers, most employ between 300 and 600, with a small number of very large farms employing up to 1,500 workers. These large workforces represent a huge cost to enterprises struggling to make ends meet in the difficult economic conditions which afflict the agricultural sector. Wage debts mount as do debts to other wage-associated statutory Funds.[10] This debt burden further reduces enterprises' capacity to acquire inputs, reducing productivity even further. Enterprises cannot afford to pay workers their full due, on time and in cash. Most pay wages late and at least partly 'in kind'. Anecdotal evidence suggests that these 'in-kind' payments are often valued at higher than market value (i.e. if one ton of grain has a market value of 100 USD, payment of one ton of grain is often valued at e.g. 120 USD against wages owed). This means that farm workers are effectively paying higher than the market price for goods, which they receive as in-kind payments for their labour. Unpaid and underpaid workers don't work, further reducing enterprise productivity. This vicious circle has become established practice on many farms.

Enterprise directors do not reduce their workforce, however, except occasionally where a worker can be proven to have repeatedly committed a sackable offence (e.g. drunkenness, absence from work without good cause or theft). The high frequency of all of these offences seems to have little effect on managers' employment decisions. Many enterprise managers claim that they 'cannot sack workers, because there is no other work for them'. This rationale is partly rooted in Soviet notions of the primacy of work, and partly rooted in a pragmatic recognition of their interdependence with the farm community. Enterprise managers recognize that their position (to which they are elected by the farm membership) depends on continued employment of the entire membership. Many also feel a moral obligation to keep people employed: 'There is nowhere else for them to go. At least they are officially employed; they are at least owed wages even if I can't pay them. They will still have a right to their pensions. What else can I do?'

The non-payment of already low wages is clearly the major cause of rural poverty, exacerbated by the need to pay market prices, in cash, for a range of services as noted above. However, people do adopt a number of strategies for coping with the non-payment of wages which characterizes the transitional period.

Diversification of incomes

In order to understand how rural populations are coping with the ongoing economic crisis in agriculture, all three studies examined the structure of household incomes. One of the major aims of all three studies was to define the role of household-plot production and sales for rural households. It was rightly assumed that rural populations increasingly rely on incomes from their household plots, as employment by large insolvent farms provides an increasingly insecure source of livelihoods. A number of both local and international observers have suggested that the increasing importance of household production indicates the de facto privatization of agriculture, and/or that these small producers are likely to develop into 'proper Private Peasant Farms'.

Throughout Ukraine (and other post-Soviet states), the development of Private Peasant Farms[11] was initially encouraged by the legalization of Private Peasant Farming as an officially recognized form of economic organization, and by a range of economic stimuli, including preferential interest rates. These changes encouraged the rapid establishment of a large number of small Private Peasant Farms during the early post-Soviet period. This growth has now stalled as the risks associated with agriculture in general and with Private Peasant Farming in particular are deemed too high in the current inclement economic climate. The World Bank/USAID (1998) study collected detailed information on the economics of household-plot production. Analysis indicates that household-plot production relies heavily on association with a large farm: the most important inputs necessary for household-plot production (specifically livestock fodder and cultivation) are acquired either as wages in kind, or 'unofficially'. The study showed that most household-plot production is not sustainable to the extent that it relies either on theft or on continued employment by a large farm for access to inputs. As noted above, current employment levels in agriculture cannot be sustained by the large farms. Cruelly, inputs for household-plot production are currently 'paid for' by unwanted and unneeded rural labour. When current levels of 'hidden unemployment' are revealed, rural populations will no longer have access to employment or to inputs for their household plots and livestock. Paying market prices for inputs will make the majority of these small subsistence farms unsustainable.

Table 9.7 shows the structure of household incomes for all respondents to the 1998 World Bank/USAID study (no. = 632).

In Donetsk and Odessa in 2000, analysis of the structure of incomes concentrated on wages, sales of products from household plots, and on returns from land/property shares, issued to farm members in the course

Table 9.7 Proportions of household income drawn from various sources

% of respondents who acquire income from this source	Source of income	average % of household income	median % of household income
38	Cash wages from all employment	47	41
12	Assistance from the state	32	26
44	Pensions	59	58
66	Sales of products from household plots	58	56
29	Return on land/property shares	25	11

Table 9.8 Structure of Incomes Donetsk 2000

% of respondents with income from this source	Source of income	average % of household income
79	Wages from all sources of employment	51
41	Sales of products from household plot	19
36	Return on land/ property shares	7

Table 9.9 Structure of Incomes Odessa 2000

% of respondents with income from this source	Source of income	average % of household income
97	Wages from all sources of employment	69
46	Sales of products from household plot	36
32	Return on land/ property shares	11

of privatization and enterprise restructuring. As pensions and other state benefits are not subject to influence by donor-assisted pilot projects, this information was not included in the analysis.

An important aspect of change in livelihoods in the transitional period has been increased reliance on both food and cash incomes from household plots. Analysis of the structure of incomes over time reveals that the sharp increase in the importance of sales of produce from household plots in the early post-Soviet period has now reversed. Where 66 per cent of respondents to the World Bank/USAID survey in 1998 reported some income from sales of products from household plots, this has decreased to 46 per cent of respondents in Odessa and to 41 per cent of respondents in Donetsk in 2000. As Table 9.10 indicates, incomes from sales of products from household plots is decreasing both as a proportion of household income and in real terms. The decrease in the value of sales is only partly due to the fall in the value of the hryvna in 1998.

Table 9.10 Changes in income from household plots in Donetsk 1998–2000

	1998	2000
% of respondents with income from sales from household plots	52	41
Average cash income from sales from household plots USD/mo.*		$13.00
Median cash income from sales from household USD/mo.	$18.00	
Average % of income from sales from household plots		16
Median % of income from sales from household plots	59	

*Exchange rate October 1998 – 1 USD = 3.50 UAH; September 2000 – 1 USD = 5.4 UAH

If we examine the importance of sales from household plots to incomes in Odessa between 1997 and 2000, we also see a steep decline in the proportion and quantity of incomes derived from sales from household plots over the four-year period. In one raion surveyed in June and July 1997, workers reported receiving on average 72 per cent of their income from sales of produce from household plots, or 263.50 UAH/ month (142.00 USD[12]). In 2000, respondents in the same raion report receiving between 42 and 51 per cent of their incomes from sales from household plots, or an average of 90.00 UAH (17.00 USD).

In another raion in Odessa, the 1998 World Bank/USAID survey found that the majority of respondents derived 100 per cent of their income from their household plots, or 42.00 to 158.00 UAH/month (12.00 to 47.00 USD). By 2000, respondents in the same raion report acquiring only 28 to 53 per cent of their income from household plots or an average of 146.50 UAH/month (27.00 USD).

There are a number of possible explanations for this decline:

- The decline in incomes from household plots may reflect the changing nature of the market for agricultural products. In 1997, there was still relatively little competition and those who produced good-quality products could demand good prices. Increasing competition among producers (large enterprises, private farms and household plots), as well as between local producers and imported products, means that prices have not risen as quickly as costs of production.
- In 1997, access to markets in major towns was not particularly difficult. Markets are now known to be 'controlled' by a variety of interests. More sales are being made to middlemen traders who visit farms to purchase produce directly from householders; many members of the rural population complain that the prices offered by these middlemen are low, but acknowledge that they have no other options.
- Further, as agriculture plunges further into crisis, payments to farm workers decrease. This entails a decrease in wage payments in kind which were a crucial source of feed for household livestock. For example in one village, 50 per cent of respondents who receive a proportion of their incomes from wages, receive **only** wages in kind. Average annual in-kind wage payments consisted of 200 kg. of grain (–0.50 UAH/kg.); 50 kgs. of flour (–1.50 UAH/kg.) and 8 kg. of oil (–3.00 UAH/kg.) – total value 16.58 UAH/month (USD 3.00). This is not enough to sustain a family and their livestock. As predicted, the further decline in large-scale agriculture is having a detrimental effect on the subsistence economies of household plots, to the extent that

access to feed for livestock is decreasing with the decrease in payments for agricultural labour. There is anecdotal evidence which suggests the numbers of head of livestock owned by households is decreasing, due to lack of access to feedstuffs.

There is also an increasing differentiation in the range of rural incomes, and in the range of incomes derived from sales from household plots. A small proportion of the rural population is increasing its income from sales of surplus household production, while the majority are falling out of the market.

If the figures above indicate increasing poverty for the majority, the following case studies give a more intimate picture of rural poverty. All three cases are from the Odessa survey 2000.

Case no. 1 A young couple in their early twenties have a three-year-old son; both parents are unemployed. Their sole income is from rental of their land shares and a small amount of state child benefit – total 69 UAH/month (USD 12.78). Total expenses equal 389 UAH/month (USD 73.00), including food (USD 30.00), clothes (USD 9.00), electricity (USD 3.00), gas (USD 8.00), water (USD 2.00), heating* (USD 8.00), transport (USD 4.00), cigarettes and alcohol (USD 9.00). These expenses may be high, and some may seem irresponsible for a household with such a low income (cigarettes, alcohol), but it is clear that this young family is in dire straits. Most services are deemed inaccessible except for kindergarten, medical consultations, and libraries/mass media (all of which are free). The costs of electricity, gas, transport, schooling are unaffordable and they have no access at all to medicine, cultural/leisure activities or household services. Not surprisingly they judge their access to a variety of goods to be worse than five years ago and think that this will only deteriorate over the next five years.

* All heating costs were averaged out over one year to give the average cost per month.

Both of the Donetsk and Odessa surveys asked people to assess their access to whatever is necessary to a good quality of life. Over 80 per cent of respondents to both surveys judged their access to self-defined 'goods'

Case No. 2 Husband and wife are both unemployed and have two sons aged 13 and 16. Their income consists of 29 UAH/month (USD 5.00) and derives from rental income from a land share (USD 3.00) and state child benefit (USD 2.00). Total expenditures equal 194 hrv./month (USD 36.00) and include electricity (USD 3.00), gas (USD 9.00), water (USD 2.00), heating (USD 4.00), school (USD 2.00), transport (USD 4.00), cigarettes and alcohol (USD 12.00). Spending nothing on food indicates that this family is subsisting only on food produced on their household plot. Access to mass media, libraries and culture/sport are the only services they can afford. All other services are too expensive. Again they assess their situation as worse than five years ago and believe that it will be worse still in five years' time.

Case No. 3 Household consists of a 72-year-old pensioner, a husband and wife aged 34 and 31, and three children aged 19,10 and 7. Only the husband works occasionally. They spend 123 UAH/month (USD 23.00), on food (USD 8.00), clothing (USD 6.00), electricity (USD 3.00), and heating (USD 6.00). Their sole regular source of income is the grandmother's pension of 49 UAH/month (USD 9.00).

to be worse than five years previously and expected the situation to be worse still in five years' time.

It is difficult to portray the despair evident in most villages. Partici-patory Appraisals and focus-group discussions were designed to elicit participants' definitions of their problems, their priorities and their suggestions as to how the situation could be ameliorated. Predicting the usual response of 'There is nothing we can do. Only the government can solve these problems . . . and they don't want to', researchers were directed to probe further, and to encourage people to attempt problem-solving, if only as a 'thought experiment'. All of the fieldworkers report the near impossibility of engaging rural populations in these problem-solving exercises. All attempts to develop 'local solutions to local problems' are met with incomprehension, as people repeat their total dependence on an uncaring government. In one village, one of the major problems was the absence of a clean water supply. It emerged that the reason for the absence of a clean water supply was the absence of a cover on the communal well. When the group facilitator asked if there was anything they could do locally to resolve the problem, the group denied that there was anything they could do, without help from the local government. The facilitator then asked to see the well. She later reported that placing a sheet of corrugated tin (which was lying about in abundance) over the well with a couple of bricks on top would have been sufficient to stop the ingress of leaves, rubbish, bird droppings and small animals.

Suggestions as to how to resolve the problem 'no money' are invariably restricted to 'pay wages', or 'the government should give the farm the money to pay wages'. If many understand why the farm is unable to pay wages (costs of inputs higher than the value of produce), few can think beyond 'going back to the way things were before'. A number of facilitators note that it can be nearly impossible to get people to talk, or even think about doing things, in the future. Even direct questions such as 'what will you do?' are often answered by reference to the past.

Such examples are, unfortunately, common and represent one of the major obstacles to the development of 'coping strategies' favoured by donors: the pessimism, cynicism, dependency and tendency to 'look backwards' of large sectors of the population impedes the development of concerted efforts to address rural poverty. If these characteristics are understandable to the extent that they shield the collective psyche from disappointment (where there is no hope, no plan for the future, there can be no disappointment), they offer a poor basis for developing a way forward.

On the other hand, the refusal to articulate problem-solving or to discuss the future does not mean that people actually sit at home with no wages and do nothing. Each individual household develops a range of coping strategies, some more creative than others! A family without sufficient income to cover basic needs may simply accumulate debts, and/or acquire small amounts of cash from casual labour, and engage in casual theft in order to survive. Others are involved in a complex of relations and activities which keep the indebtedness moving. As noted above, farm management invariably 'turns a blind eye' to the theft of produce (fodder for household livestock), and/or the use of the farms machinery, equipment and transport for non-farm activities.

If it is clear that most people 'do cope' in an ad hoc manner, it should be noted that much of this depends on continued association with and dependence on the large farms. As noted above the continued employment of such large workforces is unsustainable, and constitutes one of the major causes of farm insolvency. Should the Ukrainian government acknowledge that the current system cannot be sustained, large numbers of insolvent farms will go bankrupt, and rural unemployment will skyrocket. Avoiding the inevitable hardships that will ensue, requires concerted action now.

What to do?

One of the most obvious possible solutions to unemployment (rural and urban) would be to encourage the development of new businesses. Currently, however, rural populations are understandably extremely reluctant to confront the obstacles associated with starting a business. These include the following dilemmas.

Registering a new business of any size is time-consuming and requires an excessive amount of paperwork. Each piece of paperwork requires payment not only of the official fee, but also of additional and sometimes prohibitive fees to corrupt bureaucrats. A study conducted by the International Centre for Policy Studies (ICPS), Kiev in 1998 found that, although the time limit for registering a new enterprise is legally set at five days, the process takes on average 34.7 days, with a reported maximum of 270 days. On average, three people spend on average 3.5 hours/day actively pursuing the completion of paperwork. According to Ukrainian legislation,[13] the cost of registering a business was set at 200 UAH. The ICPS study calculated the true cost to be minimum 576 UAH (direct costs of 383 UAH plus the costed time of people pursuing registration).

Most businesses require a variety of licences in order to operate. Of enterprises in the ICPS survey, 69 per cent required on average three licences each. In order to obtain one licence, respondents had to contact 2.6 Ministries. Of the licences, 20 per cent took longer than the statutory 30 days to acquire. If the average official cost of a licence is 258 UAH, the added labour costs of chasing licences brings the total cost up to 415 UAH. The cost of a licence also varies between enterprises of different sizes, with smaller enterprises (up to 100 employees) paying over twice as much as larger enterprises (over 500 employees). Licence requirements change frequently and businesses frequently have to reapply for licences already acquired.

Once registered, businesses are vulnerable to endless 'inspections', by a wide range of agencies, most importantly the Tax Administration, the

Police, the Fire Department, the Committee for Health Protection, the Ministry for Environmental Protection, the Committee for Consumer's Rights Protection, the Committee on Standardization, the Anti-monopoly Committee and the Architecture Department. Many of these are 'partially self-financing', and acquire incomes through fines and penalties. Between 4 per cent (Architecture Department) and 32 per cent (Fire Department) of inspections result in the imposition of fines. A full 53 per cent of inspections by 'Other' agencies result in fines or penalties. The time costs of these inspections are also significant. Visits by officials from the Tax Administration averaged seven per year, lasting on average ten days. Respondents report that about 46 per cent of the time of on average 7.5 employees is spent on dealing with these inspections.

The level and complexity of taxation is a further barrier to the development of new sources of employment. Respondents to the ICPS survey report paying between ten and forty different taxes (average fourteen). These different taxes require different forms of record-keeping, accounting and reporting, and change with alarming frequency. The median number of forms which must be completed for each tax is 17. The State Tax Administration enjoys the right to deduct funds from an enterprise's bank accounts (Kartoteka).

About 37 per cent report that contracts are monitored by local officials, who can refuse to approve prices, conditions of payment, etc. if these are deemed to be associated with reducing tax liability. Similarly, the right to monitor business activity presents further opportunities for unofficial payments, as well as restricting a business's capacity to make economically sustainable decisions.

A World Bank investigation in 1995 (Kaliberda and Kaufmann 1995) reports that small enterprises spent on average 2,000 USD per year on unofficial payments for permits and licences (range 800 USD to 3,500 USD). In Kiev the average unofficial cost of doing business was an extortionate 12,000 USD per year. These fees constituted 10 to 25 per cent of gross turnover. Many enterprises pay intermediaries to resolve administrative difficulties on their behalf; this service costs on average between 500 USD and 1,300 USD for small and medium-sized enterprises respectively. Payments for 'protection' average 1,200 USD per year with wide geographical variance.

Attitudes to starting a new business were examined in Participatory Appraisals and in focus-group discussions. Participants emphasized difficulties associated with registration and with the Tax Administration as major obstacles to new business development. They were also aware of the absence of rationally distributed credit, and were convinced that banks would not lend, except to 'their friends and relatives'. Very reasonably, participants in these informal discussions also emphasized the absence of buying power (cash) among the rural population, further decreasing the likelihood of successful small-business development.

The obstacles generated by the state are complemented by fear of widespread racketeering and extortion. The combination of official and unofficial harassment of all businesses effectively impedes the development of new employment. Unfortunately, those who are in a position to change the environment (state organs) are those who benefit most from the current situation. This decreases the likelihood of improvement in the environment for generating new employment.

This chapter has presented measurable indices of rural poverty, its causes and obstacles to rural economic development. It is clear, however, that a minority of the rural population (e.g. in Donetsk where some households report much higher incomes than the majority) is managing to maintain reasonable living standards. What remain unclear are the mechanisms by which rural populations are managing in such difficult circumstances. The high proportion of unofficial economic activity makes it difficult to define these mechanisms, without long-term, in-depth fieldwork. The costs and risks of such research have so far impeded attempts to understand exactly what people do in order to survive.

The study conducted on behalf of the World Bank (Kaliberda and Kaufmann 1995) suggests that in 1993, 1994 and 1995, between 47 and 59 per cent of non-state-sector economic activity was being conducted in the 'shadow economy'. A survey conducted in the summer of 1994 indicated that 70 per cent of the (urban) sample were engaged in unofficial economic activities, and that income from these activities accounted for more than 50 per cent of income. The unofficial nature of these economic activities makes them extremely difficult to determine with any degree of certainty. It should also be noted that there are far fewer opportunities for unofficial economic activity in rural areas, especially for the majority of the population without transport. Many of the participants in the surveys noted increasing isolation as one of the untold effects of worsening poverty and decreasing services.

In conclusion, it can be stated that the uneven adoption of 'market reforms' combines with the persistence of monopolies and monopsonies and widespread corruption to create an increasingly difficult situation for the rural economy and for rural populations in Ukraine. Thankfully, the natural resources of Ukraine (excellent soils, climate) create an environment where food production is relatively easy, even with reduced inputs.

To date there is little evidence of food insecurity. However, the unsus-tainability of the current agricultural economy (with high levels of farm insolvency) indicate that there is a disaster waiting to happen. The state appears to be unable, or unwilling, to recognize the seriousness of the current situation. There were three famines in Ukraine in the twentieth century. If the first two of these were due to war (the Civil and Second World Wars), the third (resulting from collectivization in the 1930s) was not, demonstrating that it is indeed possible to create famines in what was once the 'bread basket' of Europe. Living conditions in rural areas will continue to deteriorate, unless there are significant changes in policy and practice. I would hate to predict the onset of food insecurity, but would suggest that this is not impossible.

Notes

1. *Oblast*: an administrative area similar in size and function to a county or province. Oblasts contain a number of smaller administrative areas called *raions*, which are further subdivided into rural territorial communities (*celskaya territoryalnaya obshchnina*).
2. Village Soviet is the administrative office responsible for a rural territorial community.
3. Data collection was undertaken by the following organizations: in Donetsk and Lviv, The Centre for Social Expertise and Prognosis of the Institute of Sociology, Ukrainian Academy of Sciences; in Odessa by Consult Agro; in Poltava and Zhitomir by students from the Institute for Agrarian Economy, Kiev.
4. Data collection and primary data analysis was undertaken by the Centre for Social Expertise and Prognosis of the Institute of Sociology of the Ukrainian Academy of Sciences; final analysis was undertaken with assistance from staff of the DFID-funded Donetsk AgroConsult project.
5. Data collection was undertaken by Intmar – NewBizNet. Analysis was undertaken with support from staff of the DFID-funded Farm and Rural Community Support Project in Odessa.
6. Data collection and analysis undertaken with assistance from staff at the DFID-funded Large Farm Restructuring Project.

7. These are referred to as individual subsidiary holdings (*lichnoe podsobnoe khoziyastvo* in Russian, or *osobyste pidsobne hospodarstvo* in Ukrainian) in the technical literature.
8. At the time the fieldwork was conducted (October/November 1998), the exchange rate was 3.5 UAH : 1 USD.
9. Ukrainian law prioritizes debts, so that if and when an enterprise has the capacity to pay its debts it must pay first wages, then pension fund and other social security debts, followed by tax debts followed by commercial debts.
10. These include the Pension Fund, the Employment Fund, the Chernobyl Fund and others.
11. Private Peasant Farm (*Chastnoe Krestiyanskoe Khoziyaistvo*) is purposely capitalized in order to distinguish the formal, legally recognized entity from the generic type of household farm.
12. Exchange rate June 1997: 1.86 UAH = 1 USD; data from Baseline Study for DFID's Large Farm Restructuring Project.
13. Decree of Cabinet Ministers No. 406, 3 April 1996.

References

Kaliberda, A. and Kaufmann, D. (1995), *Integrating the Unofficial Economy into the Dynamics of Post-Socialist Economies: A Framework of Analysis and Evidence*, Kiev: World Bank.

Lerman, Z. and Csaki, C. (2000), *Ukraine:Review of Farm Restructuring Experiences*, Washington, DC: World Bank.

Perrotta, L.P. (1998), *The Higher Up Don't Want To and The Lower Down Cannot: an Analysis of Focus Groups Discussions in Twenty Ukrainian Villages*, Kiev: Centre for Privatization and Economic Reform, Institute of Agrarian Economy.

—— (1999a), *Individual Subsidiary Holdings: the Micro-Economics of Subsistence in Ukraine*, Kiev: Centre for Privatization and Economic Reform, Institute of Agrarian Economy.

—— (1999b), *The Size and Structure of Rural Household Incomes in Ukraine*, Kiev: Centre for Privatization and Economic Reform, Institute of Agrarian Economy.

-10-

Mongolia in the 'Age of the Market': Pastoral Land-use and the Development Discourse
David Sneath

Introduction

In the early 1990s the Mongolian state launched a series of policies designed to establish a liberal market economy based on private property. A bright economic future was predicted – the government talked of Mongolia becoming the fifth Asian Tiger within five years (Odgaard 1996: 113). The reforms entailed the wholesale privatization of the economy, including the dissolution of the collective and state farms. The results, however, proved to be bitterly disappointing for most Mongolians, who saw a collapse in their living standards, declining public services and rising levels of unemployment and crime.

The aim of this chapter is to begin to develop a critique of international development thinking as applied to Mongolia, and in particular to examine the way in which Western economic orthodoxy is at odds with indigenous Mongolian concepts of 'property' and 'ownership'.

In doing so I argue that the notion of a discrete economic sphere, separate from and acted upon by the political structure via specific and formal means – principally legislation – can be contrasted with the more holistic socio-political traditions of Inner Asia. These traditions long pre-date the Soviet period. Although the political culture took on a new form during the socialist era, a common theme was the totalizing holistic notions of social order whereby economic and political spheres are inextricably linked.

Development and the notion of 'Transition'

The economic advice that Western experts gave to former Soviet-block nations was similar to the stabilization and structural reform packages recommended for poor countries by the IMF and the World Bank in the 1970s and 1980s (Nolan 1995: 75). It entailed price liberalization, cutting state subsidies and expenditure, currency convertibility, privatization of public assets and the rapid introduction of markets.

The conceptual basis of this new discourse was the idea of a 'transition' from what was seen as an inefficient and wasteful socialist system to the presumed dynamism of a market economy. Central to this thinking was the notion that the economic sphere could and should be emancipated from the political structure so as to allow the economy to assume its latent 'natural' form, composed of private property coupled to the market, which would tend to generate growth if given the chance. In this discourse the economy was cast as an object upon which the political system acted, and this relationship could act negatively so as to distort the economy's natural form. In Asian Development Bank literature, for example, the description of pre-revolutionary Mongolian society assumed that the economy was being prevented from attaining its true potential because it lacked certain features found in market economies – in particular the private ownership of land.

> Mongolia entered the twentieth century as an impoverished country ... an inadequate financial system hampered mobilization of savings and financial intermediation. Private wealth was stored mostly in domestic animals, and since peasants did not own the land under the prevailing system of land tenure, there was little incentive for agricultural investment and development. (Asian Development Bank 1992: 13)

Such a description presupposes an understanding of the 'natural' potential of the economy, and assumes that the reason that this potential was not attained was due to (high taxation and) a lack of things found in Western economies – an adequate financial system, and private ownership of land.

The state socialist system was also seen as precluding the growth and development of a genuine market economy. Much of the development economics literature of the time employed this sort of imagery. The World Bank (1994: 12) remarked that state controls on foreign exchange had created 'pervasive distortions'. The 'nascent private markets' and small enterprises would 'emerge', rather like natural forms, when state policy provided them with a conducive climate (see Asian Development Bank 1992: 103; World Bank 1994: 23; Nolan 1995: 82). The basis of the market was conceived of as private property, so privatization became the overriding objective of economic reform.

Acting on the advice of Western development agencies, in 1991 Mongolia began a huge programme to privatize state and collective enterprises through the issue of share coupons (*tasalbar*) (Asian Development Bank 1992: 86–8; World Bank 1994: 9). The government was also urged to withdraw from the economic sphere, so as to allow the proper play of market forces. In 1992 the Asian Development Bank complained that 'the Government continues to issue mandatory state orders under which various public agencies procure at a fixed price established by the Government. Local price commissions also continue to interfere with market forces. The Government should, therefore, abolish these commissions and phase out the system of mandatory state orders' (1992: 88).[1] The Asian Development Bank and World Bank also called for the private ownership of land, and throughout the 1990s they urged the Mongolian government to pass a highly controversial law that would allow this.

The World bank argued that 'Further development of small and medium-sized enterprises have been hampered by the lack of *land ownership legislation* and clarity on property rights. Under these conditions, private owners have been unwilling to invest their personal capital in their own companies' (World Bank, annex I: 5). It was assumed that private property rights would lead to an increase in productivity.

The Results of Economic Reform

The period of 'transition' saw Mongolia plunged into economic crisis. The worst contraction occurred in the early 1990s when incomes collapsed. The World Bank estimated that real wages halved between 1990 and 1992, and then declined by a further third in 1993.[2] The percentage of the population living below the poverty line increased rapidly. Official figures showed that income-poverty increased from zero in 1989 to 27 per cent in 1994, and this figure may well be an underestimate (see Griffin 1995: 31–3; World Bank 1994: 35). Social services were cut back; real expenditure on health services decreased by 43 per cent from 1990 to 1992, the education budget was cut by 56 per cent (World Bank 1994: 41; Robinson 1995: 4). Further reductions followed and social service spending has remained low since that time (United Nations Systems in Mongolia 1999: 5).

The official figures for unemployment increased rapidly in the early 1990s, from 10,300 in 1989 to 72,000 in 1994 – more than 8 per cent of the labour force. These figures were probably an underestimate, however, and the actual level has been estimated at 10–12 per cent (see Asian Development Bank 1994: 14; von Ginneken 1995: 47). By 1996 the official total had risen to over 80,000, and actual unemployment was

David Sneath

estimated at 15 per cent in 1997.[3] The rate of inflation shot up and stayed in triple figures from 1991 to 1993, falling only gradually since then.

In part this economic crisis was due to three external shocks – the aid shock, the trade shock, and the macroeconomic management shock (Griffin 1995). The huge flow of Soviet aid (which is thought to have amounted to as much as a third of GDP or more)[4] was reduced in 1989 and stopped altogether in 1991. At this time the Soviet trading bloc, the Council for Mutual Economic Assistance also collapsed, and Mongolian trade fell accordingly (exports declined from 832 million USD in 1989 to 370 million in 1991). Soviet advisors also withdrew from Mongolia at this time, and the government had to manage with fewer experienced planners and administrators. However, the place of Russia as an aid donor and economic advisor was taken over, to some extent, by Western nations, Japan, and international financial institutions. Between them these provided support equivalent to about 15 per cent of GDP in 1991 and 1992, about half the shortfall (Griffin 1995: 6). The three external shocks can only be held partially responsible for Mongolia's crisis. As Griffin argues, one of the reasons for the severity of the economic crisis was the inappropriate nature of the reform policies carried out at the time – in particular the rapid privatization programme, which raised unemployment, reduced saving and investment and generated a series of negative effects (ibid.: 12–13).

After this savage economic contraction, the situation improved to some extent, with GDP seeing some positive growth in 1994 and reaching 6 per cent in 1995, largely as a result of a boom in the price of copper, one of Mongolia's main exports. However, growth stalled in 1996 when the prices of copper and cashmere fell and a newly elected government embarked on an aggressive programme of economic 'shock treatment' to remove the last vestiges of the centrally planned economy, including liberalization of fuel prices and a campaign to privatize housing (United States Embassy 1999). Growth slowed to an estimated 2.6 per cent, little more than the rate of population growth.[5]

Quite early in the reform process it was seen that these reforms were not having the desired effects on the pastoral economy. In 1991, for example, Western economic advice led to the Mongolian government introducing a policy of freeing the price of milk. Liberalizing the prices, it was thought, would increase the rewards to the producer for selling more milk and increase the supply. However, after having let milk prices float for six months, it was found that the price of milk in the cities had increased to nine times the original cost, but the amount of available milk had been halved (Campi 1994: 240–1). The dramatic increase in meat prices in 1991 also failed to improve supply of that commodity.[6]

In fact the pastoral economy that had been generated by the reforms was composed of thousands of scattered households providing themselves with animal produce, only a fraction of whom were in a position to supply highly perishable produce to the urban markets. The reform policies were simultaneously dismantling the state procurement system and the institutions primarily oriented toward providing milk and meat for the cities. Without the transportation arrangements of the official procurement system, selling milk and meat represents a good deal of effort for hard-pressed pastoral families, and there was no longer any official obligation for them to do so. In rural Mongolia the reality of institutional settings and their associated methods of operation and transportation had a greater influence on pastoralists than the prices for commodities paid in distant urban markets.

Another problem with the reform process was noted by the World Bank report: 'Despite this withdrawl of marginal lands from crop production, average land productivity has *fallen* since 1989. Privatisation does not appear to have improved incentives, devolved decision making, or increased rewards to farmers. Workers on state farms are now shareholders of the enterprise.' Indeed Mongolia, which used to be self-sufficient in grain, now has to import it. The World Bank report recommends further privatization as a solution: 'for privatisation to be effective, agricultural units should be transferred to families and the enactment of the Land Law [privatizing the land] should proceed expeditiously'.[7]

Pastoralists and the 'Age of the Market'

Before the 'age of the market' (*zah zeeliin üye*), as Mongolians call it, most of the nation's 300 or so rural districts (*sum*) supported a single collective farm (*negdel*) which raised livestock in line with state planning. Some 50 districts had state farms instead (*sangiin aj ahui*), including the regions that carried out large-scale crop production.[8] The *sum* generally consisted of a central settlement of a few hundred households and a large area of grassland in which something like the same number of pastoral households kept livestock, most of them living in mobile felt yurts (*ger*) and moving to different seasonal pastures in an annual cycle. These families herded the collective or state farm livestock alongside a smaller number of their personal animals. The collectives also owned machinery for transportation and hay-cutting services that were used to support pastoralism. The dissolution of the collectives began in 1991 and was complete by 1993 with most of the livestock and other agricultural resources becoming the private property of the members of the collectives. Most of the surviving state farms and collectives become companies (*kompan*) or co-operatives (*horshoo*). In some rural areas these enterprises have been dissolved or collapsed since that time; in some districts they remain – largely as marketing organizations.

Although pastoralists gained livestock, the dissolution of the old system meant the loss of a number of important benefits that the collectives had supplied. The collectives had provided pastoralists with some guaranteed income, trucks to support pastoral movement and deliveries of winter fodder for the animals. One of the most important aspects was the security of basic food provision. The price of flour and other staple foods increased, in relative terms, much more quickly than the prices paid to pastoralists for their products (wool, meat and milk) and supplies are often unreliable in remote pastoral districts. This is of central importance to pastoral households, who have to have carbohydrates to balance their meat-rich diet, and have few alternatives to flour. The grain harvest has declined steadily since reforms began, from 718 thousand tonnes in 1990 to less than 240 thousand tonnes in 1996. The 1997 harvest was a little higher, but in 1998 the total fell to 195 thousand tonnes.[9] The shortfall has had to be filled with imported flour, and prices have risen accordingly.

The pastoral sector is now largely devoted to subsistence production: poverty increased throughout the 1990s. A survey of living standards conducted in late 1998 suggested that at least a third of Mongolia's population was living below the poverty line (United Nations Systems in Mongolia 1999: 5). The real transition that Mongolia has experienced has been from a middle-income to a poor country, as if the process of development had been put into reverse. This is certainly how pastoralists I knew saw it, describing the country as having lost decades of improvement with conditions beginning to resemble those of the 1940s!

Property and Land Use

The disappointing results of economic reform to date reveal the limitations of the thinking that informed it, and the emphasis on private property rights. The advice that was given by the international development sector appears to have been flawed by 'common-sense' presuppositions that fail to take into account the specificities of Mongolian cultural and material conditions.[10] An example of this is the notion of property.

The current Western absolutist notion of ownership generally implies total personal rights over objects. I argue that a number of indigenous Mongolian constructions could be deemed 'custodial' in that agencies have a different type of rights over objects, and always within a wider socio-political order. A particularly good example is the nature of rights to land.

Pastoralism (as opposed to ranching or mixed farming) has long offered a model of rights over resources that was an alternative to individuated private property. Our own notion of 'common land' derives from the pasturage of medieval communities; indeed, one of the very earliest uses of the word 'common' in English was a reference to common pasture in AD 1300. Pastoralism is an activity that entails a very different relationship between humans and resources than does agriculture. This relationship has usually entailed flexible access to large areas of grazing land, and this meant a different configuration of rights over resources. Rather than absolute individual ownership, pastoral operations usually depended upon public access to resources under the jurisdiction of an authority that regulated their use. In the past these authorities, and the nature of their regulation, ranged from the 'grazing councils' of the early English commons to the aristocratic lords of the Mongolian steppe.

In Mongolia, and much of Inner Asia, indigenous political institutions had combined authority over land, animals and people in the person of the lord of the local domain – the *Jasag Noyan*. There is evidence that this patrimonial form of political organization of the steppe has roots from as long ago as the third century BC.[11]

Certainly by the thirteenth century AD, the time of the Chinggisid Mongol empire, the steppe was divided into about a hundred domains, each ruled by a lord. These military-administrative units were termed *myangad* ('thousands') and were characterized as a unit from which a nominal one thousand soldiers could be levied.[12] The *myangad* were hereditary administrative units with their own territory,[13] ruled by lords who also commanded the military contingent that could be drawn from them. 'Each unit', Ch'i Ch'ing Hsiao writes, 'was assigned grazing land (*nutug*) and water sources (*usun*) for the purposes of production and self-sufficiency'.

Pasture land was assigned and regulated by the lord of the *myangan* and his officers. William of Rubruck, the observant Franciscan monk who travelled to the Mongolian capital in the 1250s, wrote that 'every captain, according to whether he has more or fewer men under him, knows the limit of his pasturage and where to feed his flocks in winter, summer, spring and autumn' (Dawson 1955: 94).

There is ample evidence as to the control exercised by the nobility and their emperor over all aspects of steppe life, economic and political. Another Christian monk sent into the Mongol empire, John of Plano Carpini, noted that 'All things are in the hands of the Emperor to such an extent that no one dare say this is mine or his, but everything is the Emperor's', he writes, 'On this point a decree has recently been issued. The chiefs have like dominion over their men in all matters, for all Tartars [the word he uses for subjects of the Khan] are divided into groups under chiefs ... The chiefs as well as the others are obliged to give mares to the Emperor as rent ... and the men under the chiefs are bound to do the same for their lords, for not a man of them is free. In short, whatever the emperor and the chiefs desire, and however much they desire, they receive from their subjects property' (Dawson 1955: 28).

In summary – as early as the thirteenth century if not before, we find that land, livestock, and even people of the commoner class were conceived of as constituant elements of an inclusivist socio-political domain under the jurisdiction of a given lord.

By the end of the seventeenth century the Manchus had gained control of Inner and Outer Mongolia, and introduced the administrative structure known as the banner system. The banner was an administrative unit ruled, in most cases, by a hereditary prince who was a vassal of the Manchu emperor – the *Jasag noyan* ('ruling lord'). The Mongolian banners were based upon the older *myangad* units ruled by nobles descended from Chinggis Khan.[14] In this sense the introduction of the banner system made few changes to the Mongolian social order, the nobility continued to rule established groups of subjects, but these units were now termed banners – *hoshuu* (Barfield 1981: 275).

There are many similarities between the two systems. Both were civil units that were characterized in terms of their military role. Like the Chinggisid *myangan*, the banner had territory allocated to it for the pasturing of the subjects' livestock, and the subjects were required to render their lord service, both military and civil. The land came under the jurisdiction of the Manchu emperor, and was administered on his behalf by his officials.[15] We know that emperors gave grants of land, both temporary and permanent, to groups who had to move from their established pastures.[16]

Ultimately, the allocation of land may have been the right of the emperor, but the actual unit for pastoral land management was the *hoshuu* ruled by the *Jasag noyan* ('banner prince') or by a lamaist monastery which had been given similar rights over a district. In everyday life the right to use pastureland was at the discretion of the officials representing the lord or monastery[17] who allocated and managed the land of the *hoshuu*.[18]

Within the banner, herdsmen were assigned to sub-units (*sum*), and to generally smaller *bag*[19] – the smallest administrative division. The herdsmen were usually required to stay within the pastures allocated to these sub-units in winter and spring. Each household had an established winter site (*övöljöö*), but the summer and autumn pastures were often utilized in common by the people of the *hoshuu* or its sub-units. The local administration enforced residence within the allocated pastures, sending men on patrol if necessary to ensure compliance. But within these administrative subunits there seems to have been a good deal of flexibility in landuse practices.[20]

The rights to land use that were held by the nobility and lamaist church at this time should not be considered to be 'ownership' in the absolute sense in which the term is now commonly used in the West. However, in practice, by the late nineteenth and early twentieth centuries rights to land seem to have been increasingly subject to commoditization, and much of the best of Inner Mongolia's land was effectively sold or rented to Chinese farmers by the banner princes. In some areas, such as the north-west, there seems to have been a form of private ownership of wheat fields. In the early twentieth century there was an increasing tendency to claim exclusivist rights of ownership over wheat and hay fields, and even over winter pastures (*övöljöö*). There were cases of the renting of winter sites, even their buying and selling. How widespread this had become is difficult to assess, but it seems to have been the exception rather than the rule.[21]

Recent studies show that even in the case of agricultural land, pre-collective Mongolian agricultural methods relied upon joint use of land, under a central authority who allocated land each year to the farming households (Erdenebaatar 1996: 101–4).

The steppeland of Mongolia has long been considered to be subject to spiritual as well as temporal authorities. The *gazariin ezed* ('masters' or 'owners' of the land) are spiritual entities that control the natural conditions of an area. Offerings were, and still are, made to them at annual *obo* ceremonies (the *obo* being a ritual cairn at which offerings are made), where they are asked to bring rain and good natural conditions: this indicates the importance of concepts of jurisdiction over land in traditional Mongolian cosmology. In the same way that, even today, officials in positions of power are often treated with deference and presented with gifts with the expectation that they will act as friendly patrons in time of need, the spiritual 'masters of the land' required similar dues. Their good nature, could not, however, be taken for granted. Pozdneyev (1971 [1892]) recorded an instance of a local *gazariin ezen* becoming angered, and interestingly the dispute centred upon the rights of foreigners to make use of Mongolian land. This is illustrated by the curious case of the burial of a certain Nemchinov in the late nineteenth century. Pozdneyev reported that when a very ordinary Russian named Nemchinov was buried in Mongolia the matter aroused great controversy. The location of this body, near the road 'is highly unpleasant for the genius, the patron of this locality, who would therefore perish from drought' (ibid.: 412). The effects of the angered *gazariin ezen* appear to have been serious. 'As though [in punishment] for a sin, there actually occurred in the next year in the hushuu of Tsetsen-beile a livestock epidemic and drought, and this was, of course, all ascribed to the burial of Nemchinov. It took the lamas a month of prayer-services to restrain the "buka"' [*bug* – evil spirit].

Far from free access to land, then, it seems clear that Mongolian culture has, for a long period of time, associated land with agencies, both spiritual and temporal, who have been considered the 'owners' or 'stewards' of it.[22]

This apparent multiple ownership of land is only confusing if we fail to discard currently dominant notions of property. If we examine indigenous Mongolian concepts carefully we see that 'owner' is a poor translation of the relationship between various authorities and the land.

A closer match is the concept of 'mastery'. The term *ezen* means 'master' (although it can be translated as 'owner') and for this reason I suggest that indigenous Mongolian notions of ownership could be described as being in a state of mastery. That the land should fall within the jurisdiction of more than one master becomes more understandable. This concept of ownership can be described as being based upon the notion of *custodial property*, a form of property that was appropriate to the pastoral productive base of the state.

In the Soviet era of Mongolia the 'feudal' social order[23] was abolished, but was replaced by another 'unitarian' socio-political order – state socialism. The pastoral districts became collectives. Most of the livestock became the property of the collective, and the officials allocated pasture to the herding households and collected a quota of produce. In some respects the conceptual shift from a 'feudal' to a collective notion of property can be seen to have been a less radical change than the one proposed at present, as the government attempts to introduce a market economy.

In both feudal and collective periods there were centralized, commandist politico-economic units that regulated residence and the use of pasture, and extracted a surplus through rights to livestock. Normally, citizens in both periods had legal duties to their leaders. In the feudal period this consisted of providing livestock and produce (tax), and might include acting as servants, or performing military service. In the collectives the duty of members was to fulfil the 'norm' for produce set by the farm.

It is significant that the everyday term used for collective or state animals is '*alban mal*' ('official' or 'duty' animals): the root of this term is '*alba*' – the feudal obligation owed by pre-revolutionary subjects to their lord. Indeed the term for a common citizen or serf was '*albat*' – meaning one with duty. Even today, if a herder cares for livestock belonging to a government institution, these are also commonly referred to as '*alban mal*', and this is often done under a contract system closely resembling the old 'norm' of the collective period.

In both collective and feudal pastoral economies, common herders were tied members of an administrative district and owed politico-economic obligations to the central authorities of that district. When the collectives were introduced to Mongolia they were widely perceived by local pastoralists as being a new form of local government, and their combination of political and economic functions was a familiar organizational form.[24]

The new concepts of collective and state property that had been introduced in the Soviet period can be seen to have been simply a new chapter in the history of the duties that subjects had long owed to official representatives of the state.

Mongolian concepts reveal the inextricable linkage between political and economic spheres, and their roots in a holistic notion of social order. The term for government, for example, is *zasaglal*. The root of this term is *zasag*, the lord of the patrimonial fief. It was at this level, (the unit of pastoral land management), then, that the notion of governance was located.

The Mongolian term for the 'economy' is *ediin zasag* – including the word *zasag*, and the term *ed* – which means both 'possessions', 'property' and 'thing', 'article' or 'item'. 'Economy' in Mongolian literally means something like the 'governance of property' or 'possessions authority'. (The other term *aj ahui* means 'living' or 'livelihood'.) We can see here that the very definition of the economic sphere depends upon the notion of political authority. This was no Soviet import: this linkage was a long-standing one.

David Sneath

Mongolian notions of 'private property' also reveal these linkages between objects and the social order, and something of the normative colouring of these connections. The term 'property' does not perfectly correspond to any single Mongolian word . . . there are several: *ed* means 'thing, object, possession'. Another – *ömch* – is often translated as property or belongings, but it also means 'inheritance' or 'legacy'. As a concept, it is closer to the other English word commonly used to translate the term – 'possession' – since *ömchilih* means to take possession of something, and *ömchihöh* means to be possessive; *höröngö* means 'seed, source, or origin', and also means capital, property, stock, estate, fund, resources.

The nuances of these words give clues as to how the social and moral order is linked to the material world of goods. There is a negative aspect to the term *ed*, and in some ways it means something closer to the English term 'loot': *ed avah* – to take *ed* – means to take bribes. *ed huvaah* – to share out *ed* – means to divide the spoils or loot. *Ed* are things that *need* governance, *ought* to be apportioned; to simply take them (*ed avah*) is illicit – a bribe.

None of these terms mean private property, of course. To mean personal belongings they have to be combined with another word – either *am'* or *huv'*. *Am* means both 'life' and 'personal', 'individual' or 'private'. An English term that begins to cover both aspects is 'self' – and the Mongolian term *aminch* means selfish or egotistical. The term *huv'* means a part, share, portion, allotment; as well as individual. The verb *huvaah* means to divide, share or apportion. The term for a third – *gurvan huviin neg* – means literally 'of three parts, one'.[25]

The most widely used term for private property is *huviin ömch* – literally it means 'apportioned possessions' or 'a share of the belongings'. Another term for private property *am'ny höröngö* might be literally translated 'funds of the self'. Private property is conceived of as shares of a whole. These are notions of social and economic order that posit a *whole*, whereas the private property of the market supposes the autonomy of the economic from the socio-political. This sort of market property is personalized, isolate, and depoliticised.

The sort of analysis that is produced by this Western notion of the 'economic' depends upon the individual – a rational and self-interested actor in the market. The behaviour of the economy can be deduced from defining the 'incentives' that these individuals have, and the strategies that they adopt to achieve aims that they can be presumed to have. The focus backgrounds the social – 'modes' of activity or institutional forms – and the cultural – value systems and dispositions. This approach is most likely to effectively model behaviour where all actors have similar motivations, and where all their production and consumption is done in line with one set of values and motivations – for example if all products are made to be sold on the market.

An alternative analysis would set out to identify modes of behaviour that correspond to social and institutional forms. This might also predict the behaviour of individuals. However, it would do so as part of broader socio-political forms, and would assume not only that the motivation and values of the actors will be specific to their culture, but that within the society the aims are diverse and specific to the context of the institutional frame within which the actor is operating.

In Mongolia the economic sphere was not distinct from the political system – the political order contained the world of things; there was, to be sure, a specialized economic part of this wider order – *ediin zasag*, the 'governance of possessions'. Historically, people and goods and resources were parts of a unitary socio-political domain (in both the feudal era and the collective one). Within this whole, land was in the custodial ownership of various authorities, and other property (and activity) was either directly subject to those authorities (*alban*), or allocations to individuals (*huviin*). Because these were allotments they were necessarily subject to the authorities who allocated them.

These two principles of custodial ownership – official and individual – have different institutional contexts and evoke different series of dispositions.

In both feudal and collective periods the large-scale pastoral operations of the district authorities (be they lords, monasteries or collectives) were official activities, obligations that subjects owed their political masters. The personal herds of animals were allotted and allowed to them for their domestic needs.

In the Mongolian context, pastoral privatization, then, meant dismantling the collectives and increasing the personal allocation of the members. Obligations to supply produce (kept alive in the form of contracts by wilier officials) were reduced, and the sales of milk and meat depended upon the needs of pastoral households. When prices increased, pastoralists could sell less of their individual portions and still manage to make ends meet. If they had been required by the authorities to sell more milk and meat, then they would have done so.

Westerners I met in Mongolia were often struck by the way in which local officials continued to be involved in almost any sort of economic activity. Traditionally, large-scale economic operations would almost have to be an 'official' rather than a 'private' matter, because the notion of private property is necessarily an individual allotment, recognized and delineated by the political system. Anything other or larger than this naturally falls under the jurisdiction of the authorities.

The privatization process, which distributed livestock to herding households, is leading to an increase in domestic subsistence orientation, and (in the short term at least) a decline in the economies of scale of the larger politico-economic units upon which pastoralism had hitherto been based: originally the feudal fief and more recently the collectives.[26]

Conclusion

The concepts of *ownership* and of *private property* are central to the models of society and economy that inform the current reform efforts in Mongolia. These concepts are not universal constants, however, not an identical and secure basis for new policies in each and every culture; indeed the equivalent Mongolian concepts form elements of a very different model of social and economic order. To try to explore these differences I have stressed the traditional unity of spheres we term 'political' and 'economic' and presented a heuristic contrast between 'custodial' and 'market' notions of ownership. I have tried to show that in Mongolia at least, this 'custodial' notion is not a Soviet import, but that it has a long history. I hope that some further detailed study of the Mongolian case will serve as a concrete illustration of this general point, and help to focus the associated critique.

Collective Mongolia adapted older notions of a hierarchical unitarian society, which was well adapted to the organization of pastoral life. In the current 'age of the market' we see that privatization neither means the same thing as it does in the West, nor does it produce the same results. Old networks continue to be used, and there are numerous 'price distortions'. The behaviour of pastoralists does not conform to the laws of supply and demand.

Whether or not the economists are right – that there is a latent potential form for economy and that this optimum state is that of private property as we know it in the West coupled to the free market – it could be argued that Mongolians had better start operating in these terms if their economy is to survive in the global market). I personally do not share this view, but I admit that it might be so. However, it seems clear to me that the problem that Mongolia faces – as many other societies have in the past – is that importing the market economy it is not an uncomplicated matter of enacting some new laws. A market system includes a whole series of related concepts which are not indigenous to this region. Indeed, the historical and environmental conditions of pastoralism in Inner Asia make it inappropriate to attempt analysis and reform by treating it like the livestock sector of a Western market economy.

Notes

1. The Government provides substantial hidden subsidies through controlled rents on public housing. ' These subsidies need also to be removed gradually, paving the way for the privatization of the housing sector' (World Bank 1994: 27).
2. See World Bank 1994: 19. Griffin (1995: viii) estimates the decline in average incomes at around 30 per cent over that period. IMF data suggest a smaller decline in average incomes of about 25 per cent, see Griffin, 1995: 5. UNDP and Asian Development Bank estimates suggested a decline of 34 per cent in GNP per capita from 1989 to 1992, see Griffin, 1995: 25.
3. The CIA World Factbook 1998 entry on Mongolia. (http://www.odci. gov/cia/publications/factbook/mg.html). A 1996 article in the Mongolian daily *Ardyn Erh* suggested that the concealed unemployment total approached 90,000. *Ardyn Erh*, No. 193 (1411), 27 September 1996.
4. The United Nations Systems in Mongolia (1999: 6) estimates that this assistance represented, on average, 37 per cent of annual GDP.
5. *Mongol Messenger*, No. 28(313), 9 July 1997.
6. The Asian Development Bank (1992: 103) notes, as a rather unimportant detail, that the increase in meat prices in January 1991 did 'not improve the supply.'
7. (World Bank 1994: 14). The report goes on to remark (with some puzzlement and exasperation) on other unexpected results of the privatization process: 'Many agricultural cooperatives and state farms continue to procure and sell their products as they did prior to privatisation. Although former arrangements have formally been abolished, many private farmers and herders continue to deal with the same official distributors' (ibid.: 38).
8. In some districts state farms have survived as companies, usually much reduced in size after large parts of their assets have been privatized. Where such companies continue to hold large numbers of

animals, these are herded by households under 'lease' arrangements that are similar to the old 'norm' by which the collective members were given production plans.

9. The *Mongol Messenger*, No. 37(271) 18 September 1996 and The Ministry of Agriculture and Industry of Mongolia, 1998, and United States Embassy, 1999.

10. An example of this is the way that the 1991 IMF report assumed that before the collective period there was an indigenous market-oriented economy in Mongolia. This is clearly quite wrong. See Campi 1994: 241.

11. The *Shih chi* states that the Hsiung-nu were ruled by an aristocracy composed of three families, and the *Shan-yü* (emperor) commanded a number of high officials, whose positions were hereditary and were defined in terms of the military force they provided. Of these leaders 'the more important ones commanded ten thousand horsemen and the lesser ones several thousand, numbering twenty-four leaders in all, although all are known by the title of "ten thousand horsemen"'. (*Shih chi* cited in Barfield 1981: 48).

12. The *myangad* were in several cases based upon older named groups that seem to have had distinct territories.

13. As Ch'i Ch'ing Hsiao notes (1978: 10), 'Thus the 95 chiliarchies in fact represented the entire Mongolian population under Chinggis Qan's control in 1206.'

14. The banners themselves seem to have existed before the Manchus, and as Natsagdorj argues, the military-administrative organization appears to be an adaptation of the earlier Mongol decimal system (see Bawden 1968: 105).

15. Sanjdorj (1980: 1) takes a Marxist line and states that in the sixteenth and seventeenth centuries 'the land . . . was the property of the feudal classes' and this may obscure the way in which the ultimate rights over land was vested in the emperor, and the *hoshuu* was administered in his name by the *Zasag noyan*.

16. The K'ang Hsi emperor did so around 1689, for refugees from Züüngar invasion (see Sanjdorj 1980: 24). The emperor also made grants of grain for these refugees – suggesting the importance of grain in the diet of the pastoralists. Manchu emperors also gave the Barga groups grants of land in what is now Hulun Buir, Inner Mongolia (zee Lattimore 1935: 158–60; also Tubshinnima of the Galzud date?:90–5).

17. Banner officials did not always have their commands obeyed without question, however. This is illustrated by an example of the difficulty

with which customary grazing rights were changed by banner officials in the nineteenth century. A noble from another banner was awarded rights to land. He was driven off, and it is probable that this was because as an outsider he had little influence among the locals (see Bawden 1968: 90–1).

18. It seems clear that it was the banner, rather than the smaller divisions within it, that was the most important unit of pastoral land management. As an official letter dated 1877 stated, 'the grass and water of a territory may be managed and assigned only by the ruler and *jasag* of the said land'. Cited by Natsagdorj (1967: 267) and also referred to by Bawden (1968: 89).

19. The *bag* was the usual civil subdivision, the *otog* was the subunit used in the ecclesiastical districts.

20. It also seems that there was some notion of a man's allotment of land (*ere-in gazar*) and there are records of an amount of territory described as 'land for fifteen men' being allocated to an official in 1805 (see Natsagdorj 1967: 268). But it seems most likely that this allotment was entirely nominal, not that each man of a banner was allocated a standard amount of land. Indeed we do not even know if this 'land for fifteen men' refers to pasture or land for farming.

21. Bawden (1968: 156–7) mentions wheat and hay fields, and (ibid.: 89–91) the renting and sale of *övöljöö*.

22. This is in contrast to the romantic notion of pastoral nomads who consider the unfenced land they move upon to belong to all.

23. There can be little disputing the many ways in which Mongolian society of the Manchu and pre-revolutionary periods resembled ones we consider feudal. There has been much discussion as to the applicability of the term 'feudal' to describe Mongolia under the Manchus. The matter has been hotly argued in Soviet literature, and is neatly summarized by Gellner (1988). I find 'feudal' an acceptable term because I consider the key criteria of feudalism to be enfiefment, the division between commoners and nobility, and a legal system which tied commoners to land administered by the enfiefed lord; all these conditions existed in pre-revolutionary Mongolia. However, as a full evaluation of the suitability of the term would require an entire book, it seems reasonable for the purposes of this debate to accept Bawden's (1968) point that 'feudal' is a useful shorthand to describe the stratified social order. Mongolian historians such as Natsagdorj (1967) and Sanjdorj (1980), drawing on the wealth of materials available to them, are able to argue convincingly that in the Manchu period, if not before, Mongolia's society was essen-

tially feudal. Rather than debate the vocabulary it seems most reasonable to accept Bawden's approach which has been to use the term 'feudal' as a useful shorthand to describe the stratified social order.

24. There was a long history of local authorities owning large numbers of livestock, and requiring the district's residents to herd them. The pre-revolutionary monasteries, for example, could own more than 60 per cent of the total livestock in a district (Lattimore 1940: 97, n. 50).

25. The oldest reference to this term dates from the Chinggisid period (twelfth century): *huv'- khubi* was the term used to mean the princely appanages. See connection between politics and social order and 'property'. These were earlier termed *ulus*: mastery over rather than possession of items, people, land, etc.

26. These two modes represent ideal-typical extremes in productive orientation, and have coexisted and been interrelated, for centuries. (The great noble and ecclesiastical herd-owners of the pre-revolutionary period organized comparable large-scale specialist pastoralism.) The 'specialist-maximizing' mode is based upon the ownership of large numbers of animals by a single agency: a company, for example, or a collective or state farm in the past. It can be characterized by the specialized herding of large herds, often of a single species, and frequently involves a relatively large amount of movement. Production is oriented toward gaining the maximum return on the herd-wealth that was kept in this way, the herders having contractual obligations to supply a certain quota of produce. This mode of production makes use of various economies of scale. The 'domestic-subsistence' mode, by contrast, is oriented toward satisfying domestic requirements, and as such is characterized by each pastoral 'family-residential group' owning and herding relatively small numbers of several species of domestic livestock, as the various species provide different necessities for the pastoralist, sheep and goats for meat and winter clothing. All pastoral households are engaged to some extent in domestic-subsistence production, particularly of milk products, but those who are primarily oriented toward this mode are those that are not part of the large-scale herding activities of a large herd-owning agency, and tend to be less mobile.

References

Asian Development Bank (1992), *Mongolia: A Centrally Planned Economy in Transition*, Oxford: Oxford University Press.

—— (1994), 'Agricultural Sector Study of Mongolia', Division 1, Agricultural Department, February.

Barfield, T.J. (1981), 'The Hsiung-nu Imperial Confederacy: organisation and foreign policy', *Journal of Asian Studies*, 41, 45–61.

Bawden, C.R. (1968), *The Modern History of Mongolia*, London, Weidenfeld & Nicolson.

Bruun, O. and Odgaard, O. (1996), 'A society and economy in transition', in O. Bruun and O. Odgaard (eds), *Mongolia in Transition: New Patterns, New Challenges*, Nordic Institute of Asian Studies, Studies in Asian Topics, No. 22, Richmond, Surrey: Curzon.

Campi, A.J. (1994), 'The Special Cultural and Social Challenges involved in modernizing Mongolia's nomadic socialist economy', in E.H. Kaplan and D.W. Whisenhunt (eds), *Opuscula Altaica: Essays Presented in Honour of Henry Schwarz*, Centre for East Asian Studies, Bellingham: Western Washington University.

Ch'i-ch'ing Hsiao, (1978), *The Military Establishment of the Yuan Dynasty* Harvard East Asian Monographs 77, Cambridge, Mass.: Harvard University Press.

Dawson, C. (1955), *The Mongol Mission*, London and New York: Sheed & Ward.

Erdenebaatar, B. (1996), 'Socio-economic aspects of the pastoral movement patterns of Mongolian herders', in C. Humphrey and D. Sneath (eds), *Culture and Environment in Inner Asia: 1. The Pastoral Economy and the Environment*, Cambridge, UK: White Horse Press.

Gellner, E. (1988), *State and Society in Soviet Thought*, Oxford: Oxford University Press.

Griffin, K. (1995), 'Economic strategy during the transition', in K. Griffin, (ed.), *Poverty and the Transition to a Market Economy in Mongolia*, New York: St Martin's Press.

Lattimore, O. (1935), *The Mongols of Manchuria*, New York: The John Day Company.

—— (1940), *Inner Asian Frontiers of China* American Geographical Society, Research Series No. 21. London and New York: Oxford University Press.

The Ministry of Agriculture and Industry of Mongolia (1998), 'Mongolian Agriculture and Agro-industry', Report published on the Worldwide Web (http://www.agriculture.mn/agroindustry.htm#2)

Mongolian Academy of Sciences (1990), *Bügd Nairamdah Mongol Ard Uls: Ündesnii Atlas* (Mongolian People's Republic: Basic Atlas), Ulaanbaatar: Mongolian Academy of Sciences publications.

David Sneath

Natsagdorj, S.H. (1967), 'The Economic Basis of Feudalism in Mongolia', *Modern Asian Studies*, 1(3).

Nolan, P. (1995), *China's Rise, Russia's Fall: Politics, Economics and Planning in the Transition from Stalinism*, Basingstoke and London: MacMillan.

Odgaard, O. (1996), 'Living standards and poverty', in O. Bruun and O. Odgaard (eds), *Mongolia in Transition*, Nordic Institute of Asian Studies, Studies in Asian Topics, No. 22, Richmond, Surrey: Curzon.

Pozdneyev, A.M. (1971 [1892]), *Mongolia and the Mongols* (translation), Vol. 1 J. Krueger (ed.), Bloomington: Indiana University Press.

Robinson, B. (1995), 'Mongolia in transition: a role for distance learning?', *Open Learning*, November: 3–15.

Sanjdorj, M. (1980), *Manchu Chinese Colonial Rule in Northern Mongolia*, London: C. Hurst.

Simukov, A.D. (1933), 'Hotoni' (Hotons), in *Sovrennaya Mongoliya* (Contemporary Mongolia), 3, 19–32.

Statistical Office of Mongolia (1993), *Mongolyn Ediin Zasag, Niigem 1992* (Mongolian Economy and Society in 1992), Ulaanbaatar: J.L.D. Gurval.

UNDP (1997), *Human Development Report, Mongolia*, Ulaanbaatar.

United Nations Systems in Mongolia (1999), *Annual Report 1998*, Report published on the internet (http://www.un-mongolia.mn/publications/anrep98.pdf)

United States Embassy (1999), 'Embassy Cable, Subject: IMI: Mongolia Shows Signs of Economic Growth: 1998 Statistics Compiled', Report published on the internet (http://us-mongolia.com/general/economy.html)

von Ginneken,W. (1995), 'Employment promotion and the social safety-net,' in K. Griffin (ed.), *Poverty and the Transition to a Market Economy in Mongolia*, New York: St Martin's Press.

World Bank (1994), *Mongolia: Country Economic Memorandum: Priorities in Macroeconomic Management*, Report No. 13612-MOG, Country Operations Division, China and Mongolia Department, Asia and Pacific Regional Office.

Broadening the Concept of Privatization: Gender and Development in Rural Kazakhstan

Rosamund Shreeves

Privatization is the very basis of rural reforms. (Esimov 1996)

All large, abstract development plans are pursued by ordinary men and women in small, concrete worlds of human relations in households, villages and peer groups, and it is on these microcosms that their outcome ultimately depends. (Massell 1974)

This chapter aims to show how an understanding of privatization in rural Kazakhstan is enriched by examining the process from the vantage of gender. Applying feminist and anthropological theories of 'public' and 'private' domains, I argue that in order to take account of gender issues – and indeed of local experiences and responses in general – it is necessary to go beyond the dominant macro-economic privatization framework to consider the process in a much broader sense. Through a case study of a specific private farm, I shall discuss some of the ways in which rural reform is changing the gender division of labour and, conversely, how local constructions of gender are shaping change.

Privatization and Rural Development in Kazakhstan

Since 1991, privatization has been the central pillar of the development programme implemented by the Kazakhstani government with the support of international agencies. The reduction of state control and introduction of private ownership has been seen as one of the key ways of producing a more efficient 'modern' market economy and stimulating growth. These processes in turn are assumed to provide economic and social benefits to individuals and communities, by opening up opportunities for participation and control over resources.

Rural development in particular has primarily been framed in terms of the need to restructure collective and state farms and encourage the formation of new agricultural enterprises based on private ownership of land and assets. Land reform and farm privatization programmes were initiated in 1991, and by 1996 were held to be almost complete. In April of that year roughly 93 per cent of Kazakhstan's approximately 2,300 state farms had been re-registered as private entities (Gaynor 1996). However, these quantitative indicators hide a more complex picture. Both government and outside consultants have recognized that rural privatization has been an ad hoc process, with considerable latitude given to local authorities and individual farm directors in shaping reform.[1] Although in some areas the majority of former collective and state farms have been dismantled and replaced by private enterprises, in other areas most have opted for little more than a change in name, with virtually no alteration in either management or production structures. Moreover, local power relations have been instrumental in shaping the outcome of reform, with local elites often 'grabbing' and consolidating control over resources.

Notwithstanding these indications that the reform process has been embedded in other relations and processes, the overwhelming majority of the critical literature on agricultural-sector reform in Kazakhstan and other postsocialist countries takes a narrow technical and economic approach, excluding the social and cultural context of transformation. Gender, in particular, is mainly conspicuous by its absence.[2] Despite the body of knowledge on the gender impact of capitalist development and agrarian reform in other parts of the world, little consideration has been given to the possible differential impact of rural privatization on women and men.[3] Neither has attention been paid to the influence of local constructions of gender in shaping responses to reform.

In this context, what makes Kazakhstan particularly interesting is its starting point to capitalist transformation. As in the other Central Asian republics, the transformation of gender relations was a key part of the modernization policies applied during the Soviet period. From the outset, the Bolshevik regime promoted emancipation of indigenous women, with attacks on practices such as veiling and attempts to bring women into the labour force and political life. Throughout the Soviet period, accounts of rural development used indicators of women's education levels and employment as evidence of successful modernization and progress. However, critiques of Soviet development point to its mitigated success in changing the position of women, evoking the perpetuation, or even reinforcement, of gender inequality under the Soviet regime, especially in rural areas.[4] The history of Soviet intervention in Kazakhstan therefore raises questions about gender and socio-economic inequality and the ways that local identities and practices may serve as obstacles to engineered change or may shape it in particular ways, that are equally salient in relation to the current development project.

Defining public and private spheres

If mainstream accounts of privatization tell us little about gender, then this is partly because the frameworks they employ obscure its salience. In particular, the mainstream definition of the public/private dichotomy, which has been central to the debate around the 'transition' of state socialist societies and the development policies implemented there, effectively masks the social and cultural – including gender – aspects of change.

The economic/political science definition

According to this conceptualization, society is divided into a public (state) sphere and a private (non-state) sphere of the market and civil society, which was 'submerged' in the USSR, hence stagnation. The restructuring process initiated by perestroika and accelerated since the dissolution of the USSR, can be seen as the forging of a new social contract: the 'private' (non-state) realm is to be 'reborn' through the creation of a deregulated economy and civil society, thereby increasing efficiency and liberating individual initiative and participation. The creation or restoration of the 'proper' relationship between public and private spheres, in this instance through restructuring of state and collective farms, is presented as a 'gender neutral' process.

At macro level, this conceptualization is reflected in development policy and programmes. Both Government and the international community draw a distinction between *developing* and *transition* countries, where the main priority is seen as the move from plan to market, rather than wider issues of social and human development. During my fieldwork from 1996 to 1998, few of the many aid programmes being implemented in the agricultural sector considered the social impact of agrarian reform in project design, implementation or assessment, and none had a specific gender component. Even when organizations did have a gender and development programme, because Kazakhstan was a 'transition' state this was not generally deemed applicable or had not yet been applied (USAID 1996).[5] However, 'transition' policy may not be so much gender-neutral as gender-blind.

Rosamund Shreeves

The feminist definition

Western feminist analysis points to the need to critique this first definition for obfuscating or ignoring a more fundamental public/private division. According to this analysis, both the state and non-state spheres described above are 'public', since they are implicitly built on the exclusion of another 'private' sphere of family and kinship relations. It is argued that Western democracies have been built on a gendered association of men/ public/production and women/private/reproduction, which has led to the marginalization of women in both state and market spheres and their exclusion from full citizenship (Pateman 1989). In these terms, the espousal of a Western, liberal model based on the withdrawal of the state and the (re)emergence of the market and civil society may well not benefit women and men equally as citizens and individuals. This may be particularly true in postsocialist societies. The socialist state altered the relation between gendered domestic and public spheres familiar from nineteenth-century capitalism, socializing significant elements of repro-duction and drawing women into the labour force, even as it left them responsible for the rest (Verdery 1994: 232). Women and men are therefore likely to stand in different positions in relation to the retraction of the state and the emergence of the market, and women may be particularly vulnerable. Since the perestroika period, this framework has been used to shed light on the gendered aspects of 'transition' ideology and policy, suggesting that women have been particular losers, with market reform forcing them out of the labour market and into the domestic domain (Bridger et al. 1996).

From this perspective, gender was a salient factor in the division of labour, reward and entitlement on state farms. Women and men engaged differently in socialized labour, with a tendency for women to be engaged less and in the lower-status sectors (Bridger 1987). Further, a state farm was not just an economic unit of production but a 'total social institution' (Humphrey 1995: 7) and a microcosm of the socialist gender regime. In other words, it was not only the primary – and in many cases the only – employer, but also the provider of the basic infrastructure, along with services ranging from shops to childcare, culture and leisure facilities and opportunities for political and social activity. With privatization, these 'social-sphere assets' are perceived to be a major brake on economic efficiency, and are to be divested to local authorities or private enterprises. Since women stood in a particular relationship to them, both as primary employees and users of services, many of which had been specifically introduced to help them combine work and family responsibilities, this

– 214 –

is not a gender-neutral process. Lastly, the transfer from state to private ownership also means a shift from a collective to a household form of agricultural production. To analyse this only in terms of economic efficiency is to miss the particular impact on women of the division of labour and power within the household (Hivon 1995: 78).

The anthropological definition

Anthropologists suggest that it is necessary to unpack both these conceptualizations of the public/private dichotomy. Since they can obscure the culturally specific ways in which public and private domains are constituted and valued in different, particularly non-Western, societies, such conceptualizations therefore may hamper an understanding of change.

From this perspective, it is argued that socialist development led to a specific construction and interrelation between public and private spheres, and that the 'private' domain was actually *more* significant than the 'public' domain dominated by the socialist state (Hann 1993). It was in the private domain of kinship and informal networks that people found ways to cope with endemic shortages as well as positive values and identities lacking in socialism, and these may be playing a key role in people's current strategies.

It is also argued that the feminist conceptualization of public and private spheres needs to be problematized, since it imposes Western concepts of value on 'native' explications of gender domains. Yanagisako's work on two generations of Japanese immigrants in America shows how the overarching 'public/private' dichotomy hides a transition over several generations from a socio-spatial (inside-outside) conceptualization of male and female roles to a functional model of labour specialization in production and reproduction, with different implications for gendered relations of authority and power (Yanagisako 1987).

From this perspective, without taking account of the value which people attached to public and private spheres in specific local contexts, it is difficult to understand how they are responding to, and may be shaping the outcome of, the current reforms. Thus we can ask, 'what light do these three definitions shed on decollectivization in rural Kazakhstan?' That the classic political-science definition of the relationship between public and private spheres fails to capture either the nature of collective farming communities under socialism or the specific nature of the private enterprises which are emerging from them is clear if we turn to a closer analysis of material from one of my fieldwork communities.

Rosamund Shreeves

Complicating privatization: Kairat's 'private farm'

Although economic and productive forms are now changing, this is not necessarily in the direction intended by the reformers. According to the reform programme, privatization means surveying the land and other assets of individual state and collective farms and dividing them among their members in the form of shares (*pai*). Members can then decide either to take their shares and start an independent 'peasant' farm (*krestyanskoe khozyaistvo*), or become shareholders in a larger cooperative or joint stock society, to be run on a market basis. Although there is some argument about which is the more economically valid alternative, ideologically the role of the individual family farmer has been promulgated as a symbol of the new model of capitalist development and modernity. However, in the region I shall discuss, this model has both failed in its own terms and been resisted and shaped by local communities in particular ways.

Although state farms have ostensibly been restructured, the majority have chosen to remain as large entities, with very few independent private farms.[6] Further, the experience has been less one of withdrawal of the state and emergence of a new sphere of private enterprise than one of withdrawal and collapse of services and living standards. Households have been thrown back on their own safety net of subsistence production and ties of kinship and mutual aid. In this sense, in comparison with urban areas, rural communities as a whole are not so much being developed or marketized as relocated to a subsistence domain. These are not just economic processes but also social and cultural ones, as reform undermines the established moral accommodation of state and domestic domains. The new private farms are caught up in these processes. From the perspective of state ideology, they are the vanguard of the new values of entrepreneurship and economic efficiency. Locally, they also represent the arrival of the market, but practical necessity and perceptions of proper conduct mean that they are also embedded in kinship strategies of obligation and reciprocity. A close reading of one particular private farm illustrates how the new 'market' sphere is intertwined with both the public and domestic domains. More specifically, it shows how reform is disrupting patterns of gendered labour and, conversely, how what I term the 'rural gender contract' is influencing the roles men and women are playing in the family and the new sectors of the economy.

In my first talk with Kairat about the farm, my impression was that it operated as just the kind of entrepreneurial, commercially-oriented private enterprise which the reforms hoped to produce. He told me that he had created the enterprise in 1995 and officially registered it with the authorities as a private farm. After a false start in the first year, when he had sowed grain with disastrous results, he had moved into vegetable production and now produced mainly potatoes and carrots on 6 hectares of land near the canal. He had some technical equipment, including a lorry, a tractor and an irrigation pump. The enterprise was one of only seven private farms set up on the sovkhoz, which has now reorganized as a joint stock company, and Kairat was proud of the fact that the new enterprises were more productive and efficient than the parent farm. He was happy to be 'his own master' (*sam khozyain*), able to make his own production decisions, and was keen to tell me that his farm was making money. The main problem was to market the farm's produce and to find credit for further development. However, once past this initial interview, I began to realize that the situation was more complex than it appeared.

Complicating the 'individual entrepreneur' model

First, the term 'Kairat's farm' is a misnomer since, although Kairat was registered as its director, he was not a single entrepreneur. Two brothers and a close Russian friend were also formal members, had contributed their land shares and were involved in production and marketing. This pattern of male kin, typically brothers or a father and sons pooling their assets to set up a farm, was a characteristic one in my research communities.[7] So, although by law a private farm must be registered in the name of one person who has formal leadership status, the actual structure is generally much more complex.

This complexity is often not formally recorded and still less so when it comes to women's involvement in the creation and operation of the new private farms.[8] When I went to the oblast' authorities in Karaganda to find figures on women-headed farms, I was told that my question was ridiculous. Of course there were none – first because women 'were not farmers' and secondly because their husbands would 'naturally' be the head of the enterprise. These reactions point both to the gender structure of labour in the local farming system, and to the local 'normative model' for decision-making. In the sense that they tended to participate less in the socialized agricultural sector than men, women 'were not farmers' – although most played a key role in the household subsidiary farm. 'Being a farmer' is also equated with the local model of authority, which conceives headship in terms of male kinship, hierarchy and obligation, and ascribes overall authority to the most senior male. In this region, even where senior women did have as much agricultural or managerial experience as men, they were generally not considered as potential or actual 'heads' of farms.[9] However, looking beyond the notion of formal registration, the picture of women's involvement is more complex.

When I asked Kairat and his partners whether their wives were members of the farm, they initially treated my question as a great joke. However, in talking to Kairat's wife Madina, I began to see that her contribution was considerable. Characteristically, the redistribution model used on the sovkhoz meant that, as a 'social-sphere worker', her land share had been calculated at a lower coefficient than that of agricultural workers and she had not been eligible to receive an asset share of machinery or livestock.[10] However, she had received a land share, which she contributed to the private farm. She also contributed her labour on a frequent basis. Especially at the beginning, when they were just getting off the ground, she and two of the other wives had worked in the fields alongside their husbands, weeding, irrigating and harvesting. Although – now that they were able to hire workers – she did less fieldwork, during harvest time she still went to the fields most evenings, together with Kairat and sometimes with the children, to harvest carrots and potatoes. Apart from this direct involvement in agricultural production, Madina was now responsible for organizing the labour of the mainly female workers the farm seasonally employed (mostly neighbours, friends, relatives and former colleagues) and for selling produce from home. And not least, their household served as 'host' for the farm, which involved cooking and caring for the frequent guests, such as visiting traders and suppliers. So, although Madina's work was 'formally' invisible, she was actually making an important contribution to the private enterprise.

I also began to realize that the enterprise could not be considered in isolation. Kairat and the other male partners described the farm as the main input to their households, but when pressed for details, were reticent about specifying its actual contribution to household income. What gradually became clear was that the enterprise was part of what has been termed a 'livelihood jigsaw'.[11] In other words, each of the four households directly involved was pursuing a range of different – and essential – subsistence and income-generating strategies, in which women played the major role.

With the closure of the kindergarten, Madina had been made redundant and was now putting increasing time and energy into work on the domestic smallholding, which provided the bulk of the household's meat, dairy products, eggs and vegetables and occasionally a small surplus which she bartered or traded for other goods. The task of managing the domestic economy fell to Madina, although Kairat would 'help out' with the heavier work such as mucking out the stable and forking hay. All three of the other wives were employed 'off farm', one as a teacher and the others in the administration of the joint stock company. This work brought various benefits – the school was by then one of the few employers to pay money wages, if in arrears; and, while the joint stock company did not often pay in cash, employment did give entitlement to goods 'in lieu of wages' and to vital social benefits, including medical care and pensions. In addition, two of the wives occasionally traded in goods from home and one sometimes produced a particularly lethal home-brew vodka for sale. So, the private farm was only one of a range of different inputs to the households involved. Public-sector employment, the domestic smallholding and informal trade were vital alternative sources of (relatively) steady money, food and social security.

Moving beyond the four households directly involved 'officially' or 'formally' in the enterprise, the picture becomes even more complicated. A much wider circle of kin had been involved in the creation of the farm, were still involved in its operation and benefited from it in various ways. Kairat's sisters had been instrumental in establishing the farm. The director of the joint stock company had been hostile to members separating from the enterprise and refused to hand over the asset shares that were due. It was only because two sisters were able to use their positions to obtain all the machinery, together with seed and fertilizer, from their sovkhoz, that the farm became a viable concern.[12] They continued to 'obtain' resources in this way on a regular basis. They also organized sales of the farm's produce through their own networks of neighbours, colleagues and friends. On learning that their brothers were planning to drive the lorry over with potatoes and carrots for sale, they would begin to spread the word. By the time the lorry actually arrived, the village would be primed. The men would leave the women in charge of the proceedings. Kairat would decide whether goods were to be available for barter, but apart from this, they acted at their own discretion in setting prices, generally after checking with a former colleague, now a trader, as to the going rates in the local town. The sale would take the good part of two hours – time 'stolen' from official jobs in the sovkhoz administration. Later, the sister who lived in the local town would take charge of sales there, using her networks in a similar way. So, while the four men formally involved in the farm were responsible for long-distance sales, on the markets in Karaganda and further afield, along with local sales to formal structures such as wholesale dealers, close female kin were largely responsible for local and informal sales of produce. The two areas were associated with specific moral values and meanings. Local sales were felt to be less lucrative but more secure, being based on existing relations of trust and solidarity; on the other hand, the market was seen as a cut-throat arena where one was likely to be cheated. The brothers' accounts of their travels were heroic tales of affronting an alien outside world, pitting their wits and daring against the 'immoral' middle-men who produced nothing of their own, and returning with money for their families.

Moving even further outward, the fact that Kairat had been able to bypass the Farm Director to get the good land he wanted and to get the farm officially registered at all was at least partly due to the influence of high-placed relatives and networks in the rayon and oblast administration. As he put it, 'you need both a good head and connections to make it as a private farmer'.

These connections were not built up by Kairat himself, but developed by his parents through everyday and ceremonial acts of hospitality and exchange.[13] Kairat's parents had invested a good deal of energy in nourishing their household's social networks, his father through his official position as head accountant and his mother through managing ritual obligations with kin, neighbourhood and community. In this case, the wife of a key oblast' official had been adopted into the family on the death of her mother and put through college at its expense. The rayon Akim had come to the farm as a young specialist and had been taken under the family's wing – eating at their house most days. So, although Kairat's parents had come to live on a 'Russian' sovkhoz, they had maintained strong links with the Kazakh community on which Kairat was able to draw in founding the farm. This resource was a key advantage in terms of start-up and viability over the majority of Russian private farmers in the community.

So, the first 'complicating' factor to emerge from my fieldwork was that the model of 'individual entrepreneurship' did not fit the actual situation. In the context of rural Kazakhstan, the creation and functioning of the new private farms cannot be understood without taking a much wider perspective and looking at the ways they are intertwined with and reliant on kin relationships beyond the individual entrepreneur or even household itself. In terms of gender, the model of 'individual entrepreneurship' obscures women's contribution to the emerging private enterprises and marginalizes the other household survival strategies in which they play a crucial role. This is especially true in communities such as these, where women are rarely registered officially as heads or members of private farms and their labour is therefore informal and invisible. This model also fails to take account of the way in which men's and women's roles in the family and wider social networks impact on their economic behaviour.

Complicating the 'market/profit-oriented' nature of the enterprise

The 'privatization model' assumes that the new enterprises will be profit- or market-oriented. This was certainly the way that Kairat presented the farm to me initially. However, when I began to investigate further, it became clear to me that this was only part of the picture. Like the majority of the private farms in my research communities, this one actually had a dual orientation – both toward market production and toward subsistence. Although it did produce food for the market, much of the produce was not actually destined for outside sale but for direct consumption by the four households officially involved and a much wider circle of kin.

In fact, it is impossible to consider the private farm in isolation from this wider network of kin and the interdependencies this involves. By the sisters and other kin, the farm is viewed primarily as an 'extended family resource': a source of food, particularly in times of trouble, such as the drought which struck the region two years running, and for more vulnerable family members such as the youngest sister, unemployed and pregnant, and the divorced sister with a child to support. For both the extended families of the male partners and the extended families of their wives, the farm is therefore primarily part of a wider network of kin reciprocities.

This situation sets up conflicts and tensions: between 'commercial' and 'kinship' orientations, between the extended family and the four households 'directly' involved as partners in the farm, and between and within these four households themselves. Who is the farm 'for'? Is it a profit-making commercial enterprise or part of a kinship survival strategy? What is the place of money and other exchanges? What is the value of the different contributions and how should they be rewarded?

These conflicts are increasingly evident in the day-to-day running of the farm. One of the signs of this is the increasing tension over the meaning of work for the enterprise. Two of the main issues have been what – or whose – activities should be classed as work and how work contributions should be measured and rewarded. What seems to be emerging is a growing tension between two concepts of work: first, work as a commodity, whose quantity and effectiveness should be measured and rewarded accordingly in the interests of the efficiency of the enterprise; and second, work seen as part of a whole, as just one contribution to household and kin strategies, which cannot – and indeed should not – be measured in terms that would split household and family unity or disrupt long-term kin reciprocities. Here we can see both how values and practices connected with kinship and ethnicity are shaping work practices and how market values are beginning to penetrate and undermine values based on kinship and solidarity.

Let me explain what I mean with some concrete examples. As Kairat admitted during my last fieldwork visit in 1998, production decisions are not based on 'efficiency' criteria alone and, as head of the enterprise, this was causing him increasing problems. Until then, he had been dividing subsistence produce and the cash or goods from sale of the surplus produce equally among the four households directly involved. In 1997, his major headache was his eldest brother, who had taken to drink and was doing less and less work for the farm. In the interests of the enterprise, he would have liked to pay him a smaller share. However, he felt obliged to put family solidarity above efficiency and to continue to reward each member equally. In addition, according to Kazakh custom, he told me, as the middle brother he was traditionally bound to 'defer' to his oldest brother, and to act against this in his capacity as head of the enterprise would be strongly criticized by the extended family. So, until then, production decisions had been shaped and circumscribed by kin commitments and authority relations within the family – to the detriment of the enterprise, as Kairat was increasingly coming to feel.[14]

However, kin solidarities are being increasingly stretched by its existence. Although everyone associated with the farm expressed the idea that 'we do everything in common' (*vsye obshchee*) and that 'we do not measure individual contributions', there were now increasingly bitter wrangles over which of the four men worked harder and who was actually pulling his weight. Each thought that he was working the hardest but that the others were being paid better. Similarly, among the extended kin, there were increasing complaints about some family members receiving preferential treatment and others being passed over when produce was given out. So, although relationships within the enterprise continued to be expressed in the idiom of kinship, their content was in the process of changing.

One incident in particular shed light for me on the way in which gender ideology was operating in this context to make the women the upholders of the kinship idiom and the 'glue' holding the enterprise together. I was sitting in the kitchen with Madina and one of Kairat's sisters, drinking tea and talking about the farm. Madina was explaining how she and two of the other wives had worked alongside their husbands in the fields and how hard it had been. She said that for her, it was natural to help with the private farm, it was just one of the things that were there to be done, like looking after the family smallholding and taking care of the children. She helped her husband and he helped her. They didn't keep count. Kairat had asked her if she wanted to become an official member of the farm, but she had said no. Why would she? The only reason to do so would be if she did not trust him. She went on to say that the youngest brother's wife, Aigul, was the only one who hadn't done any work in the fields. Yes, interjected Mainur, with some disapproval – she thought she ought to be paid for her work like the men. They both went on to criticize her for this : she thought her work was so valuable that she should be paid for it, did she? She was too big for her boots. She didn't realize that her contribution to the household was worth nothing in comparison to what her husband brought in through the farm. She only worked short hours and brought in 1,200 tenge a month. She didn't appreciate how hard Mischa worked and the fact that everything in the house, including her precious TV, had come from him. The only thing that she had brought in her dowry was the wall unit (*stenka*). And she was greedy and grasping and wanted new things all the time. Given the sheer vituperativeness of the criticism, Aigul was clearly breaking important norms, as follows.

First, for a wife to bring up the idea of payment for labour 'for the family' was clearly unacceptable, even in the context of a private enterprise. Although agricultural labour is organized and rewarded according to relations of reciprocity rather than on a contractual basis, there is a further gender distinction in the division of labour. Kairat talks about sharing the produce and profits equally among the four households, but it is primarily the men's work which counts, with the women's counted as subsidiary 'help'. Aigul's behaviour in asking for an individual monetary appreciation of her contribution was heavily criticized not just because it was a direct challenge to the kinship-based organization of labour but also because it transgressed women's proper position within it.

Second, the fact that the criticism was framed in terms of Aigul's failure to recognise Mischa's primary breadwinning role takes us to the 'rural gender contract' created by the accommodation between indigenous and socialist practice and values. According to this local narrative, which was strikingly consistent across the community, a husband's role was to be '*glava sem'i*' (head of the family), to '*obespechit*' (provide), to '*kormit' semyu*' (feed the family), to '*dostat*' (obtain goods), and to '*dogovorit*" (do deals in pursuit of the latter); a wife's role, on the other hand was to *'kontrolirovat' sebe'* (be self-controlled) and to *'byt' zhenshchinoi'* (be a woman) which entailed being the 'guardian of the hearth', managing the domestic sphere of childcare, cooking, cleaning, gardening and looking after some aspects of the smallholding (milking, caring for young animals and poultry, feeding the livestock) as well as managing the 'public' face of the household.[15] A key contrast here is the difference between the male role of 'feeding the family', in the sense of materially and financially providing for the family's needs, and the female role of 'feeding the family' in the sense of growing food, raising livestock and producing meals. Although this was presented as a partnership – running the household was conceived as a common enterprise, with separate but complementary roles for husband and wife and different roles for children according to age – the 'mainstay' of the household was generally perceived to be the male wage, reflecting and reinforcing the consensus that the husband was the *'khozyain doma'* (head, literally master, of the household). One of the main signs of the changing relationship between the former sovkhoz and the household has been the erosion of the 'male wage' – both through increasing layoffs and because work for the joint stock company is paid in kind, if at all, and is therefore bringing less and less financial benefit. On the other hand, women working in the social sector are, along with pensioners, some of the few to be paid in money. This shift has threatened men's position as main breadwinners and heads of household and undermined the gender contract.

In fact, far from experiencing market reform as the herald of new entrepreneurial labour opportunities, many rural men have felt it as a kind of emasculation and overturning of their role and status. In the countryside, men as well as women are being marginalized from the public and forced into the domestic domain, into unemployment or what is commonly termed 'sitting at home'. For men in particular, this experience is complicated by the new discourses surrounding national identity, work and success in the market sphere. Reinvented models of manliness, of hero-entrepreneurs conquering the market and making good are, for most, unattainable dreams. Instead, economic reform is making it difficult for rural men to maintain the performance of masculinity, whose 'threshold is in the eye of the beholder, a fuzzy demarcation always in need of testing' (Gilmore 1990: 66). This critical threshold, which must be seen to be crossed, is 'the point at which the boy produces more than he consumes and gives more than he takes' (ibid.: 266). In this sense, economic reform is creating painful divisions between men who are able to provide, and others, labelled as 'misadapted' or 'lazy' who cannot do so.[16] Private farming, initially rejected by many men as 'not being real work', is now being embraced as a productive activity which socially re-establishes men as providers. However, its combined commercial and subsistence status makes this new identity an ambiguous and unsteady one.

Women who worked for the state farm also experience 'sitting at home' as a painful situation of becoming marginal or invisible, losing the security of state protection and their position in society.[17] However, local models of work have allowed them to validate their activities in a way that men cannot. Discourse analysis of conversations about reactions to the changes in the community produced a series of gendered qualities: women are said to be *gibkie* (flexible), *shustrie* (quick on the uptake), *pobystree prisposablivayutsya* (more adaptable), whereas men are lazy, jealous, drunk and *skandalyut doma* (make scenes at home). In effect, women are locally perceived not as the main 'losers' from reform, but as 'winners', and this is profoundly disruptive to the local economic and moral order. The depth of anxiety felt by both sexes was reflected in the anecdotes circulating among men about the new dominance of women, wives berating their husbands for failing to provide and increasing levels of domestic conflict and violence.[18] From this perspective, the reaction to Aigul's demands is one of the characteristic patterns of responses to the undermining of the gender contract. With the exception of Aigul, the wives saw one of the functions of the private farm as to reaffirm their husbands' role as provider, rather than as an opportunity for themselves to formally become entrepreneurs. The definition of women's new activities in private farming and trade as part of their family-oriented caring responsibilities, and men's as part of their productive obligations, therefore reaffirms the previous cultural construction of gender domains. What this means in terms of relative power and inequality is not straight-forward. On the one hand, conflicts of interest are negotiated within a framework which ascribes men and women separate domains, and both draw social recognition and leverage from their different cultural reper-toires.[19] On the other hand, the perception that male work is economically important and women's economically subsidiary, if morally or spiritually central, is being carried over into the new market environment. Women who, like Aigul, overtly claim economic recognition of their work are seen as transgressing the proper boundaries of the female domain.

Third, criticism of Aigul focused on the fact that she was greedy (*zhadnyi*) and selfish and thought about consumer goods all the time. In fact, both Madina and Mainur were equally fascinated by this topic and could talk endlessly about the new status symbols such as linoleum for the floor or a wall unit, their prices and where they could be obtained. On other occasions, Mainur berated Madina herself for being greedy and persuading Kairat to stop sharing the proceeds of the farm with his sisters. This, I think, is the crux of the issue. In a microcosm of what is happening in the community at large, the private farm is heightening the inequalities between the individuals and households who are involved in relations of mutual support. As such, it is putting strain on these relationships at a time when the erosion of wages and services is making them more vital than ever before – at least for some members of the family. By evoking the 'greed' and 'selfishness' of the new entrepreneurs, people are bringing them into the normative atmosphere of the moral economy, asserting the 'proper' limits of individualistic and money-making behaviour and the claims of love, kinship and solidarity. What particularly interested me about the example of Aigul was the light it shed on the gendered aspects of this process. The underlying tensions between the farm as commercial enterprise and the farm as family resource were largely played out not between the men – which might have split the enterprise – but in emotional conflicts between sisters-in-law or sisters and sisters-in-law. In this sense, women's criticism of each other is playing a vital role in defusing or drawing attention away from conflicts and potential divisions that threaten unity. Just as women's 'invisible' productive labour is actually an important contribution to production as a whole, their invisible 'emotional' labour 'contains' or 'manages' the underlying contradictions and is therefore vital to the survival of the enterprise and family solidarities.

The question must now be, for how long? In 1998, the sisters no longer received shares of the harvest, as Kairat decided that the farm could no longer support the whole extended family on a regular basis. In turn, they were beginning to 'account' for their own contributions to the farm, and were extremely upset that their work was not recognized. It was in this year that they told me for the first time about their involvement in the start-up of the enterprise. Rather than deflecting deeper conflicts onto conflict with their sisters-in-law, they were also beginning to criticize their brothers themselves, contrasting their own attitude that they 'would jump out of their skins' for their brothers, with their brothers' neglect of them. The farm, and the profit relations it had introduced, were perceived as an undermining, foreign element in relations of reciprocity. Relations of reciprocity remained important for the sisters, who were respectively divorced and single, whereas they were becoming less so for their brothers. With the increasing commercial success of the farm, the latter could now 'buy in' hired labour and were no longer so dependent on the extended family. My fieldwork therefore captured a particular moment in the creation of the new enterprise, as its initial reliance on kinship reciprocities has shifted towards greater reliance on market relations. However, this is not to say that Kairat's farm and others in my research communities will necessarily end up 'fitting' the macro-level model of entrepreneurship and private enterprise. This model is in itself flawed, even in relation to Western society, and it is likely that the domestic sphere will continue to influence its further transformations in specific ways (Wheelock, Ljunggren and Baines 1999).

Conclusions

The political science approach to the public/private dichotomy fails to capture the specific ways in which the introduction of the market is intertwined with public (state) and private (kin, domestic) spheres in 'transitional' societies such as Kazakhstan. To understand the nature of private farms, and especially to get a fuller picture of women's role in their creation and functioning, we need to look a good deal further than the idea of an individual entrepreneur, driven by ambition, establishing a business for profit. One of the impacts of government reforms in Inner Asia has been to strengthen the economic importance of kinship relations (Humphrey and Sneath 1999: 137). As collective and state farms relinquish ownership of livestock and other rural resources, the role of families in productive activity increases in importance. Moreover, since families are not clearly bounded units, but part of networks of social obligation, private farms such as Kairat's also enter into wider relations of obligation and reciprocity. At the same time, they represent the entrance of new market and commercial relations into families and social networks. As such they are disrupting and shaping family and kin relations in new ways.

For the moment, the idiom of kinship is masking the emergence of new forms of inclusion and exclusion, visibility and invisibility and inequality. However, commercial relations are introducing new ways of valuing family members' labour and other contributions, stretching generalized relations of reciprocity to breaking point and heightening the differences between haves and have-nots within the extended family. Gender ideology is playing a key role both in keeping these contradictions from rising to the surface and in structuring new working and social relations. What is particularly striking is the continuity in meanings across socialist and postsocialist forms of rural economy. Despite the challenges to it, the 'rural gender contract' is perpetuating the association of men with the 'outside' and women with the 'inside' economy, with men primarily linked with market production and women with the domestic/subsistence domain. However, interpretation of this is problematic. In the short term, the fact that the domestic economy is now playing a key role in household survival gives women's 'inside' role increased value. On the other hand, both the macro-economic and local models misrecognize the value of women's work, in terms of both their actual contribution to production and the added value of their reproductive labour. In the long term, this may pose important questions about formal recognition of women's labour, property rights and access to resources that need to be taken into account in further development interventions.

Acknowledgements

This chapter is based on fieldwork conducted on two former state farms between 1996 and 1998, as part of a research project for the Centre for International Development and Training and Russian and Eastern European Research Centre at the University of Wolverhampton. Early versions were presented at the Workshop on Anthropology in Post-Socialist Societies and at the Conference on Gender and Rural Transformations in Europe, in 1999. I am grateful for the helpful insights offered by participants and by colleagues in Wolverhampton and Cambridge. Most of all I would like to thank my respondents for their unfailing hospitality and patience. I hope that this account will go some way to bringing their difficulties and resilience in the face of rapid and profound economic and social change into the public domain.

Notes

1. Legislation on land reform and farm restructuring evolved in a piecemeal way between 1991 and 1995 leading to a state of confusion and flux. Particularly in the early stages, no clear process for implementing it was defined. There was, for example, no standard nation-wide model of farm restructuring.
2. Some notable exceptions are Sue Bridger's (1993) and Myriam Hivon's (1995) work on women and agrarian reform in Russia. More

recently, the Conference on Gender and Rural Transformations in Europe, organized by Wageningen University from 14–17 October 1999, made agrarian reform in postsocialist countries a central theme. For Kazakhstan in particular, gender issues have not been specifically addressed in the technical literature on agricultural sector reform, but some findings are presented in the United Nations Development Programme (UNDP)'s annual development reports and in the special study on *Women and Gender Relations in Kazakhstan: the Social Cost*, commissioned by the Asian Development Bank (Bauer et al. 1997).

3. Since Esther Boserup's groundbreaking (1970) study on women's role in economic development, a considerable literature on women and/or gender and development has been built up. For a discussion, see for example Moore (1998). Analyses of agrarian reform (cf. Palmer 1985) provide a useful springboard for comparative analysis in a Kazakhstani context. However, in that they investigate the introduction of market systems into traditional forms of subsistence production, their applicability to Kazakhstan, which is moving from one 'modernizing' system to another, remains at issue.

4. Bridger (1987) gives a detailed account of women's role in rural development in the Soviet Union, while Massell (1974) and Warshofsky Lapidus (1978) are useful sources on the role of gender in Soviet development policy in Central Asia. An excellent critique of the arguments around change and continuity can be found in Kandiyoti (1996).

5. In 1996, the only international organization to have established a specific WID programme in Kazakhstan was the United Nations Development Programme (UNDP), which was operating with a broader 'human development' framework. In this context, an interesting comparison can be drawn between Kazakhstan and neighbouring Kyrgyzstan, where other agencies were implementing development policies with a strong social and gender focus. This seems to have been connected with the strategic positioning of the two countries on the development spectrum, with Kazakhstan classified (and positioning itself) as a major, resource-rich economy requiring mainly economic and technical aid and Kyrgyzstan as a poor, low-income country, requiring poverty-alleviation and other classical 'development' interventions. The correlation between the incorporation of gender and broader definitions of development is borne out by the fact that, in Kazakhstan, there have been moves since 1996 to incorporate gender in 'social' sectors, notably civil society development, where

resources are now being allocated to women's NGOs and leadership programmes.

6. This outcome was characteristic of the rayon as a whole, where the overwhelming majority of state farms had opted to remain as large entities, with relatively few independent private farms formed. The local authorities explained this in terms of agricultural conditions (inadvisability of splitting up large, grain-producing enterprises, lack of small-scale equipment, credit and training) and the 'laziness' or 'backward mentality' of local people. Donor organizations pointed to the lack of information and democracy in the reform process. In the community itself, private farmers explained that the local and farm administrations actually preferred to maintain the status quo in order to safeguard their own power bases, and had made it difficult for them to form and operate their enterprises. Others also raised the question of power relations but primarily the priority of getting their basic needs met and fear that the creation of private enterprises would lead to a breakdown of community and 'everybody being out for themselves' (*kazhdii sam po sebe*).

7. Kairat often said that this particular friend was like a brother to him. They had known each other since childhood and the friend had also once saved his life. Historically, the use of kinship to incorporate incomers was a feature of the Kazakh *aul* (nomad encampment) where newcomers often became part of Kazakh patrilineages.

8. Records on all *krestyanskie khozyaistva*, including the names of all those who contributed shares to the enterprise or who are officially listed as members are supposed to be held by the oblast' land registration offices (*Goskomzem*). However, given the rapidly evolving situation, particularly the conflicting processes of amalgamation and disintegration of private farms, these are not always up to date. In fact, many farmers never go through the full process of obtaining an official registration, since the cost is beyond their means. In addition, many private farms do not register all their members, since taxes and contributions have to be paid for each person.

9. The picture in my other research community was rather different. Here, the former sovkhoz had completely split into independent private farms and a significant proportion were officially headed by women. On the one hand, this can be explained by the privatization model, which allocated specific land plots rather than paper share certificates to each sovkhoz member, simplifying the process of establishing an enterprise for everybody. However, women here were also more heavily involved in socialized agriculture. The sovkhoz had had

a mixed profile, with dairy, beet cultivation and horticulture all female-dominated sectors. Further, the land is fertile and irrigated, meaning that small-scale, mostly non-mechanized, labour-intensive cultivation is a viable option. Although women and men are both registered as farmers, differences are emerging, with the perception of male-headed farms as 'commercial' enterprises and female-headed ones as 'subsistence' enterprises, primarily designed to 'feed the family'.

10. This was a common factor across all the communities I studied. The question of share allocation to different categories of sovkhoz member was decided by the farm membership. It was generally felt that social-sector workers had not contributed to agricultural production and therefore should receive a lower share. In addition, under the reform, these branches now came under the responsibility of the local authorities and were beginning to be seen as 'separate'.

11. This term is used by Wheelock, Ljunggren and Baines (1999) in their comparative analysis of rural entrepreneurs in Norway and England. They suggest that behaviour is rarely 'enterprising' in the individualistic sense put forward in small business policy, but that small enterprises are more usually part of a 'jigsaw' of livelihood sources for rural households. The construction of such 'jigsaws' takes place within the household and draws on individual and community understandings of what is right and expected of women and men when it comes to income-generating and caring responsibilities. As such, it draws on existing gendered power relations, but may on occasion disrupt them.

12. The practice of joint stock company directors seizing control of resources and preventing shareholders from withdrawing their shares is widespread. It is locally known as *'prikhvatisatsiya'* from the verb *'khvatat"* – to seize. In this way, although production structures appear to have remained 'the same', there is increasingly a shift in relations from collective membership and entitlement to an employer/ employee relationship.

13. As Cynthia Werner (1997) describes in her study of household networking strategies in a village in southern Kazakhstan, feasting and gift exchange were a particular 'Central Asian' form of the Soviet-era practice of using personal connections (*blat*). As such, they are a visible sign of the networks of reciprocal exchange and mutual indebtedness which provided a form of insurance for individuals and households.

14. On Lenin sovkhoz, one of the only private enterprises, a shop, was purportedly bankrupted because its head gave too much on credit or as gifts to his many relatives in the community. In the village, he was often praised to me for his solidarity.
15. To draw a parallel with the situation described by Ingrid Rudie (1994: 151), marriage and motherhood turned a woman into adult and wife and gave her a role in local ceremonial life, the 'arena where women cooperate, exchange services, create and maintain local network ties' which was 'a substantial portion of women's public space'.
16. One statistical study (Buckley 1997) pointed to the rising suicide rate among Kazakhstani men between 1990 and 1996 and put forward the hypothesis that men were experiencing an identity crisis: whereas their identity had been more closely tied to work in the public sphere, women's had been constructed in various different sites and was therefore less threatened by loss of employment.
17. One major contrast in the community was the use of the terms 'sitting at home' and 'taking care of the domestic economy' (*zanimatsya khozyaistvom*). This second, much more active and positive, term was used by Kazakh men and women in the outlying villages and pointed to the continued importance there of the indigenous model of labour and value which perceived work in the domestic sphere as a valid and valuable activity.
18. The most widespread goes like this: a man meets an acquaintance, whom he has not seen for some time. He asks him what he is doing now. 'Oh, you know, Zh.K.O', he replies. 'What's that then, some kind of new enterprise?' 'No, "*zhena kormit, odevaet*" (my wife feeds and clothes me).'
19. The ways in which women may use the cultural construction of gender domains to their own advantage is illustrated in the case of Mainur herself. To divorce her husband because of his infidelity and her desire to pursue her career would not have been acceptable. On the other hand, her husband's inability to fulfill his 'breadwinner' role was perceived as an acceptable motive for divorce by kin and the wider community. Similarly, the metaphor of 'feeding the family' gave Madina a morally acceptable way of trading and entering the market, which is otherwise perceived as immoral, individualistic and divisive. The eldest brother's wife was able to use the equation between men and private farming to avoid leaving her job in the administration, which gave her a separate public identity and economic independence.

References

ADB (1996), *Strengthening the Implementation of Agriculture Sector Reforms*, T.A. No. 2356, September, Final Report. Volume 1: Main Report. Danagro Adviser a/s and Landell Mills Ltd.

Anderson, D.G. (1995), 'Hunters, Herders and Heavy Metals in Arctic Siberia', in D.G. Anderson and F. Pine (eds), *Surviving the Transition: Development Concerns in the Post-Socialist World, Cambridge Anthropology*, 18(2): 35–46.

—— (1996), 'Bringing civil society to an uncivilised place: citizenship regimes in Russia's Arctic frontier', in C.M. Hann and E. Dunn (eds), *Civil Society: Challenging Western Models*, London: Routledge, 99–120.

Bauer, A., Boschmann, N. and Green, D. (1997), *Women and Gender Relations in Kazakstan: The Social Cost*, Manila: Asian Development Bank.

Boserup, E. (1970), *Women's Role in Economic Development*, London: Allen and Unwin.

Bridger, S. (1987), *Women in the Soviet Countryside: Women's Roles in Rural Development in the Soviet Union*, Cambridge: Cambridge University Press.

—— (1993), 'Women and the Farming Campaigns of Perestroika', in M. Liljeström, E. Mäntysaari and A. Rosenholm (eds), *Gender Restructuring in Russian Studies*, Conference Papers, Helskinki, August 1992, Tampere, Finland: University of Tampere, 29–38.

——, Kay, R. and Pinnick, K. (eds) (1996), *No More Heroines? Russia, Women and the Market*, Routledge: London.

Buckley, C. (1997), 'Suicide in post-Soviet Kazakhstan: role stress, age and gender', *Central Asia Survey*, 16(1), March,: 45–52.

Esimov, A.S. (1996), 'Privatizatsiya – osnova reformy sel'skogo khozyaistva (Doklad na soveshchanii rabotnikov agropromyshlennogo kompleksa strany 25 dekabrya 1995)', *Sayasat*, 1 (January), 3–18.

Gardner, K. and Lewis, D. (1996), *Anthropology, Development and the Post-Modern Challenge*, London: Pluto Press.

Gaynor, R.M. (1996), *Study on Market Reforms in the Agricultural Sector*, Asian Development Bank T.A. No. 2448-KAZ, Legal and Institutional Reform in the Agricultural Sector, Report No. 7, October, Abt Associates Ltd.

Gilmore, D.G. (1990), *Manhood in the Making: Cultural Concepts of Masculinity*, New Haven and London : Yale University Press.

Hann, C.M. (ed.) (1993), 'Introduction', *Socialism: Ideals, Ideologies, and Local Practice*, London: Routledge.

Herman, R., Johnson, C. and Estes, V. (1997), 'Gender Considerations in the Central Asian Republics: A Preliminary Assessment', Report of TDY team visit, 1–14 December 1996, prepared for USAID/CAR, Almaty.

Hivon, M. (1995), 'Rural Women and Agrarian Reform', in S. Bridger (ed.), 'Women in Post-Communist Russia', *Interface: Bradford Studies in Language, Culture and Society*, 78–93.

Howe, L. (1998), 'Scrounger, Worker, Beggarman, Cheat: The Dynamics of Unemployment and Resistance in Belfast', *Journal of the Royal Anthropological Institute*, 4(3), 531–50.

Humphrey, C. (1995), 'Introduction', in D.G. Anderson and F. Pine (eds), *Surviving the Transition: Development Concerns in the Post-Socialist World, Cambridge Anthropology*, 18(2), 1–12.

—— and Sneath, D. (1999), *The End of Nomadism? Society, State and the Environment in Inner Asia*, Cambridge: White Horse Press.

Kandiyoti, D. (1996) 'Modernization without the market? The case of the "Soviet East"', *Economy and Society*, 25(4), 529–42.

Kor'be, O. (1950), 'Kul'tura i byt Kazakhskogo kolkhoznogo aula', *Sovetskaya Etnografiya*, 4, 67–91.

Massell, G. (1974), *The Surrogate Proletariat: Moslem Women and Revolutionary Strategies in Soviet Central Asia, 1919–1929*, Princeton, New Jersey: Princeton University Press.

Moore, H.L. (1988), *Feminism and Anthropology*, Cambridge: Polity Press.

Palmer, I. (1985), *The Impact of Agrarian Reform on Women*, West Hartford: Kumarian Press.

Pateman, C. (1989), *The Disorder of Women*, Cambridge: Polity Press.

Pine, F. (1994), 'Privatization in Post-Socialist Poland: Peasant Women, Work and the Restructuring of the Public Sphere', *Cambridge Anthropology*, 17(3), 19–42.

Pine, F. (1996), 'Redefining Women's Work in Rural Poland', Abrahams (ed.), *After Socialism: Land Reform and Social Change in Eastern Europe*, Providence and Oxford: Berghahn, 133–56.

Rai, S., Pilkington, H. and Phizacklea, A. (eds) (1992), *Women in the Face of Change: The Soviet Union, Eastern Europe and China*, London: Routledge.

Rogers, S.C. (1975), 'Female forms of power and the myth of male dominance: a model of female/male interaction in peasant society', *American Ethnologist*, 2(4), 727–56.

Rudie, I. (1994), 'Visible Women in East Coast Malay Society: On the Reproduction of Gender in Ceremonial, School and Market', *Oslo Studies in Social Anthropology*, Oslo: Scandinavian University Press.

USAID (1996), 'Women in Development (WID) in Central Asia', Information Leaflet from USAID Office, Kazakhstan.

Vasileva, G.P. (1975), 'Zhenshchina respublik srednei azii i Kazakhstana i ikh rol' v preobrazovanii byta sel'skogo naseleniya', *Sovetskaya Etnografiya*, 6, 17–27.

Verdery, K. (1994), 'From Parent-State to Family Patriarchs: Gender and Nation in Contemporary Eastern Europe', in J. Borocz and K. Verdery (eds), 'Gender and Nation', *East European Politics and Societies*, 8(2), Spring, 225–55.

Warshofsky Lapidus, G. (1978), *Women in Soviet Society: Equality, Development and Social Change*, Berkeley, Los Angeles, London: University of California Press.

Werner, C.A. (1997), 'Marketing Gifts: Economic Change in a Kazakh Village', *Central Asia Monitor*, 6, 1–7.

Wheelock, J., Ljunggren, E. and Baines, S. (1999), 'Between the household and the market: a comparative study of rural entrepreneurs in Norway and England.' Paper presented to the Conference 'Gender and Rural Transformations in Europe: Past, Present and Future Prospects', 14–17 October, Wageningen, The Netherlands.

Yanagisako, S.J. (1987), 'Mixed Metaphors: Native and Anthropological Models of Gender and Kinship Domains', in J. Fishburne Collier and S.J. Yanagisako (eds), *Gender and Kinship: Essays Toward a Unified Analysis*, Stanford: Stanford University Press, 86–118.

Index

Index

ideas of 22, 107
money 5, 25, 69–70, 75–97
  exchange rates 75, 84
  morality and 89–91
Mongolia 10–11, 12, 191–210
morality 4, 33–34, 46, 89–91
  collective 5
  market and 4–5, 39–46, 220
  moral norms 223
  moral obligation 179
multinationals 26

networks 27–28, 83, 227
  household 220, 231
  neighbours 219
Nolan, P. 191–2, 210
'normality' 8, 13, 127, 131–136, 139

officials 28, 199, 203–204

passivity 60, 134, 184–185
pastoralism 11, 194–196
paternalism 35
peasantry 34, 53, 56, 79–80
  'arkhangelskie muzhiki' 61, 64, 70
  'kresvanskie khozyaistva' 230
  'peasant farms' 64, 179–180
perestroika 2, 60, 68
Perotta, L. 4, 11, 12, 13, 169–190
pilfering 81, 185
Pine, F. 4, 5, 10, 13, 15, 31, 35, 51, 75–97, 234
Poland 5, 12, 75–97
politics 13
  indigenous political institutions 197–200
pollution 49
'postsocialism' 3, 13, 91–94, 102
post-modernity 8
poverty 11–12, 79, 128, 171, 177–179
  poverty line 193, 196
prestige 26, 93, 136, 159
practices 12, 47, 121–122
prices 7, 39, 44–46, 84, 91, 150
pride 41–46
  centrally determined 34
  price commissions 193
  price setting strategies 45–46
private farms 216–217
privatization 6, 9, 19–20, 49, 128, 169,

177, 192–3, 195, 204, 211–235
'privatikhatsiya' 6, 231
production 35, 66–67
  on private plots 37, 42
  co-operative 49
profiteering see 'speculation'
progress 8, 102, 108–109
property
  common 11, 13
  custodial 11, 197, 203–204
  multiple ownership 199–202
  private 12, 191, 196, 202, 204
  protection 12
public and private spheres 213–215, 227
Rausing, S. 4, 8, 13, 127–142
religion 20
  Christianity 86
  Islam 22
Romania 7–8, 101–125
Russia 5–6, 9, 53–74, 73
  nationalism 58
  'New Russians' 53, 105, 120
  Russian-ness 8, 54, 127

Sampson, S. 115, 125
service sector 26
shame 4, 7, 25, 33–51
'shock-therapy' 2, 9, 11, 193–194
shops 129–131
Shreeves, R. 4, 10, 211–235
small business 19–20, 68
smuggling 79
Sneath, D. 4, 10–11, 12, 191–210, 227
socialism 35, 57, 104
'social biography of things' 43–44
'speculation' 7, 25, 72
Stalinism 6, 57, 80, 135
state 5, 35, 41, 47, 67, 192, 213–214
  hostility to 90
suicide 232
surplus 43

taxation 187
trading 1, 4
  informal 219
  morality of 232
  routes 38, 79
  sea trade 55
  shuttle-trade 24, 38

Index

Lightning Source UK Ltd.
Milton Keynes UK
11 May 2010

154025UK00001B/62/A